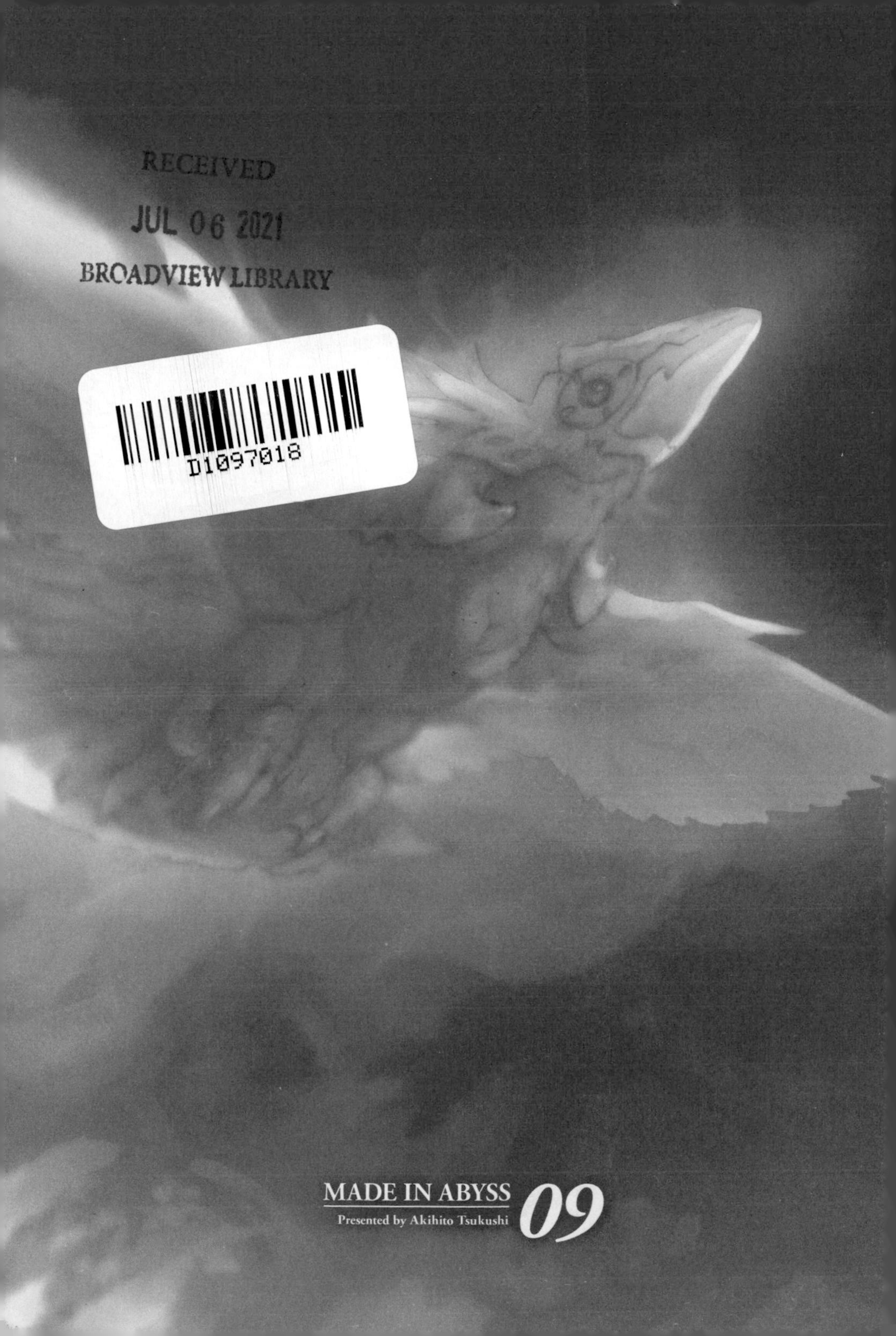

MADE IN ABYSS 09
Presented by Akihito Tsukushi

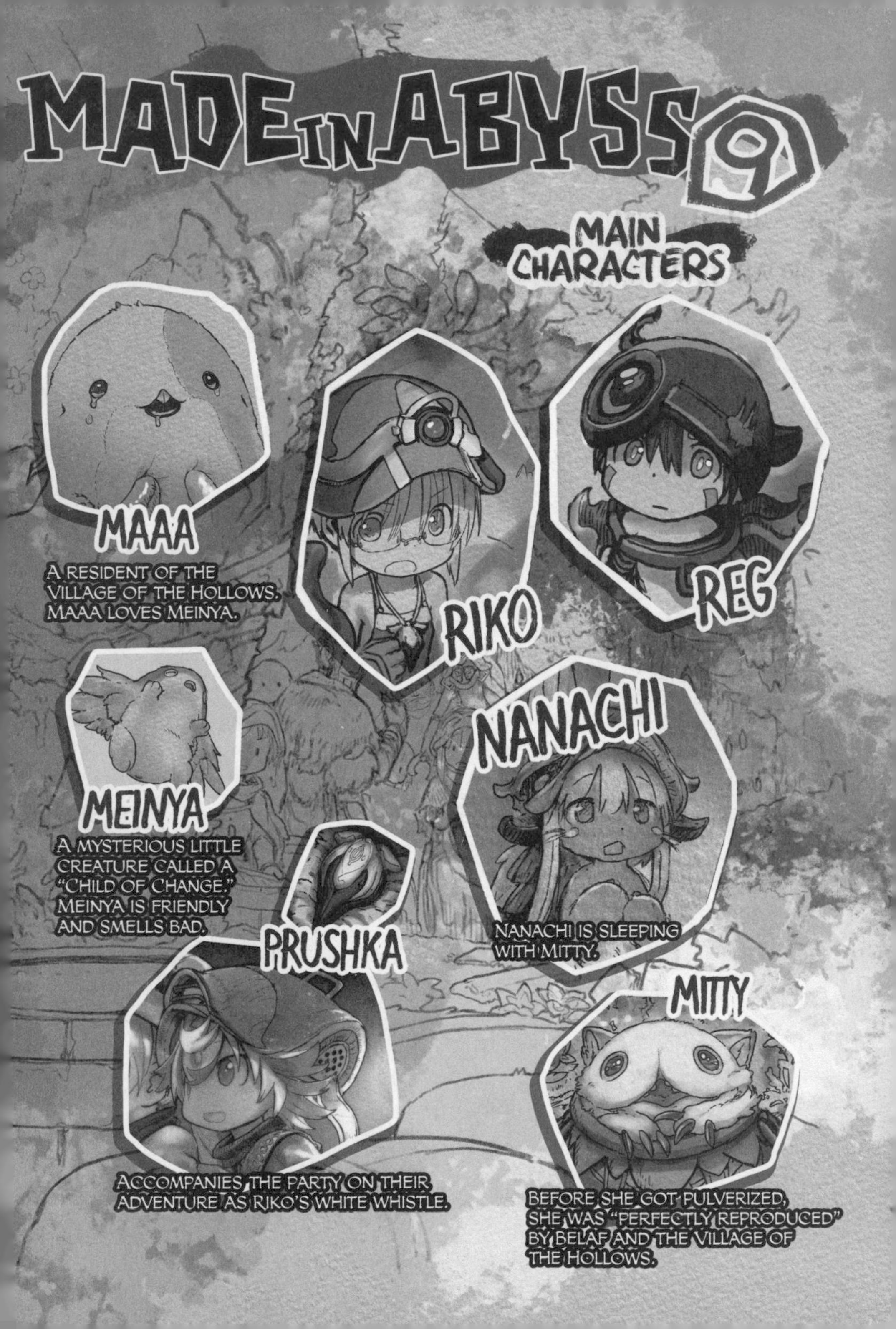
MADE IN ABYSS 9
MAIN CHARACTERS
MAAA
A RESIDENT OF THE VILLAGE OF THE HOLLOWS. MAAA LOVES MEINYA.
RIKO
REG
MEINYA
A MYSTERIOUS LITTLE CREATURE CALLED A "CHILD OF CHANGE." MEINYA IS FRIENDLY AND SMELLS BAD.
NANACHI
NANACHI IS SLEEPING WITH MITTY.
PRUSHKA
ACCOMPANIES THE PARTY ON THEIR ADVENTURE AS RIKO'S WHITE WHISTLE.
MITTY
BEFORE SHE GOT PULVERIZED, SHE WAS "PERFECTLY REPRODUCED" BY BELAF AND THE VILLAGE OF THE HOLLOWS.

THE THREE SAGES

THE EMINENT INDIVIDUALS CONSIDERED TO HAVE CREATED THE VILLAGE OF THE HOLLOWS. THE RESIDENTS CALL THE VILLAGE IRUBURU.

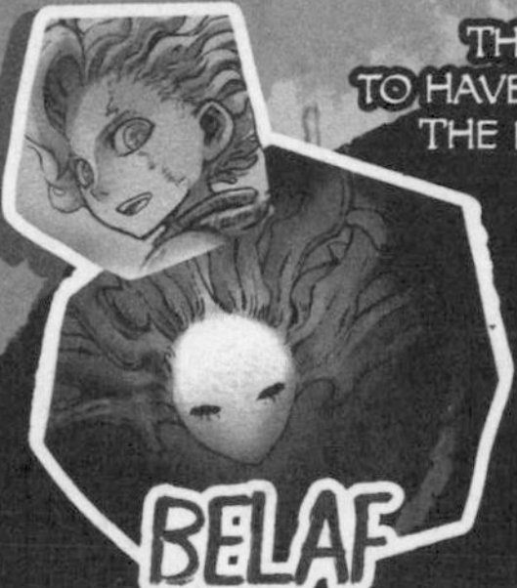

BELAF

HAS A REALLY LONG BODY. BELAF HAD BEEN ABSORBING THE REPRODUCED MITTY, BUT NANACHI WAS HORRIFIED BY THIS AND BOUGHT MITTY FROM BELAF. HOWEVER, BELAF WAS HAPPY TO RECEIVE NANACHI THEMSELF IN EXCHANGE.

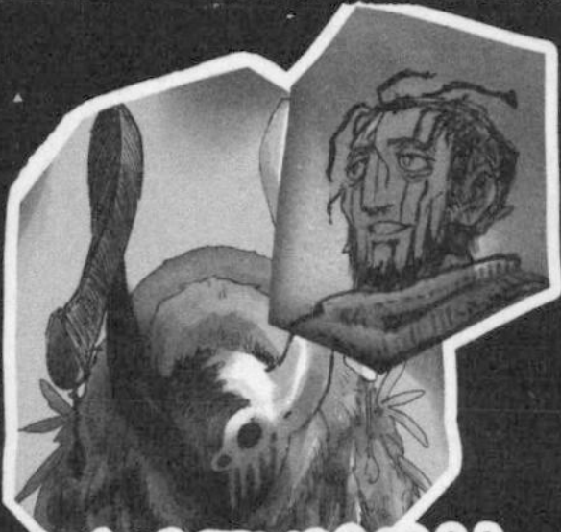

WAZUKYAN

ACTS LIKE A KNOW-IT-ALL BUT IS PRETTY LIGHTHEARTED. BE THEY ARMS OR BE THEY FINGERS, HE HAS LOTS OF THEM.

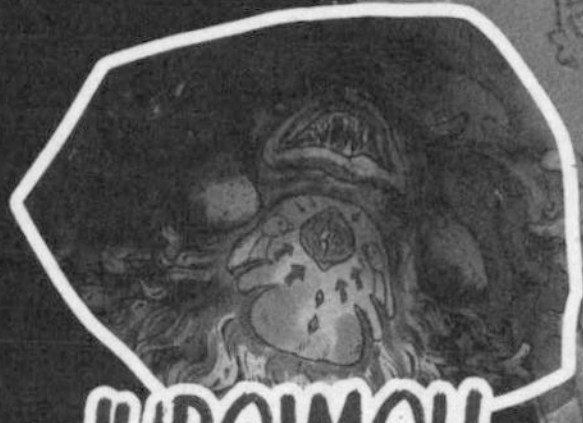

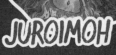

JUROIMOH

VALUES BATTLING THE STRONG. EXUDES A LONG SLIME-COVERED OBJECT CALLED THE "GREAT SWORD."

THE THIRD ONE

WAZUKYAN USED IT ON HIMSELF, BUT THE ATTEMPT FAILED. WHEN HE TURNED INTO A HOLLOW, IT WAS CONFISCATED BY IRUMYUUI, WHO HAD TRANSFORMED INTO THE VILLAGE.

THE SECOND ONE

AFTER IRUMYUUI BECAME SWOLLEN, WAZUKYAN MADE AN OFFERING TO HER SCAR WHERE THE CRADLE BROKE AND FURTHER INCREASED THE POTENCY.

THE FIRST ONE

VUEKO GAVE IT TO IRUMYUUI TO HELP HER RECOVER FROM A DEADLY ILLNESS.

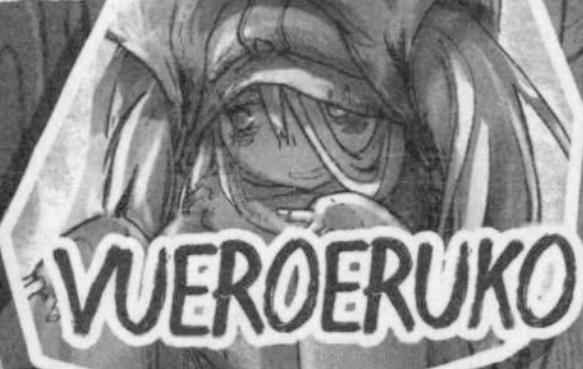

VUEROERUKO

COMMONLY KNOWN AS VUEKO. DUE TO CERTAIN CIRCUMSTANCES, SHE WAS CONCEALED IN THE DEPTHS OF THE EYE. SHE USED TO BE ONE OF THE THREE SAGES AND KNOWS THE ORIGINS OF THE VILLAGE.

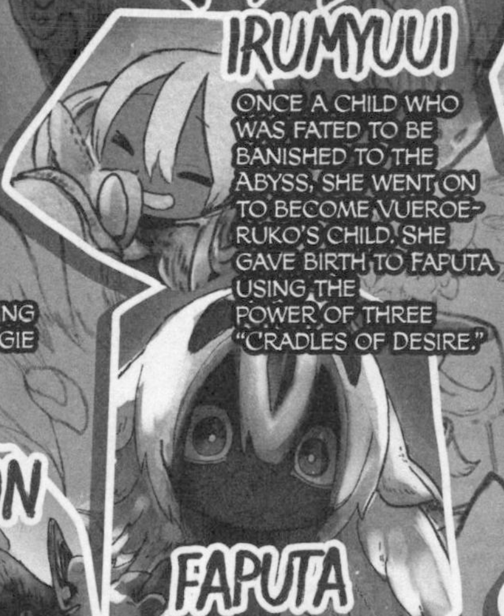

IRUMYUUI

ONCE A CHILD WHO WAS FATED TO BE BANISHED TO THE ABYSS, SHE WENT ON TO BECOME VUEROERUKO'S CHILD. SHE GAVE BIRTH TO FAPUTA USING THE POWER OF THREE "CRADLES OF DESIRE."

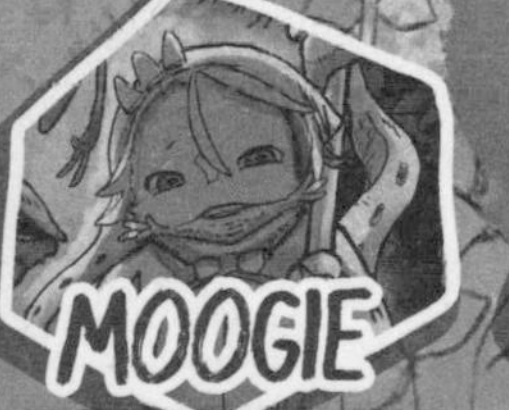

MOOGIE

THE OWNER OF THE RESTAURANT. GENDER UNKNOWN. DUE TO WORKING IN THE RESTAURANT, MOOGIE HAS LEARNED--TO SOME EXTENT--A VARIETY OF LANGUAGES.

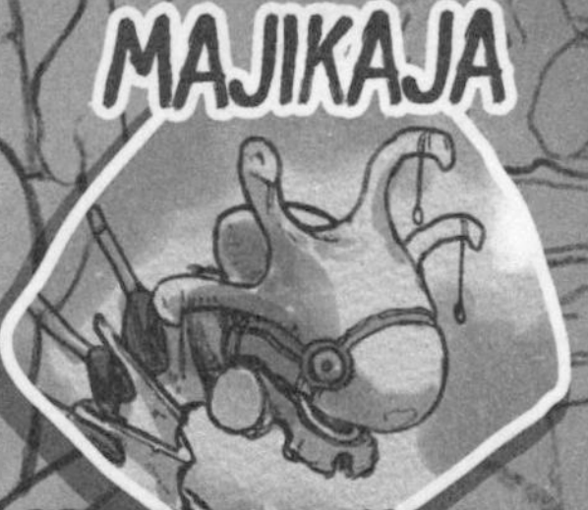

MAJIKAJA

WHAT LOOKS LIKE MAJIKAJA'S BODY IS REALLY JUST A VESSEL. MAJIKAJA SAYS THEIR BODY IS ACTUALLY GASEOUS. THEY ARE A BUSYBODY WHO LIKES TO SHOW NEW ARRIVALS AROUND THE VILLAGE.

FAPUTA

IMMORTAL. SHE IS IRUMYUUI'S FINAL CHILD AND IS CALLED THE "EMBODIMENT OF VALUE." PRINCESS OF THE HOLLOWS. SHE DESIRES TO ERADICATE THE VILLAGERS, WHO EAT AWAY AT HER MOTHER'S BODY. SHE SEEMS TO HAVE A DEEP CONNECTION WITH REG AND IS VERY ATTACHED TO HIM.

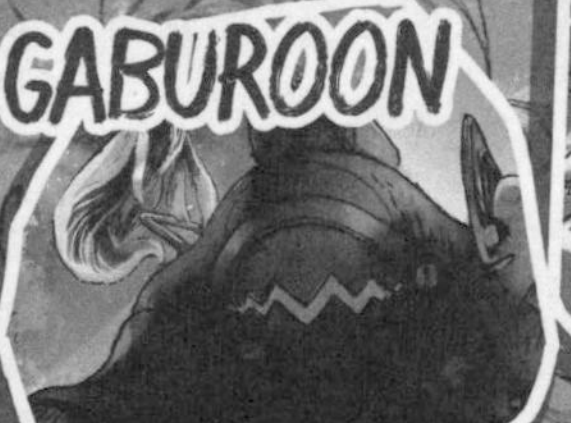

GABUROON

A SO-CALLED "INTERFERENCE UNIT," ONE OF THE MYSTERIOUS DOLLS THAT HAVE EXISTED IN THE ABYSS SINCE ANCIENT TIMES. THEIR NAME IS SAID TO MEAN "GUARDIAN."

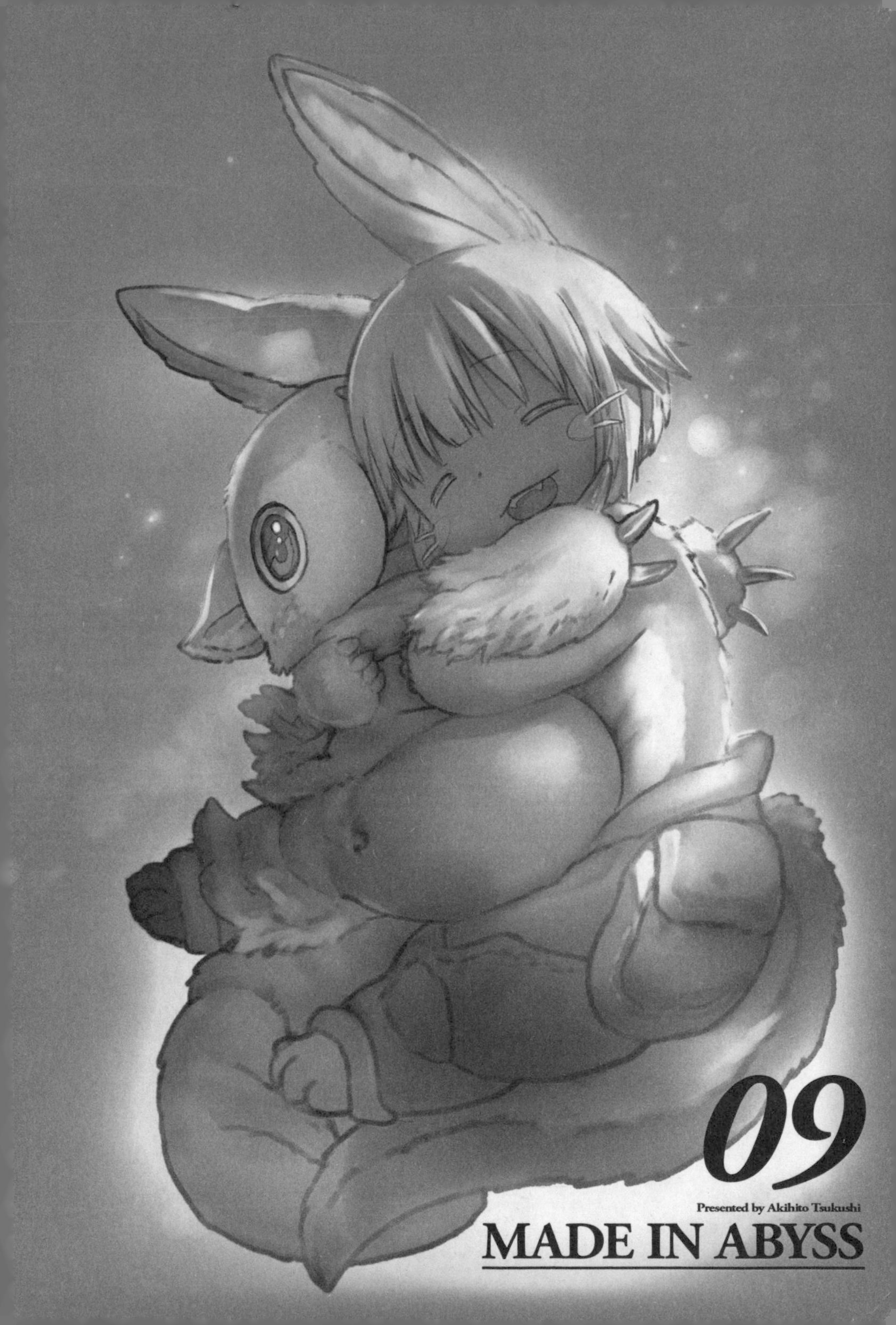

09

Presented by Akihito Tsukushi

MADE IN ABYSS

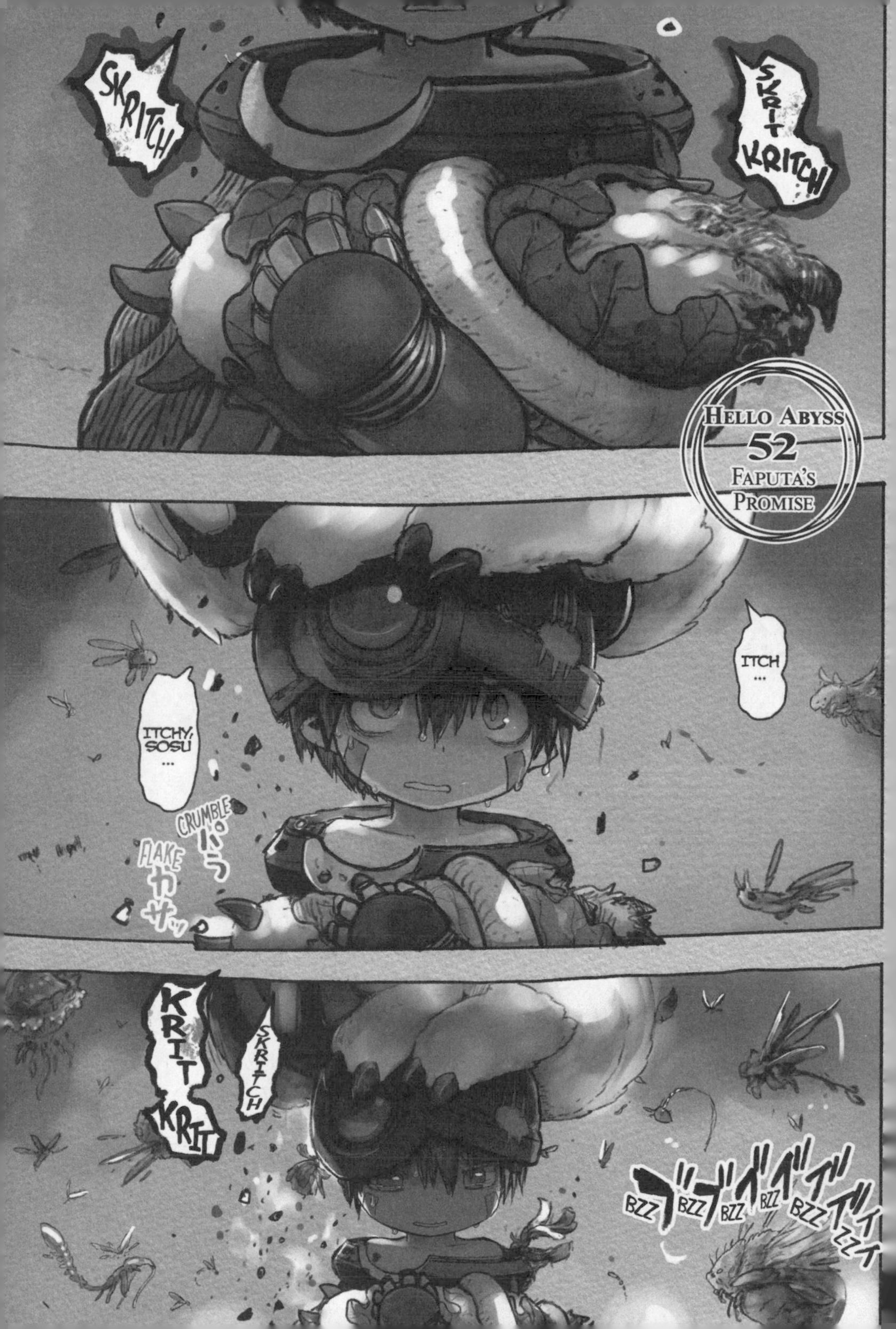
SKRIT KRITCH
SKRITCH
HELLO ABYSS
52
FAPUTA'S PROMISE
ITCH ...
ITCHY, SOSU ...
CRUMBLE パラ
FLAKE カサッ
BZZ ブ BZZ ブ BZZ イ BZZ イ BZZ ブ ブ イ ZZZ イ
SKRITCH
KRIT KRIT

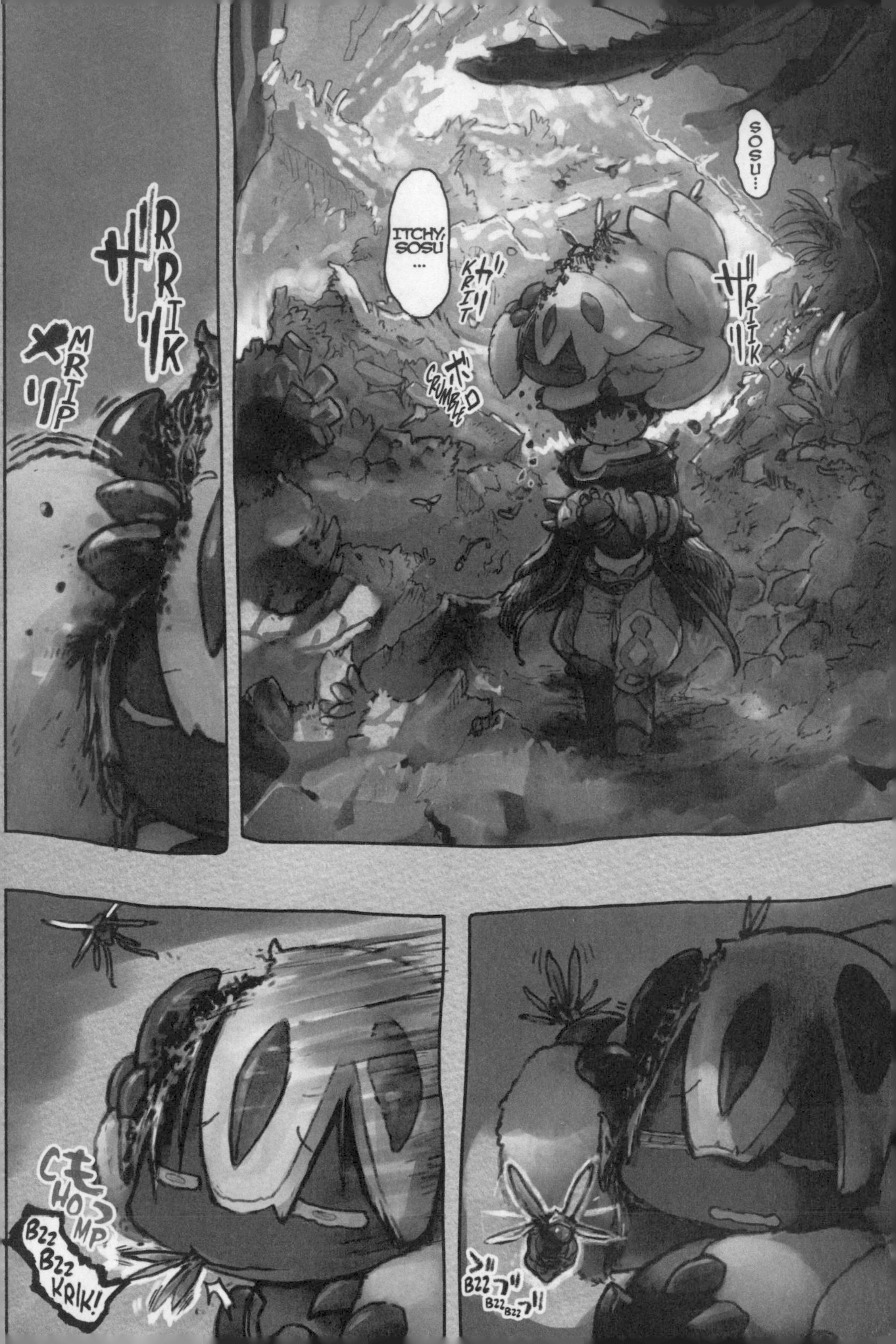

SOSU...
RRIIK
ITCHY, SOSU...
KRIT
CRUMBLE
RRRIK
MRRIP
BZZ
BZZ BZZ
CHOMP
BZZ BZZ KRIK!

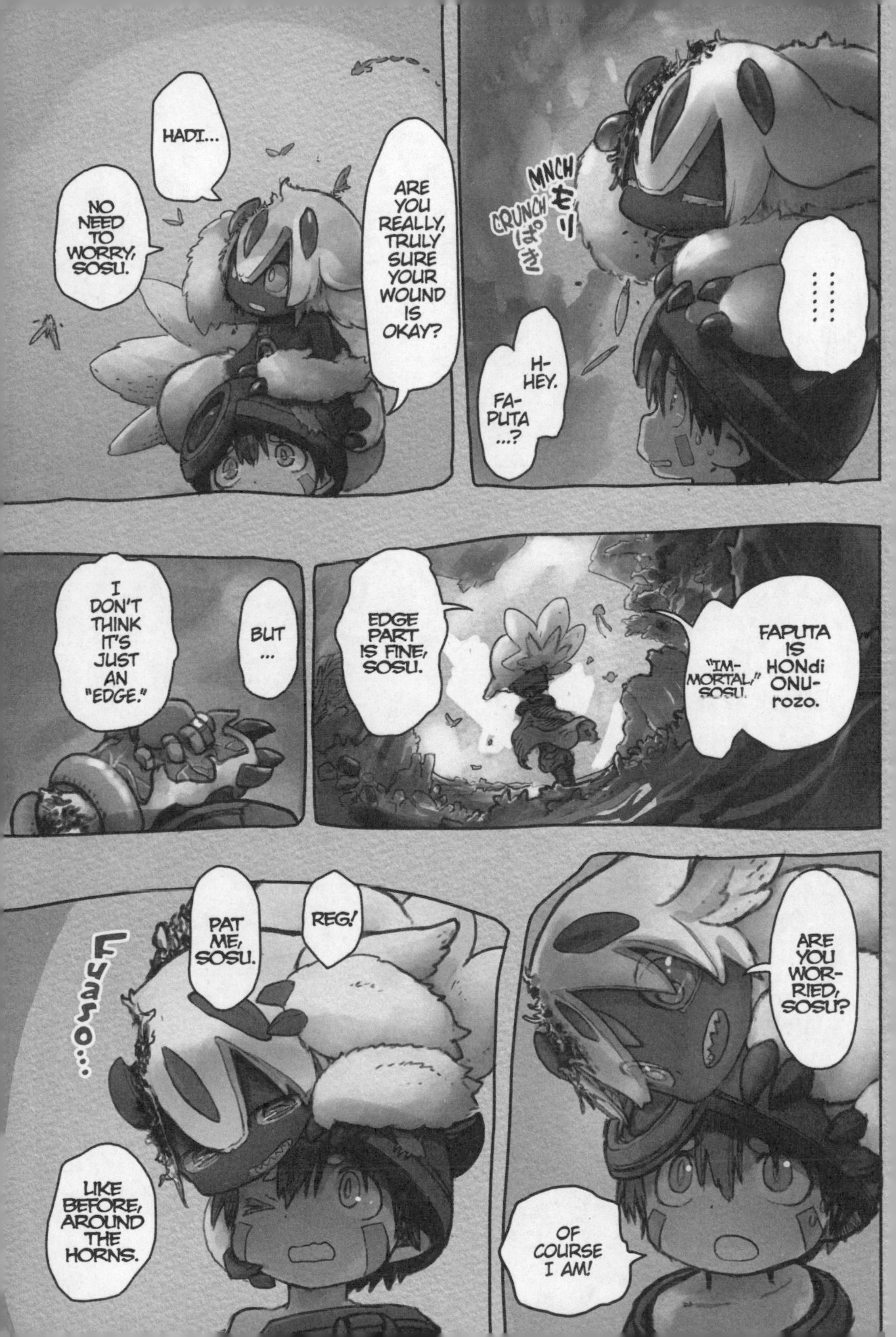
MNCH モリ
CRUNCH ぱき
……
H-HEY. FAPUTA ...?
ARE YOU REALLY, TRULY SURE YOUR WOUND IS OKAY?
HADI...
NO NEED TO WORRY, SOSU.
FAPUTA IS HONdi ONU-rozo.
"IM-MORTAL," SOSU.
EDGE PART IS FINE, SOSU.
BUT ...
I DON'T THINK IT'S JUST AN "EDGE."
ARE YOU WOR-RIED, SOSU?
OF COURSE I AM!
REG!
PAT ME, SOSU.
Fuaso...
LIKE BEFORE, AROUND THE HORNS.

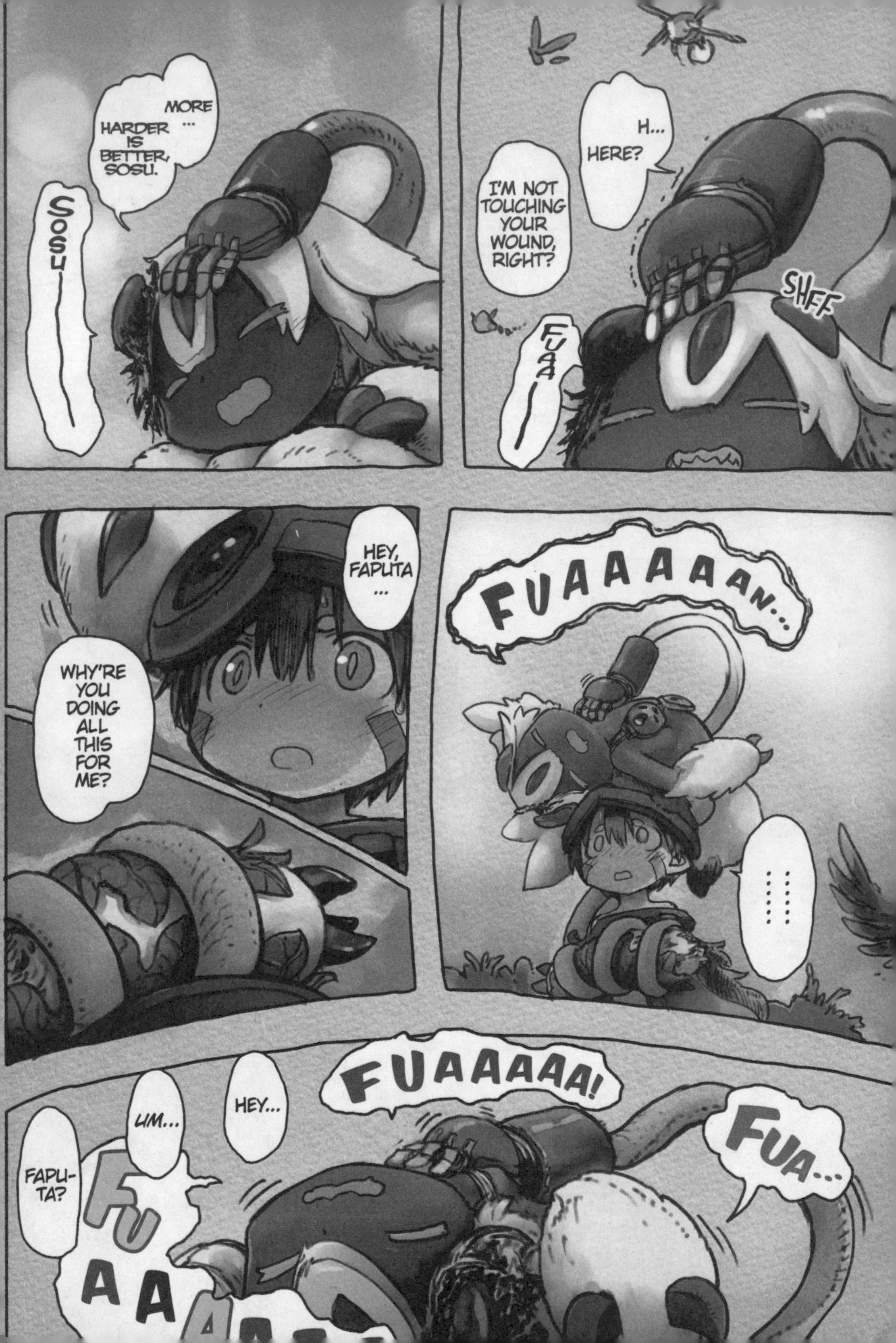
H... HERE?
I'M NOT TOUCHING YOUR WOUND, RIGHT?
SHFF
FUAA—
MORE... HARDER IS BETTER, SOSU.
SOSU—
FUAAAAAAN...
......
HEY, FAPUTA...
WHY'RE YOU DOING ALL THIS FOR ME?
FUA...
FUAAAAAA!
HEY...
UM...
FAPUTA?
FUAAA

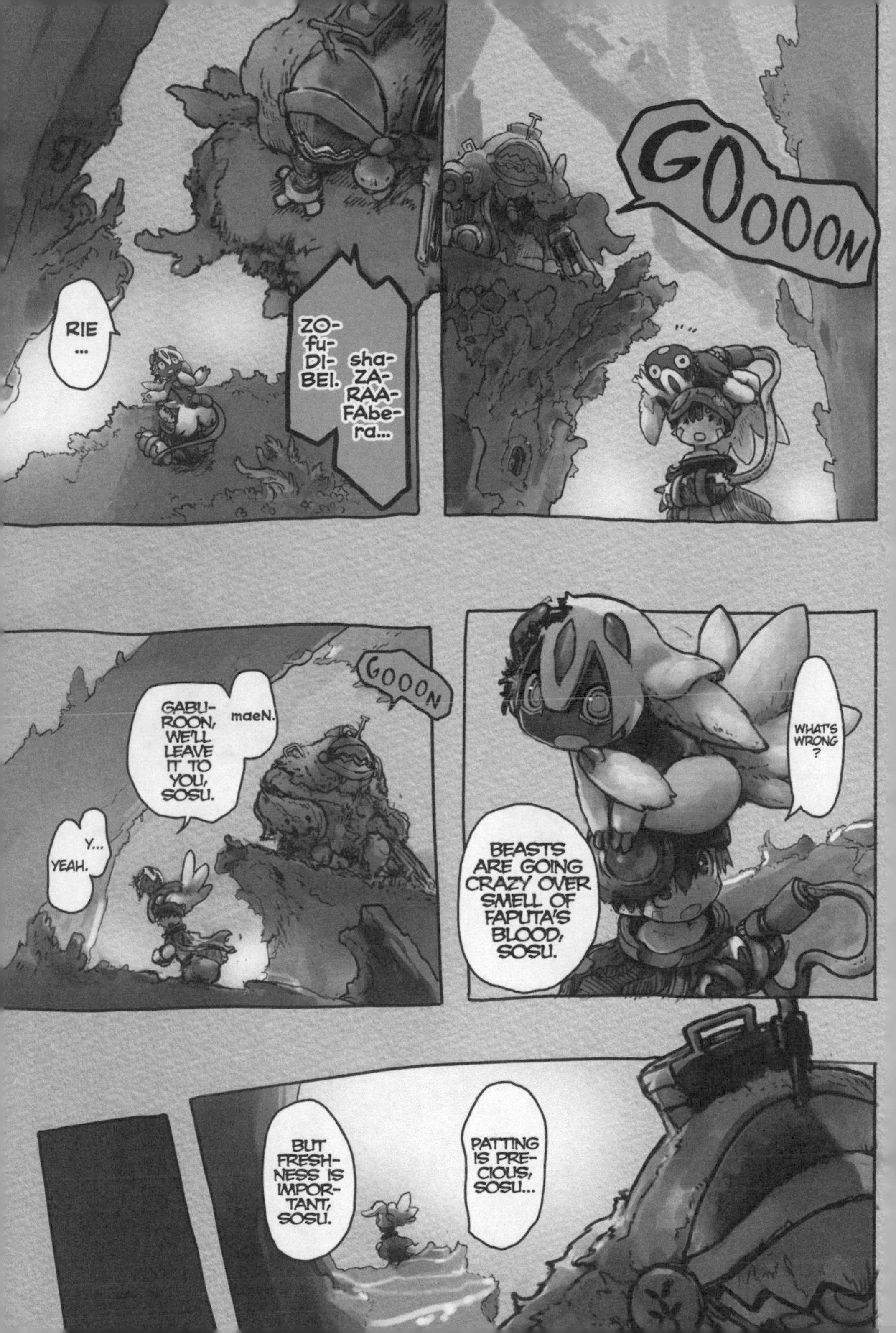
GOOOOON
ZO-fu-DI-BEI. sha-ZA-RAA-FAbe-ra...
RIE...
WHAT'S WRONG?
BEASTS ARE GOING CRAZY OVER SMELL OF FAPUTA'S BLOOD, SOSU.
GOOON
maeN.
GABU-ROON, WE'LL LEAVE IT TO YOU, SOSU.
Y... YEAH.
PATTING IS PRE-CIOUS, SOSU...
BUT FRESH-NESS IS IMPOR-TANT, SOSU.

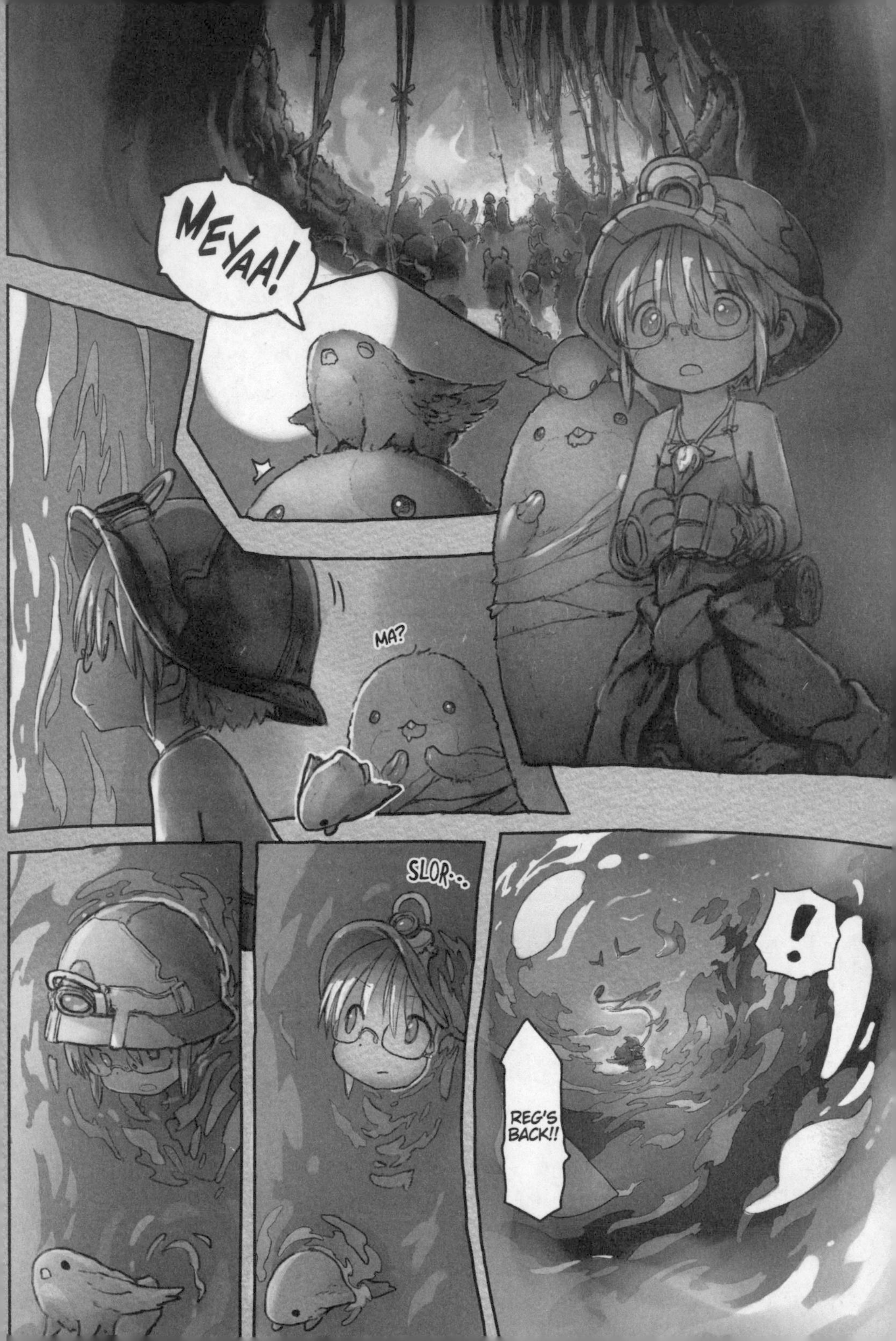
MEYAA!
MA?
!
REG'S BACK!!
SLOR...

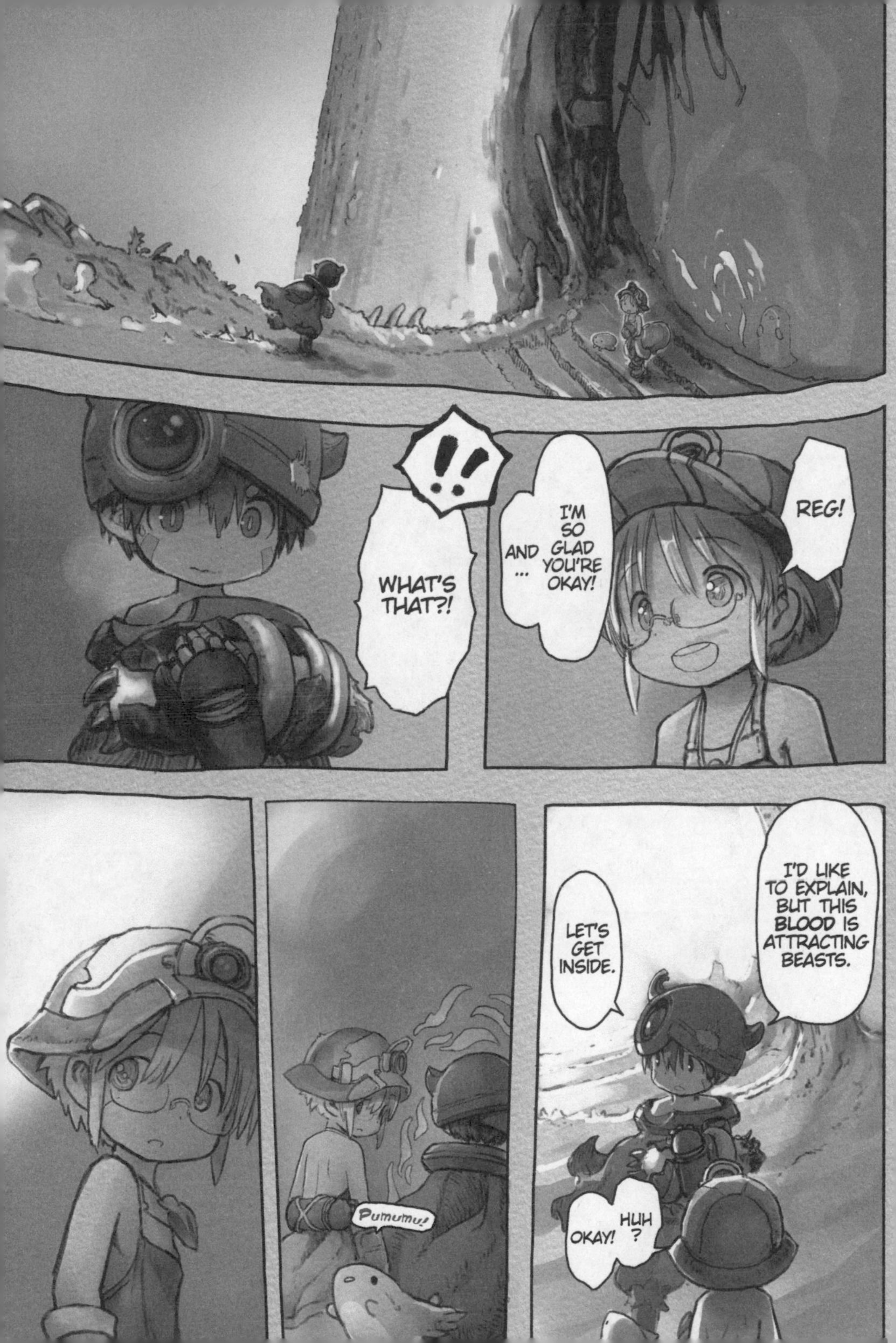
REG!
I'M SO GLAD YOU'RE OKAY!
AND ...
!!
WHAT'S THAT?!
I'D LIKE TO EXPLAIN, BUT THIS BLOOD IS ATTRACTING BEASTS.
LET'S GET INSIDE.
HUH ?
OKAY!
Pumumu!

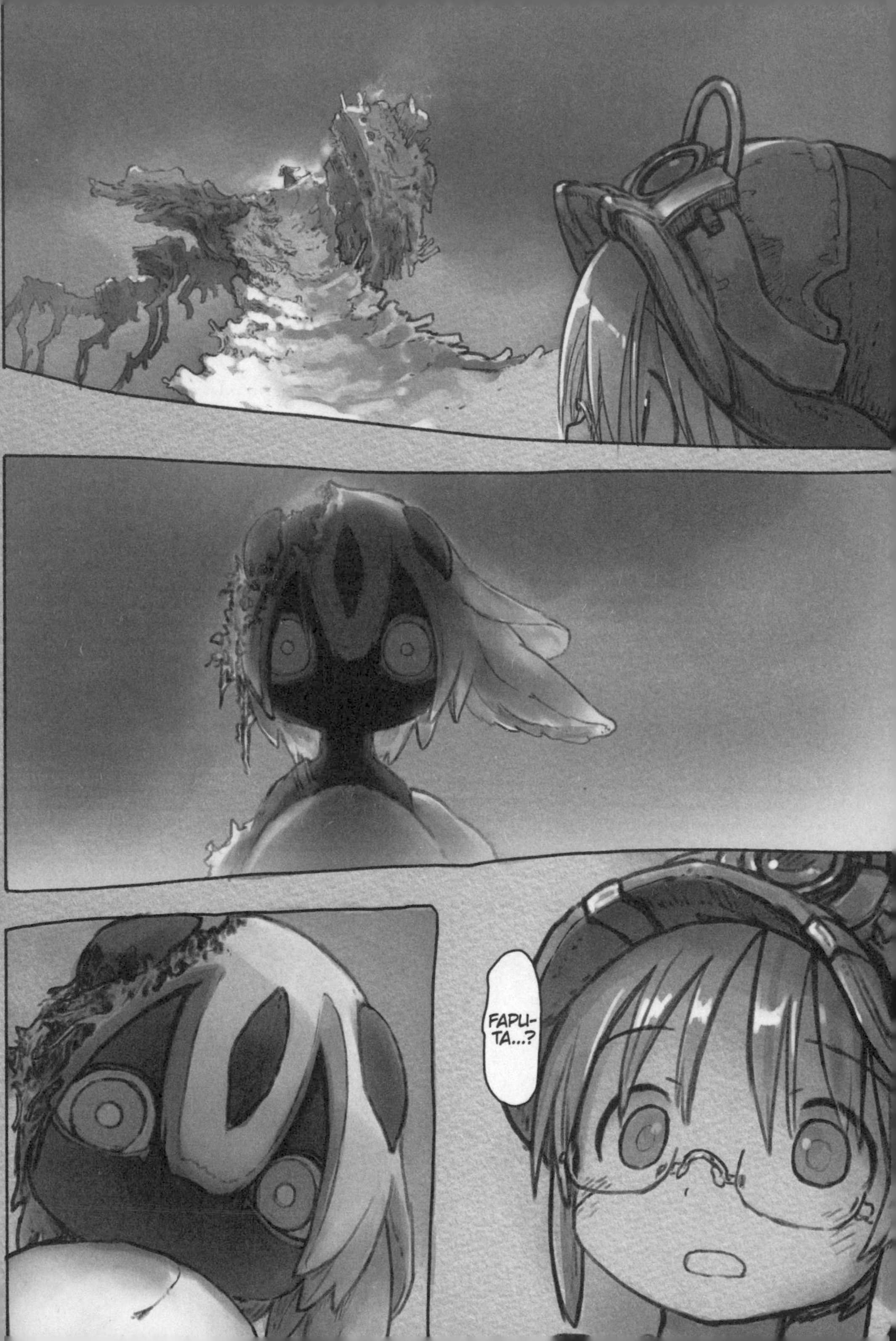
FAPU-TA...?

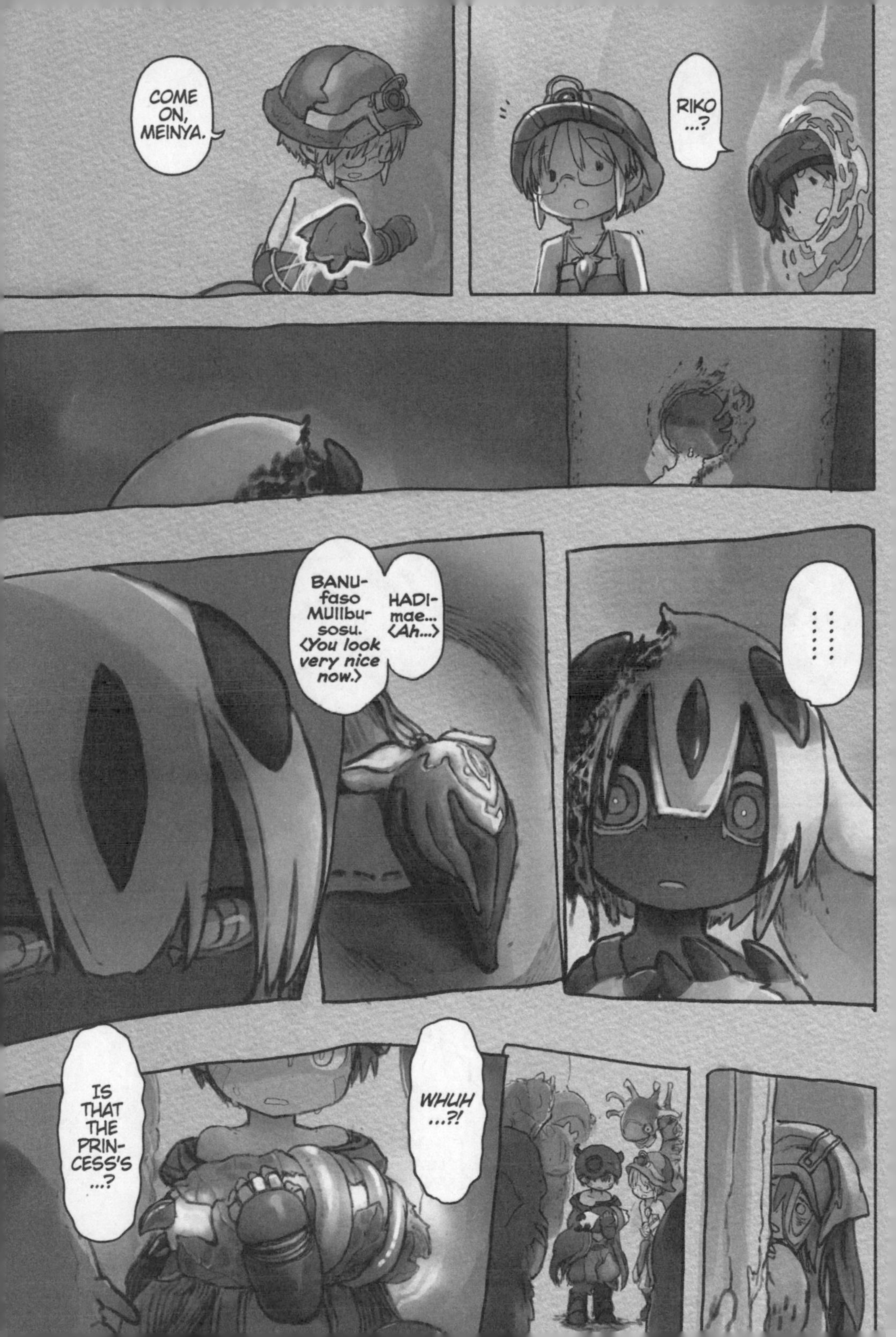
RIKO ...?
COME ON, MEINYA.
......
HADI-mae... <Ah...>
BANU-faso Mullbu-sosu. <You look very nice now.>
WHUH ...?!
IS THAT THE PRINCESS'S ...?

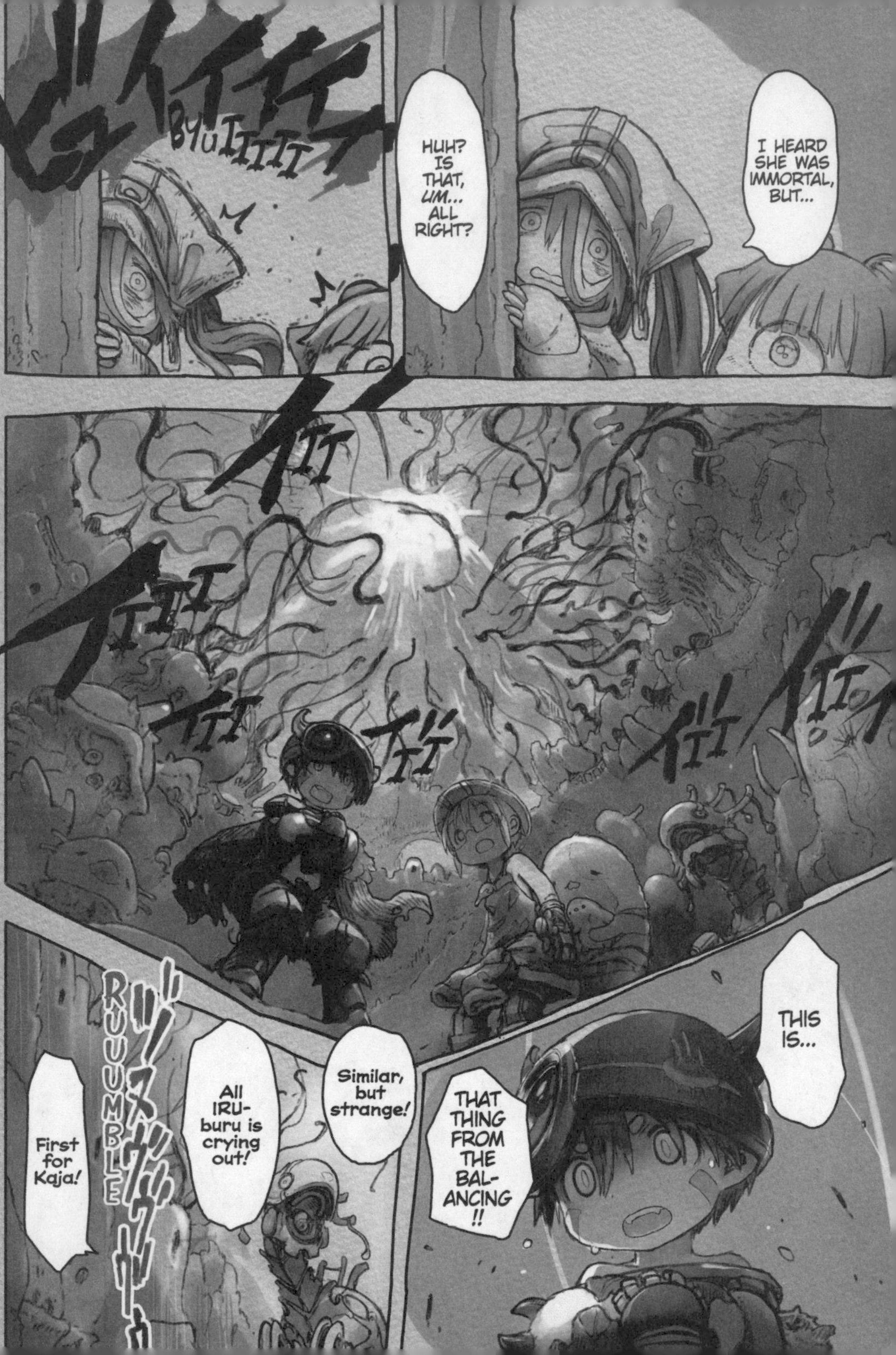
I HEARD SHE WAS IMMORTAL, BUT...
HUH? IS THAT, UM... ALL RIGHT?
BYUIIIIII
THIS IS...
THAT THING FROM THE BAL-ANCING!!
Similar, but strange!
All IRU-buru is crying out!
RUUUMBLE
First for Kaja!

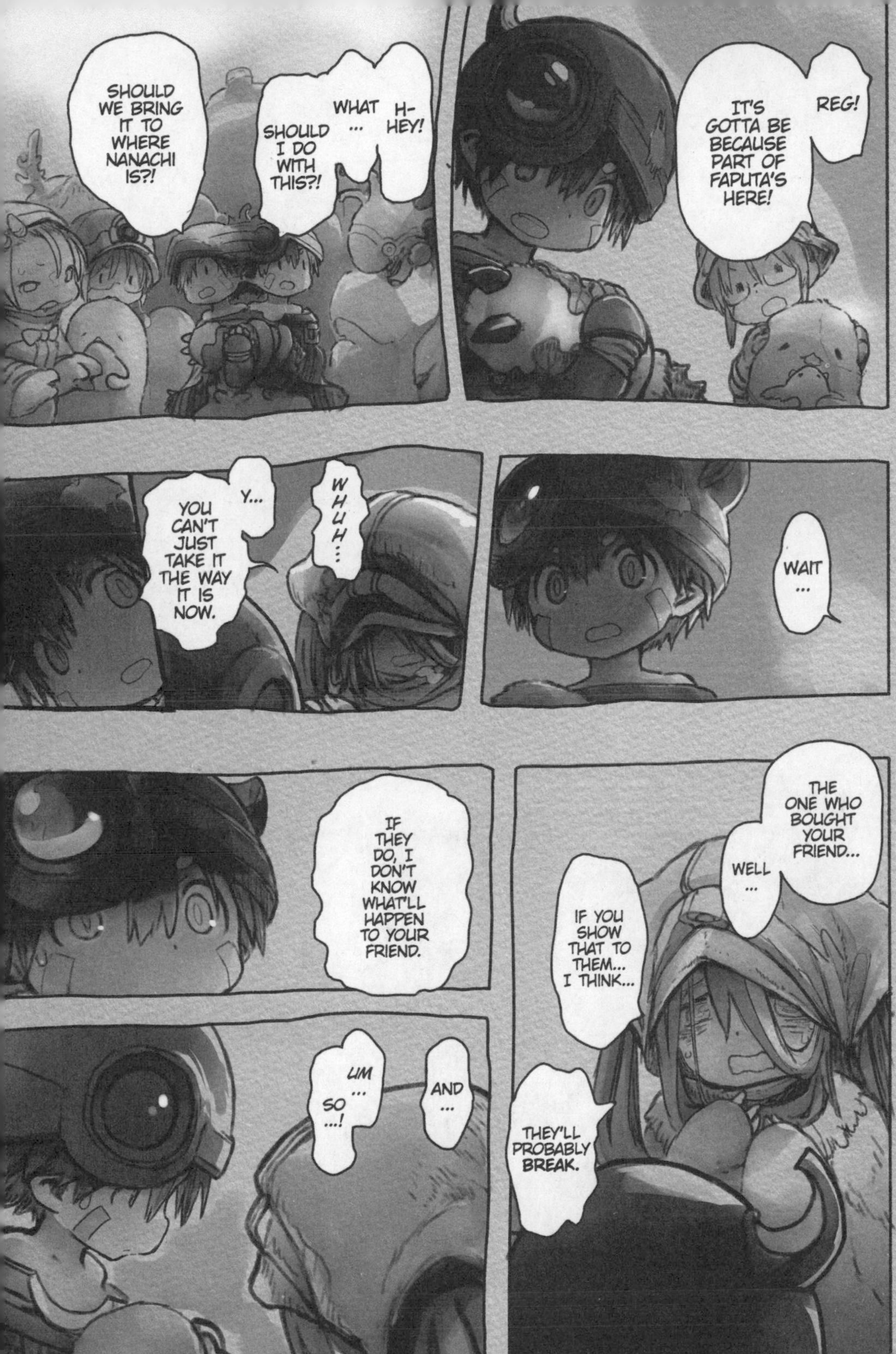
REG!
IT'S GOTTA BE BECAUSE PART OF FAPUTA'S HERE!
H- HEY!
WHAT ... SHOULD I DO WITH THIS?!
SHOULD WE BRING IT TO WHERE NANACHI IS?!
WAIT ...
WHUH...
Y...
YOU CAN'T JUST TAKE IT THE WAY IT IS NOW.
THE ONE WHO BOUGHT YOUR FRIEND...
WELL ...
IF YOU SHOW THAT TO THEM... I THINK...
THEY'LL PROBABLY BREAK.
IF THEY DO, I DON'T KNOW WHAT'LL HAPPEN TO YOUR FRIEND.
AND ...
UM ... SO ...!

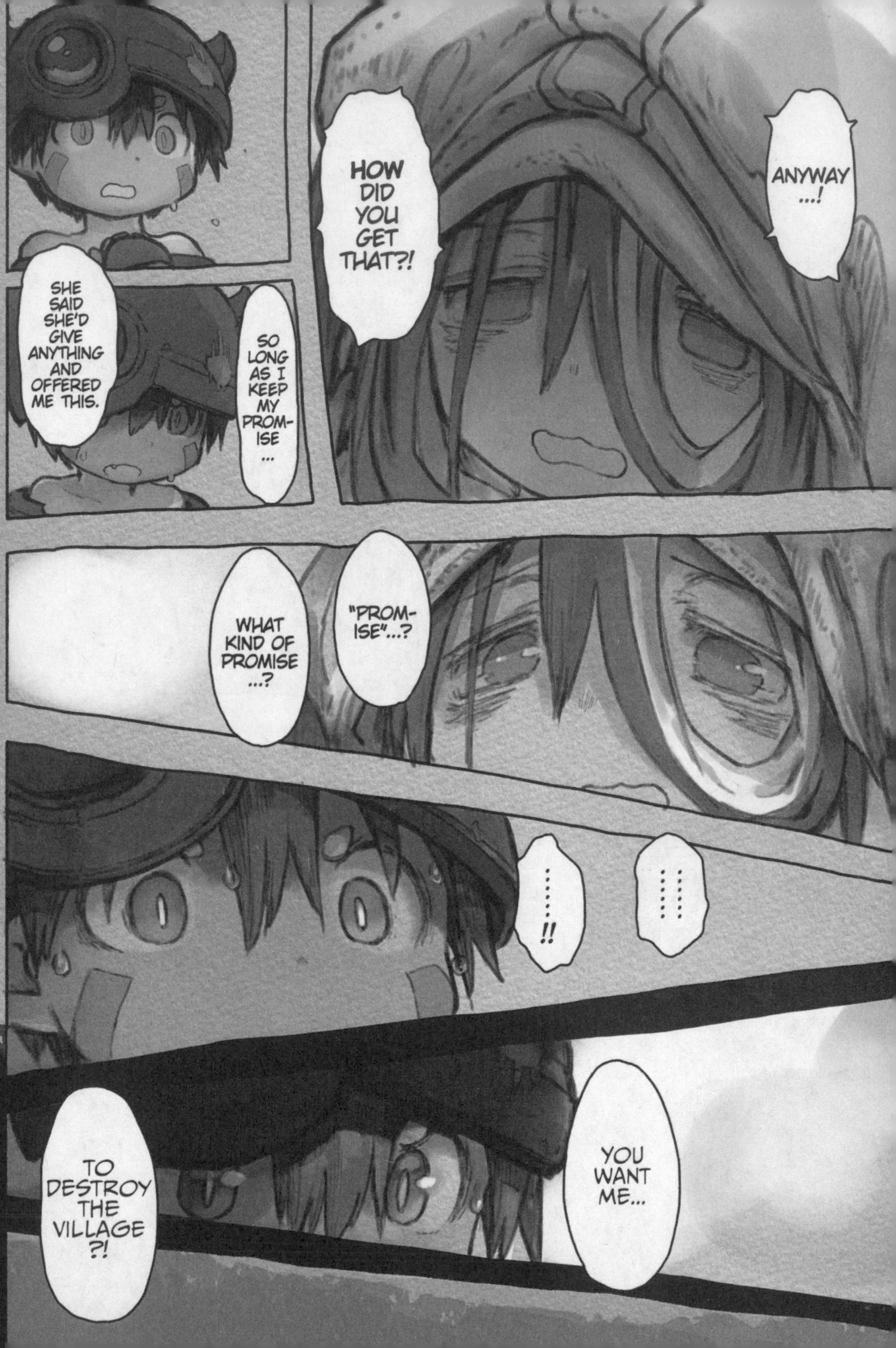
ANYWAY...!
HOW DID YOU GET THAT?!
SO LONG AS I KEEP MY PROMISE...
SHE SAID SHE'D GIVE ANYTHING AND OFFERED ME THIS.
"PROMISE"...?
WHAT KIND OF PROMISE...?
......!!
......!!
YOU WANT ME...
TO DESTROY THE VILLAGE?!

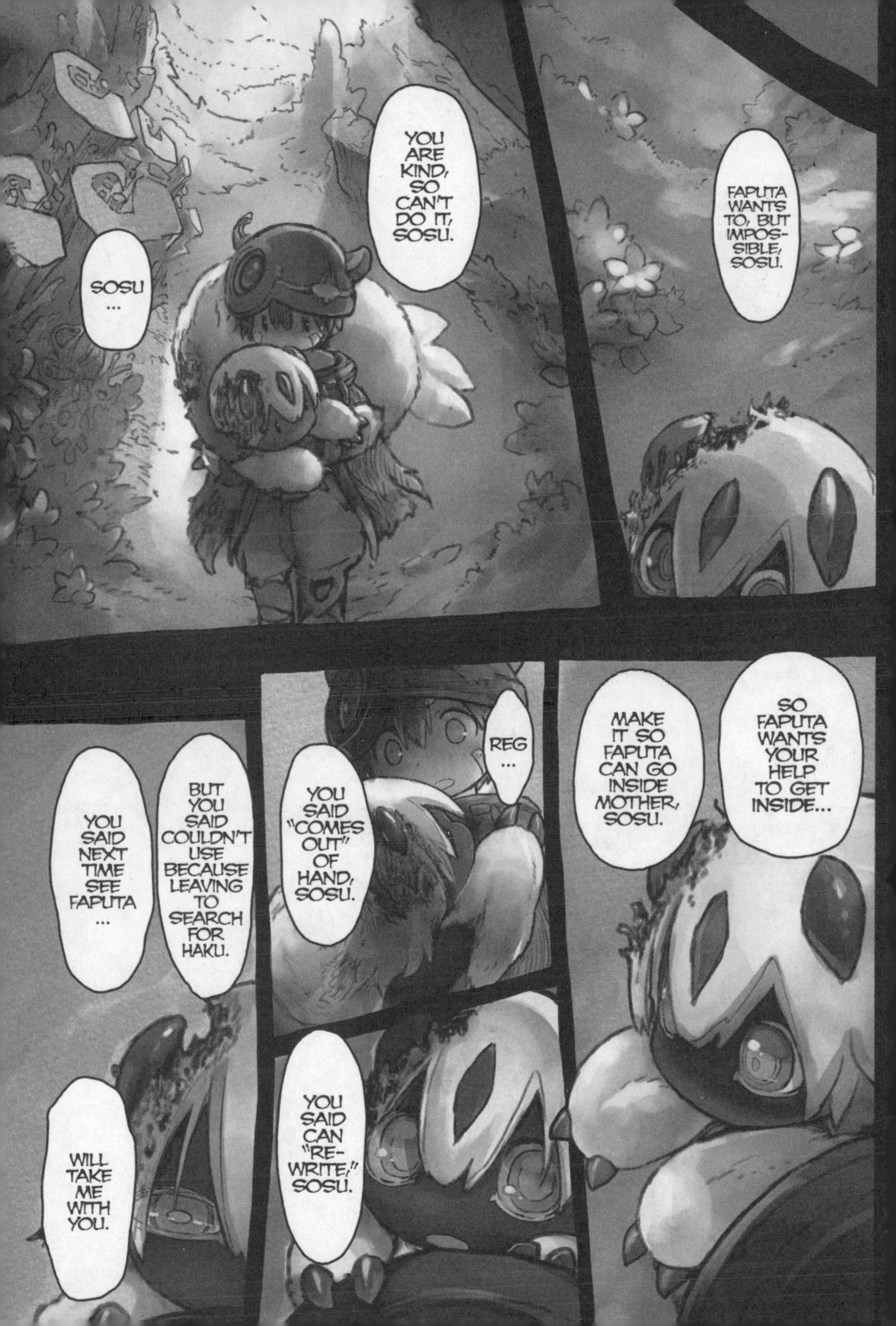
FAPUTA WANTS TO, BUT IMPOSSIBLE, SOSU.
YOU ARE KIND, SO CAN'T DO IT, SOSU.
SOSU ...
SO FAPUTA WANTS YOUR HELP TO GET INSIDE...
MAKE IT SO FAPUTA CAN GO INSIDE MOTHER, SOSU.
REG ...
YOU SAID "COMES OUT" OF HAND, SOSU.
YOU SAID CAN "RE-WRITE," SOSU.
BUT YOU SAID COULDN'T USE BECAUSE LEAVING TO SEARCH FOR HAKU.
YOU SAID NEXT TIME SEE FAPUTA ...
WILL TAKE ME WITH YOU.

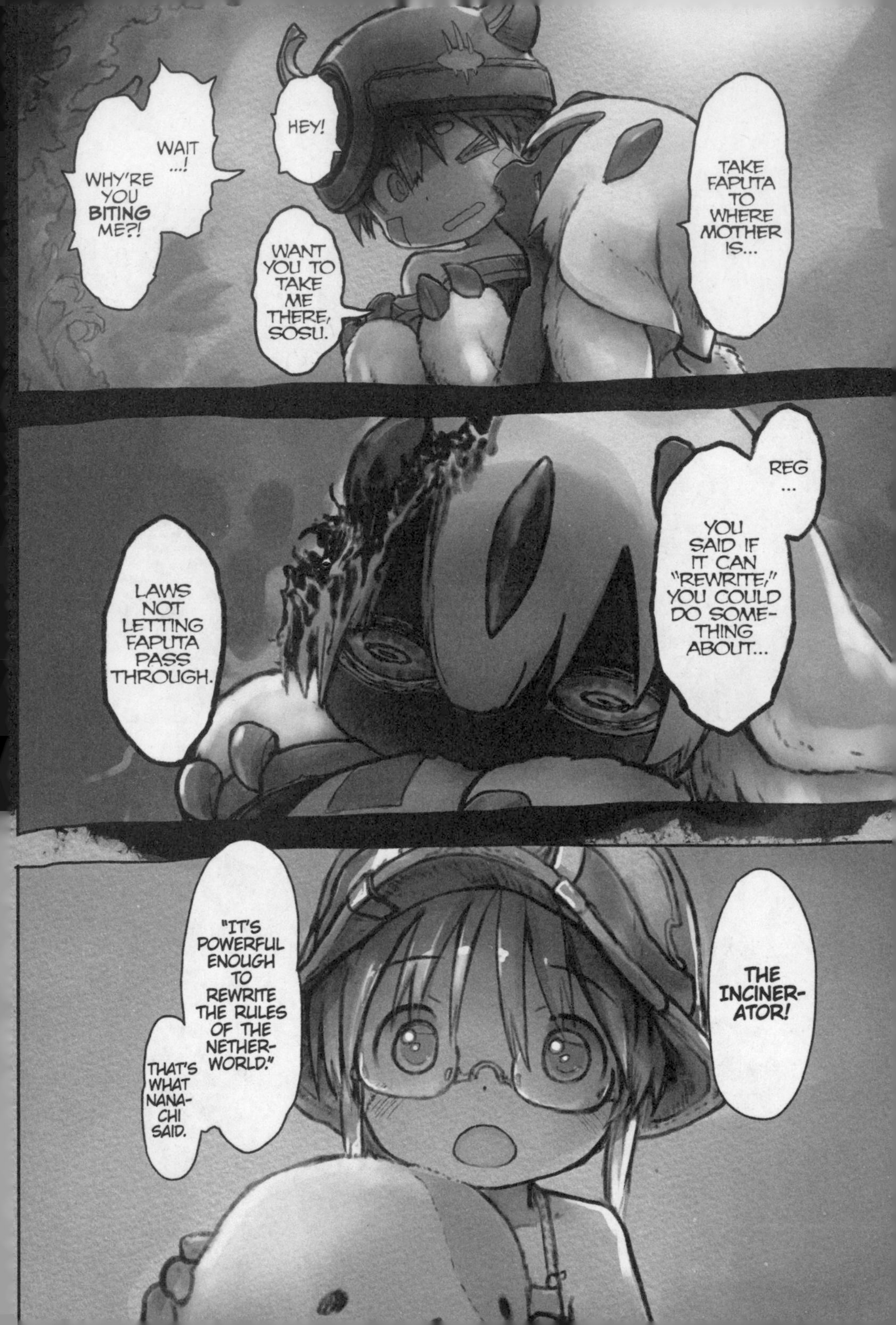
TAKE FAPUTA TO WHERE MOTHER IS...
HEY!
WAIT ...! WHY'RE YOU BITING ME?!
WANT YOU TO TAKE ME THERE, SOSU.
REG ...
YOU SAID IF IT CAN "REWRITE," YOU COULD DO SOME-THING ABOUT...
LAWS NOT LETTING FAPUTA PASS THROUGH.
THE INCINER-ATOR!
"IT'S POWERFUL ENOUGH TO REWRITE THE RULES OF THE NETHER-WORLD."
THAT'S WHAT NANA-CHI SAID.

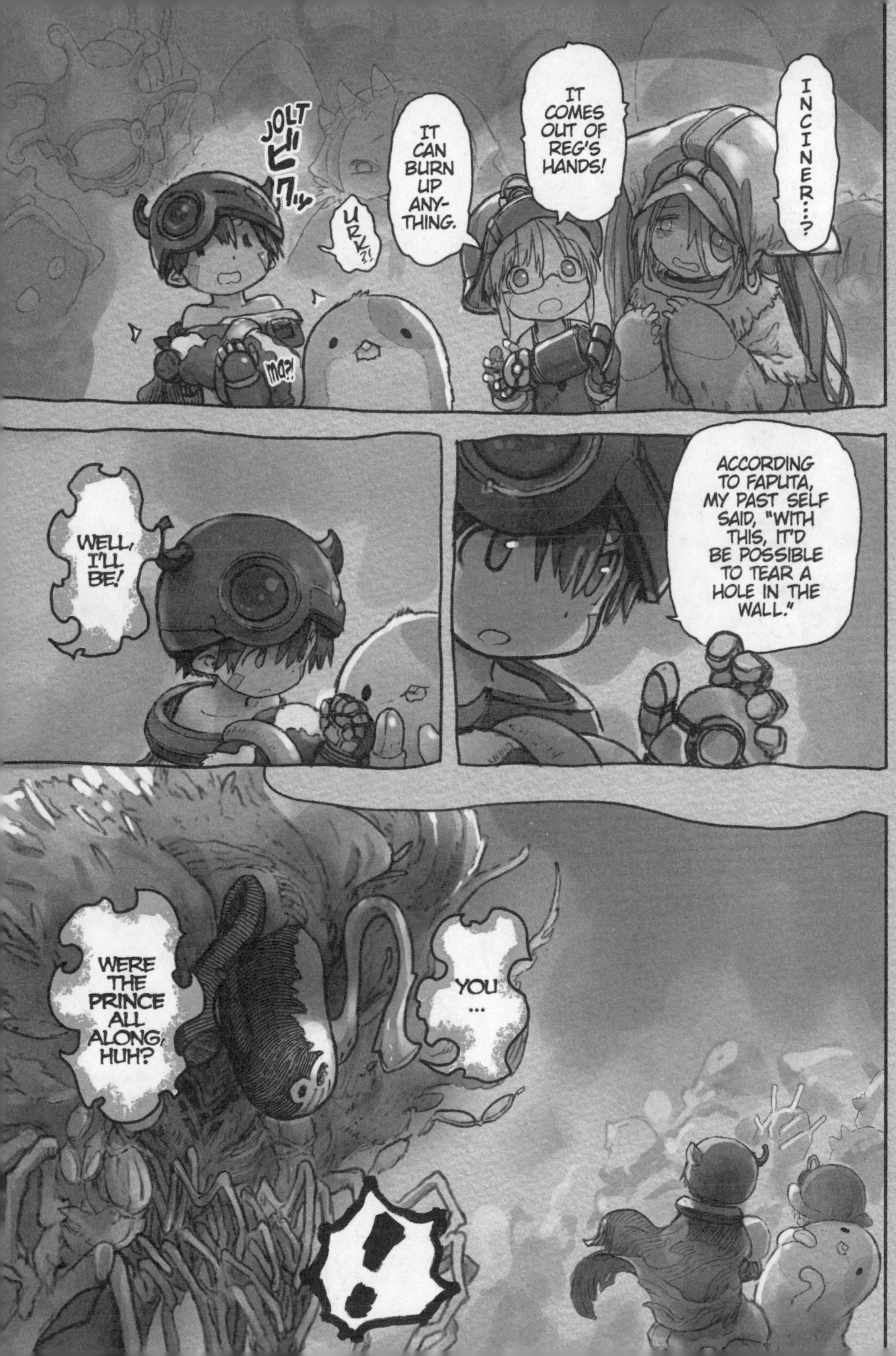
INCINER...?
IT COMES OUT OF REG'S HANDS!
IT CAN BURN UP ANYTHING.
URK?!
JOLT
ma?!
ACCORDING TO FAPUTA, MY PAST SELF SAID, "WITH THIS, IT'D BE POSSIBLE TO TEAR A HOLE IN THE WALL."
WELL, I'LL BE!
YOU ...
WERE THE PRINCE ALL ALONG, HUH?
!

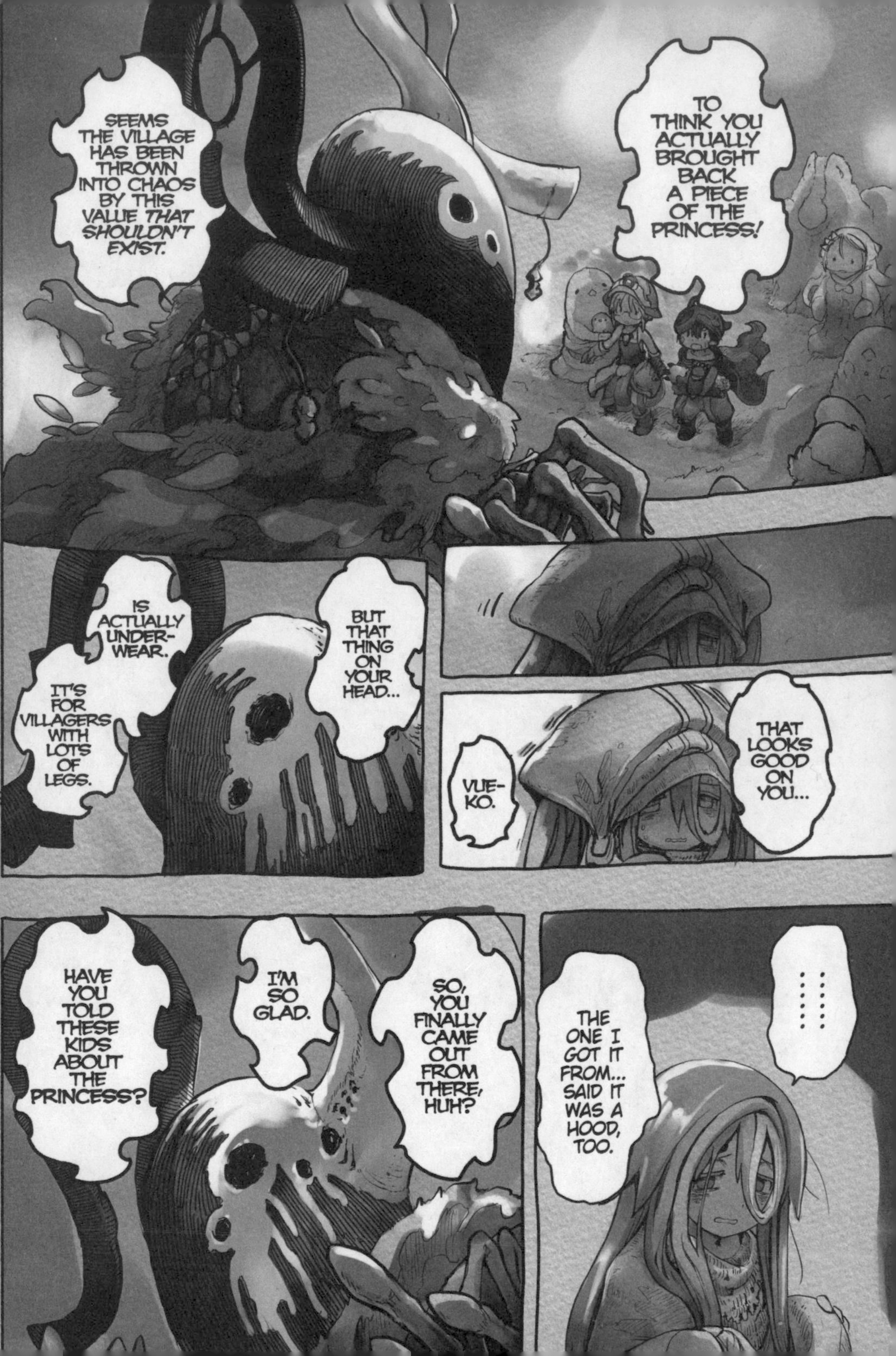
TO THINK YOU ACTUALLY BROUGHT BACK A PIECE OF THE PRINCESS!
SEEMS THE VILLAGE HAS BEEN THROWN INTO CHAOS BY THIS VALUE *THAT SHOULDN'T EXIST.*
THAT LOOKS GOOD ON YOU...
VUE-KO.
BUT THAT THING ON YOUR HEAD...
IS ACTUALLY UNDER-WEAR.
IT'S FOR VILLAGERS WITH LOTS OF LEGS.
......
THE ONE I GOT IT FROM... SAID IT WAS A HOOD, TOO.
SO, YOU FINALLY CAME OUT FROM THERE, HUH?
I'M SO GLAD.
HAVE YOU TOLD THESE KIDS ABOUT THE PRINCESS?

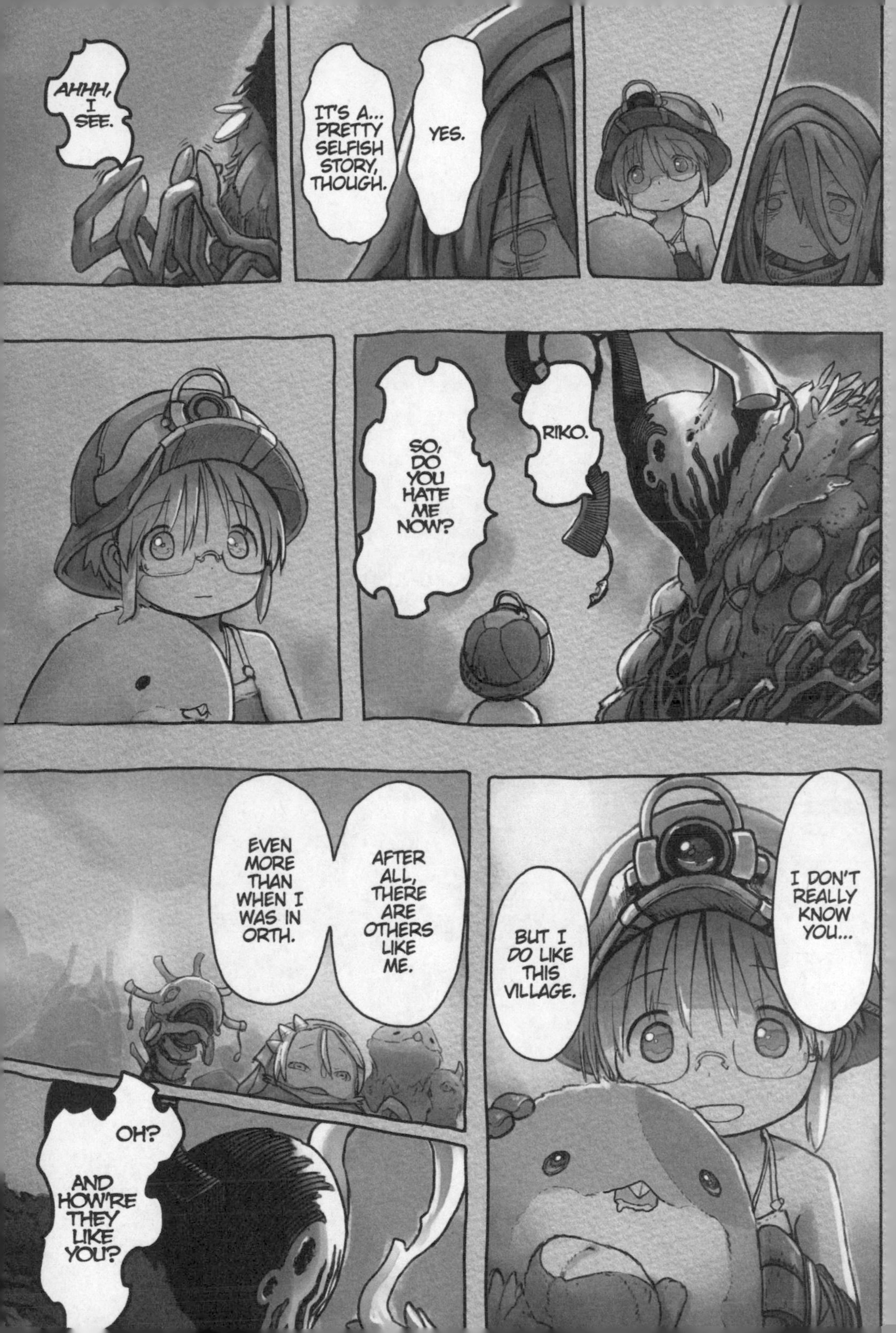
YES.
IT'S A... PRETTY SELFISH STORY, THOUGH.
AHHH, I SEE.
RIKO.
SO, DO YOU HATE ME NOW?
I DON'T REALLY KNOW YOU...
BUT I DO LIKE THIS VILLAGE.
AFTER ALL, THERE ARE OTHERS LIKE ME.
EVEN MORE THAN WHEN I WAS IN ORTH.
OH?
AND HOW'RE THEY LIKE YOU?

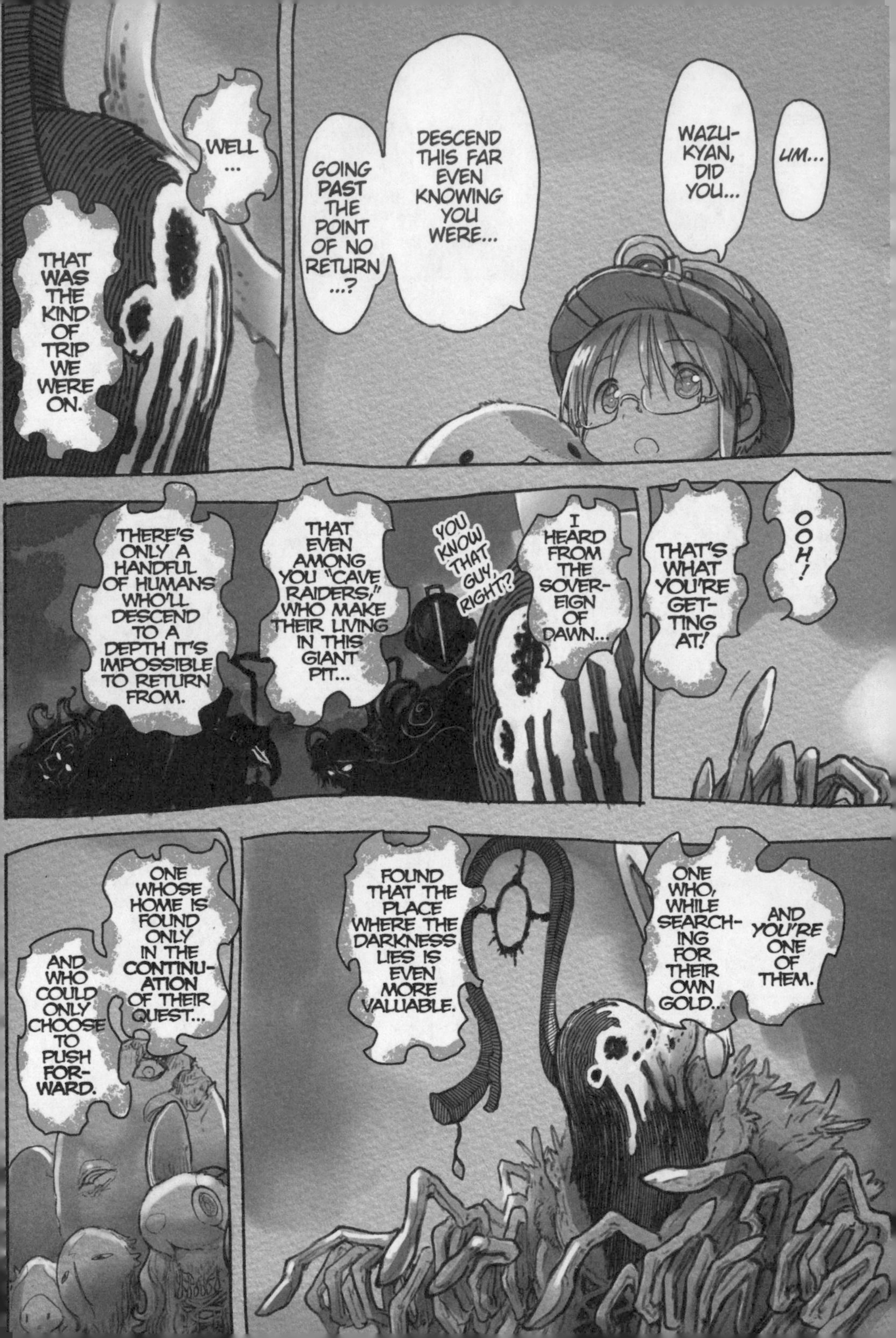
UM...
WAZU-KYAN, DID YOU...
DESCEND THIS FAR EVEN KNOWING YOU WERE...
GOING PAST THE POINT OF NO RETURN ...?
WELL ...
THAT WAS THE KIND OF TRIP WE WERE ON.
OOH!
THAT'S WHAT YOU'RE GETTING AT!
I HEARD FROM THE SOVEREIGN OF DAWN...
YOU KNOW THAT GUY, RIGHT?
THAT EVEN AMONG YOU "CAVE RAIDERS," WHO MAKE THEIR LIVING IN THIS GIANT PIT...
THERE'S ONLY A HANDFUL OF HUMANS WHO'LL DESCEND TO A DEPTH IT'S IMPOSSIBLE TO RETURN FROM.
AND YOU'RE ONE OF THEM.
ONE WHO, WHILE SEARCHING FOR THEIR OWN GOLD...
FOUND THAT THE PLACE WHERE THE DARKNESS LIES IS EVEN MORE VALUABLE.
ONE WHOSE HOME IS FOUND ONLY IN THE CONTINUATION OF THEIR QUEST...
AND WHO COULD ONLY CHOOSE TO PUSH FORWARD.

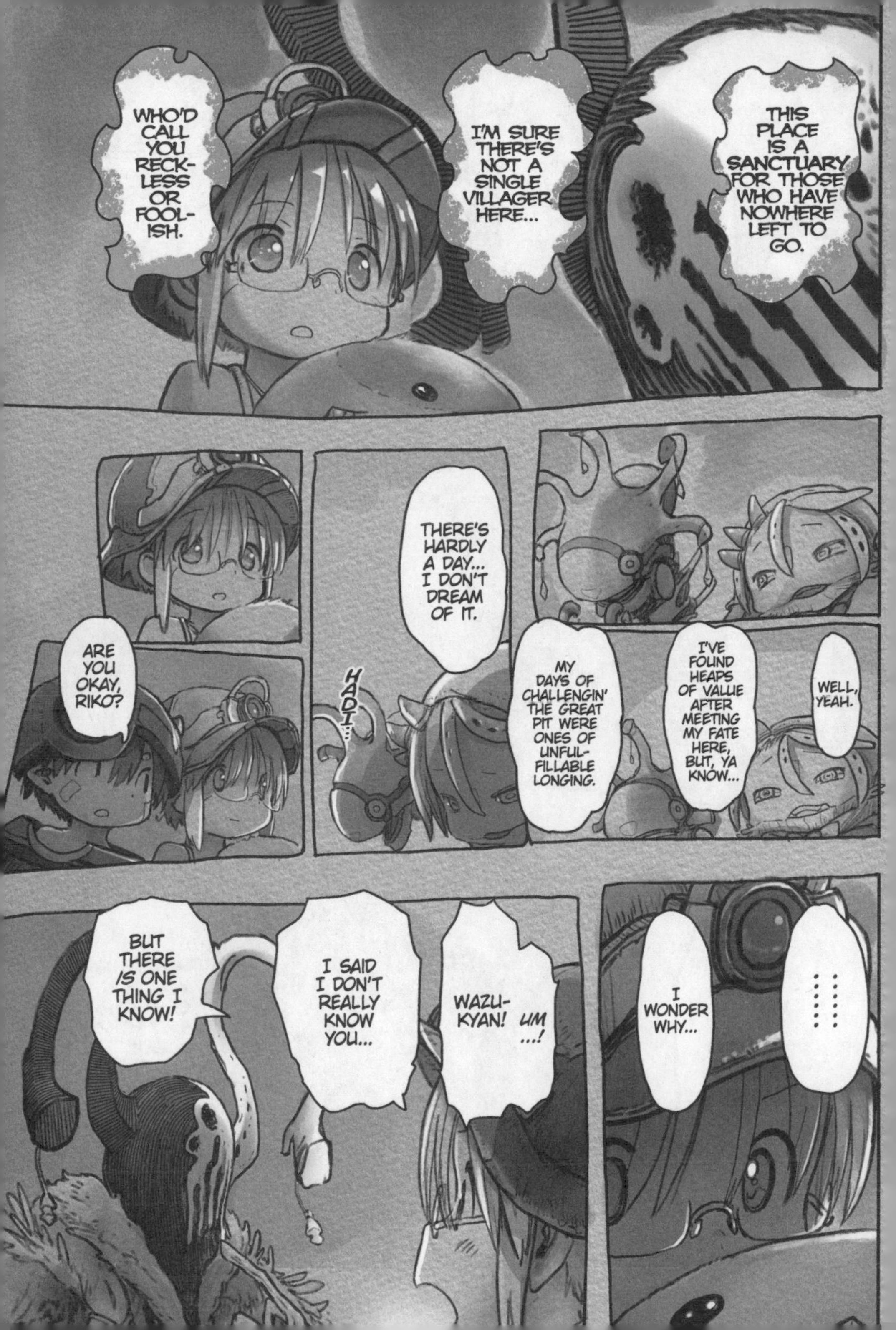
THIS PLACE IS A SANCTUARY FOR THOSE WHO HAVE NOWHERE LEFT TO GO.
I'M SURE THERE'S NOT A SINGLE VILLAGER HERE...
WHO'D CALL YOU RECKLESS OR FOOLISH.
WELL, YEAH.
I'VE FOUND HEAPS OF VALUE AFTER MEETING MY FATE HERE, BUT, YA KNOW...
MY DAYS OF CHALLENGIN' THE GREAT PIT WERE ONES OF UNFULFILLABLE LONGING.
THERE'S HARDLY A DAY... I DON'T DREAM OF IT.
HADI...
ARE YOU OKAY, RIKO?
......
I WONDER WHY...
UM...!
WAZU-KYAN!
I SAID I DON'T REALLY KNOW YOU...
BUT THERE IS ONE THING I KNOW!

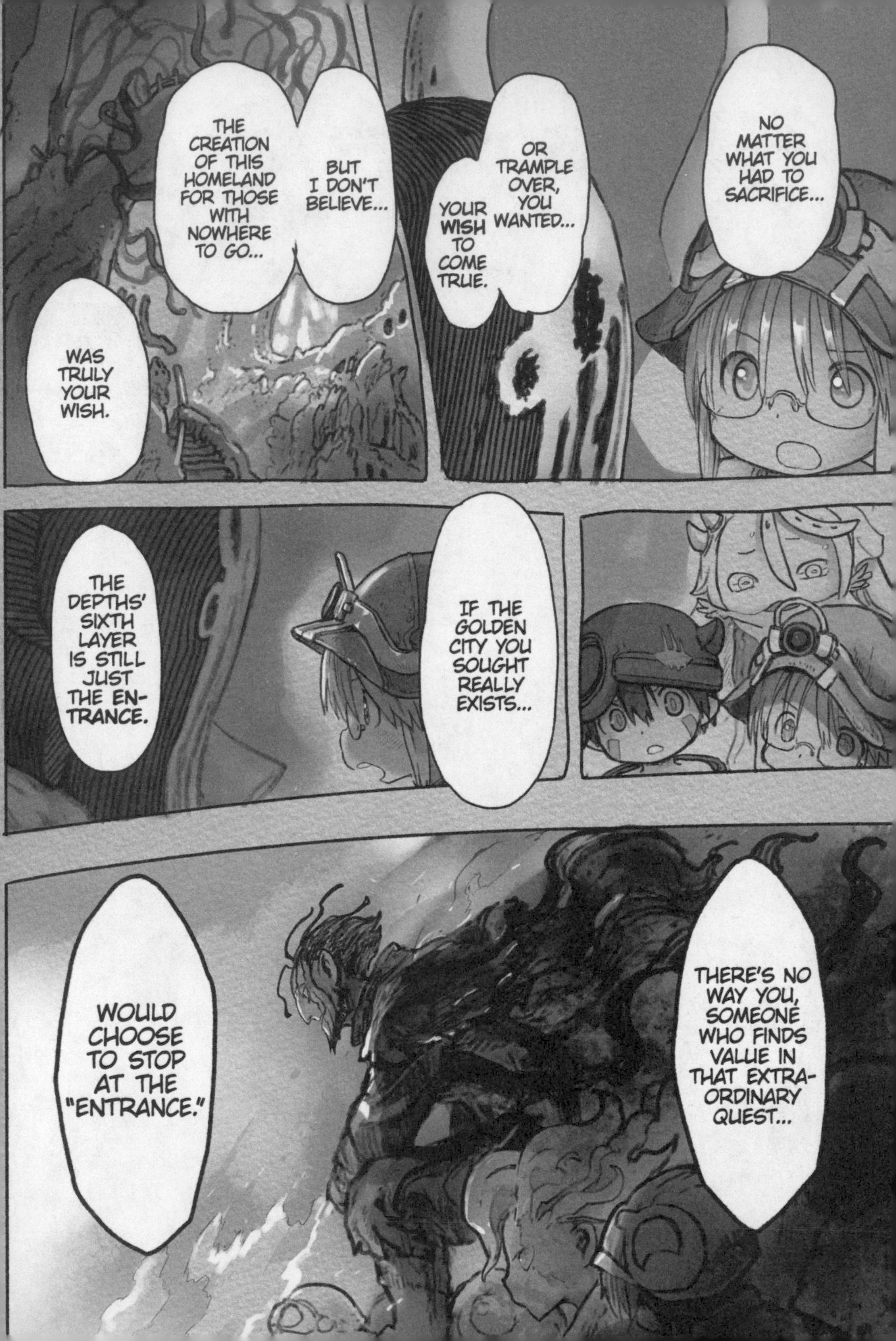
NO MATTER WHAT YOU HAD TO SACRIFICE...
OR TRAMPLE OVER, YOU WANTED...
YOUR WISH TO COME TRUE.
BUT I DON'T BELIEVE...
THE CREATION OF THIS HOMELAND FOR THOSE WITH NOWHERE TO GO...
WAS TRULY YOUR WISH.
IF THE GOLDEN CITY YOU SOUGHT REALLY EXISTS...
THE DEPTHS' SIXTH LAYER IS STILL JUST THE ENTRANCE.
THERE'S NO WAY YOU, SOMEONE WHO FINDS VALUE IN THAT EXTRA-ORDINARY QUEST...
WOULD CHOOSE TO STOP AT THE "ENTRANCE."

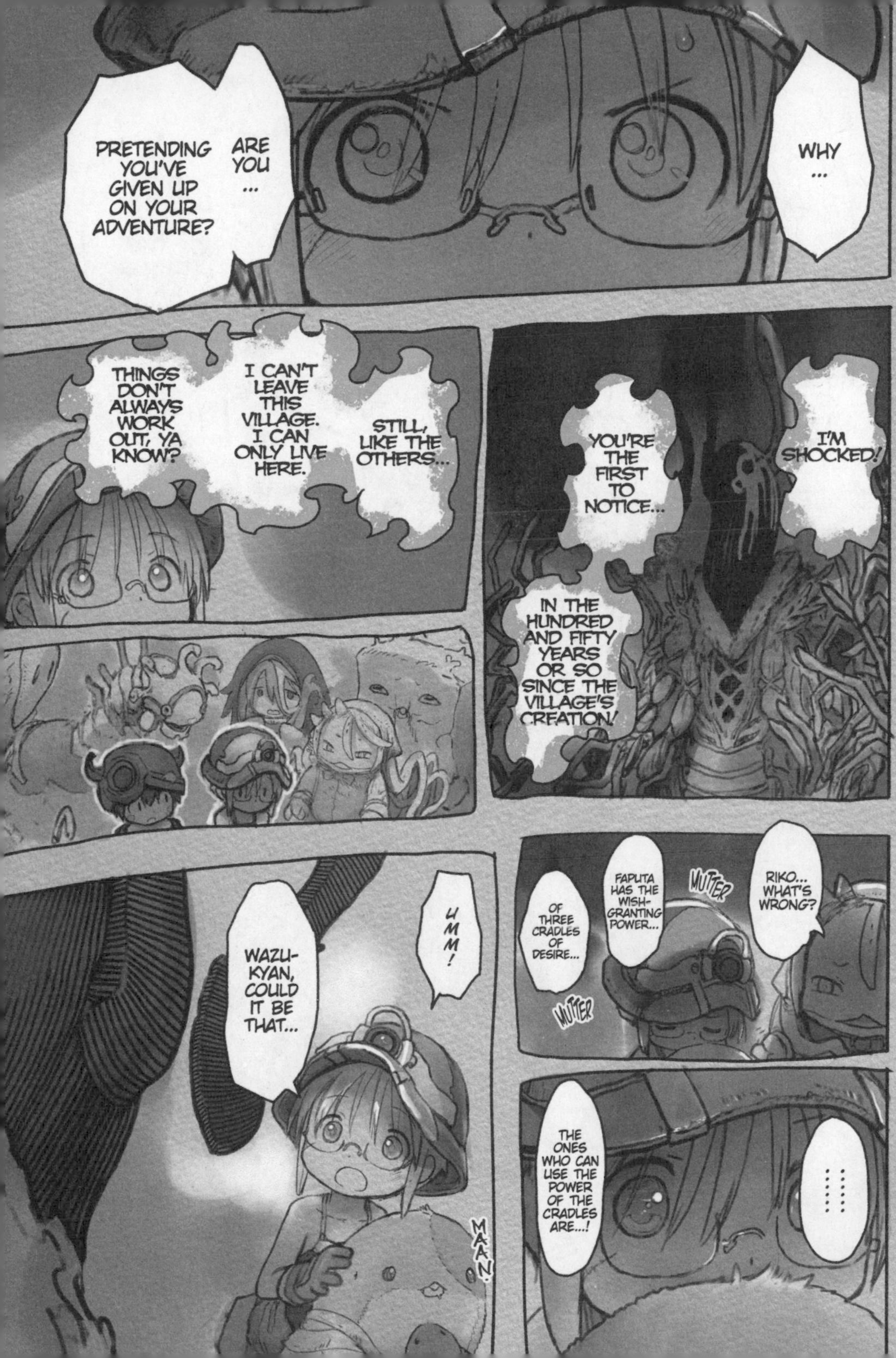
WHY ...
ARE YOU ...
PRETENDING YOU'VE GIVEN UP ON YOUR ADVENTURE?
I'M SHOCKED!
YOU'RE THE FIRST TO NOTICE...
IN THE HUNDRED AND FIFTY YEARS OR SO SINCE THE VILLAGE'S CREATION!
STILL, LIKE THE OTHERS...
I CAN'T LEAVE THIS VILLAGE. I CAN ONLY LIVE HERE.
THINGS DON'T ALWAYS WORK OUT, YA KNOW?
RIKO... WHAT'S WRONG?
MUTTER
FAPUTA HAS THE WISH-GRANTING POWER...
OF THREE CRADLES OF DESIRE...
MUTTER
......
THE ONES WHO CAN USE THE POWER OF THE CRADLES ARE...!
UMM!
WAZU-KYAN, COULD IT BE THAT...
MAAN.

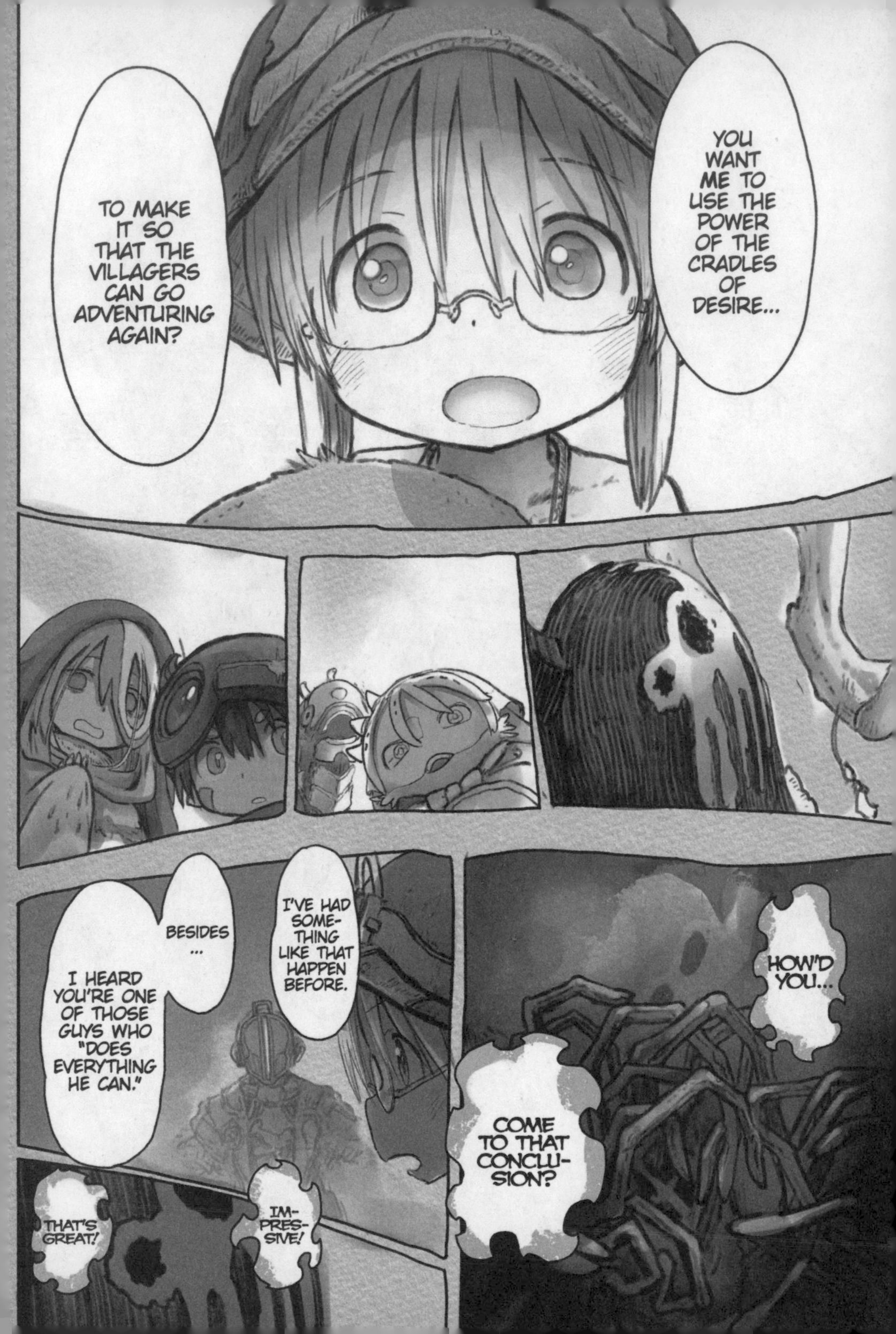
YOU WANT ME TO USE THE POWER OF THE CRADLES OF DESIRE...
TO MAKE IT SO THAT THE VILLAGERS CAN GO ADVENTURING AGAIN?
HOW'D YOU...
COME TO THAT CONCLU-SION?
I'VE HAD SOME-THING LIKE THAT HAPPEN BEFORE.
BESIDES ...
I HEARD YOU'RE ONE OF THOSE GUYS WHO "DOES EVERYTHING HE CAN."
IM-PRES-SIVE!
THAT'S GREAT!

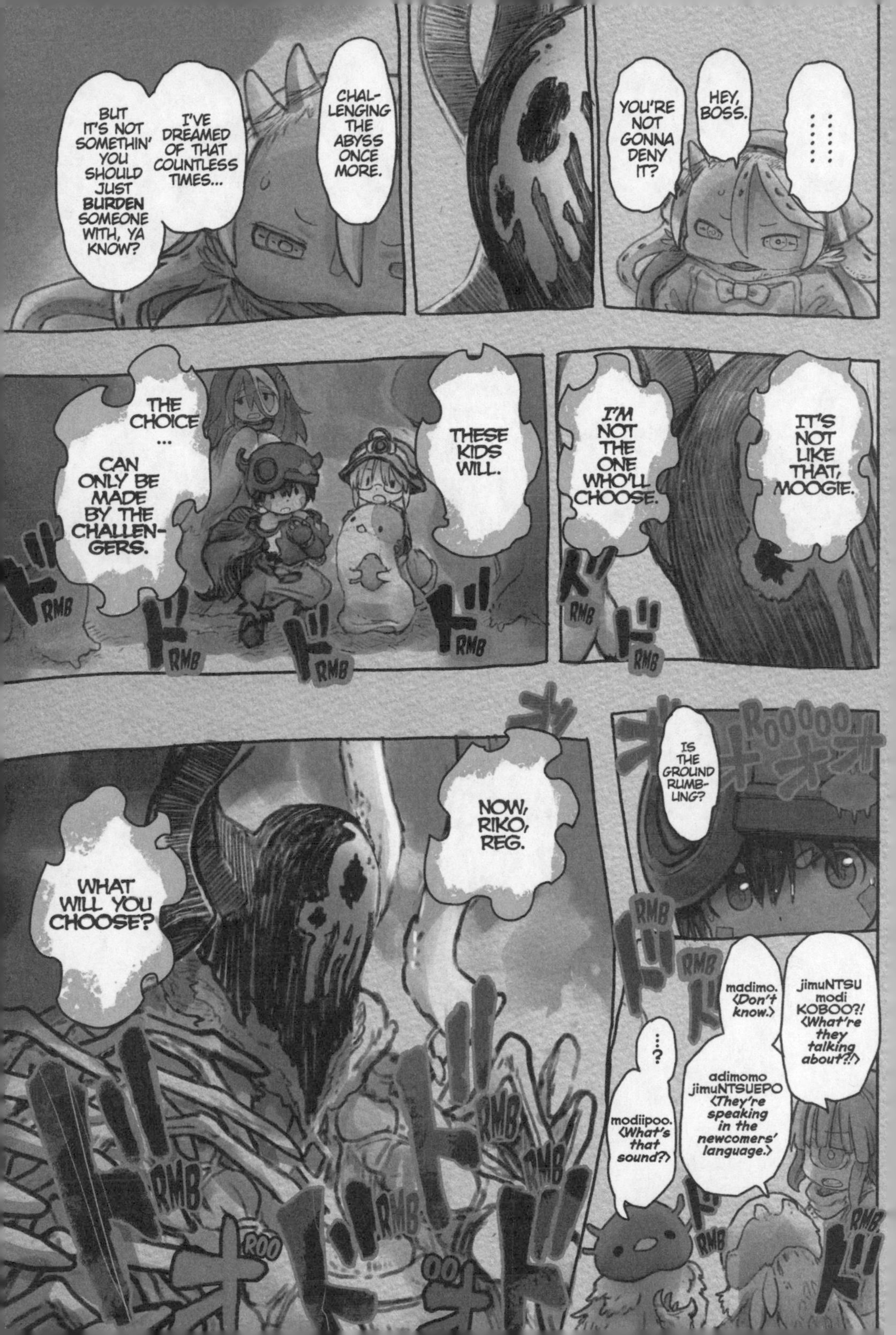
......
HEY, BOSS.
YOU'RE NOT GONNA DENY IT?
CHAL-LENGING THE ABYSS ONCE MORE.
I'VE DREAMED OF THAT COUNTLESS TIMES...
BUT IT'S NOT SOMETHIN' YOU SHOULD JUST **BURDEN** SOMEONE WITH, YA KNOW?
IT'S NOT LIKE THAT, MOOGIE.
I'M NOT THE ONE WHO'LL CHOOSE.
RMB
RMB
THESE KIDS WILL.
THE CHOICE ...
CAN ONLY BE MADE BY THE CHALLEN-GERS.
RMB
RMB
RMB
RMB
ROOOOO
IS THE GROUND RUMB-LING?
RMB
jimuNTSU modi KOBOO?! ⟨*What're they talking about?!*⟩
madimo. ⟨*Don't know.*⟩
adimomo jimuNTSUEPO ⟨*They're speaking in the newcomers' language.*⟩
...?
modiipoo. ⟨*What's that sound?*⟩
RMB
RMB
RMB
NOW, RIKO, REG.
WHAT WILL YOU CHOOSE?
RMB
RMB
RMB
RMB
ROO
OO

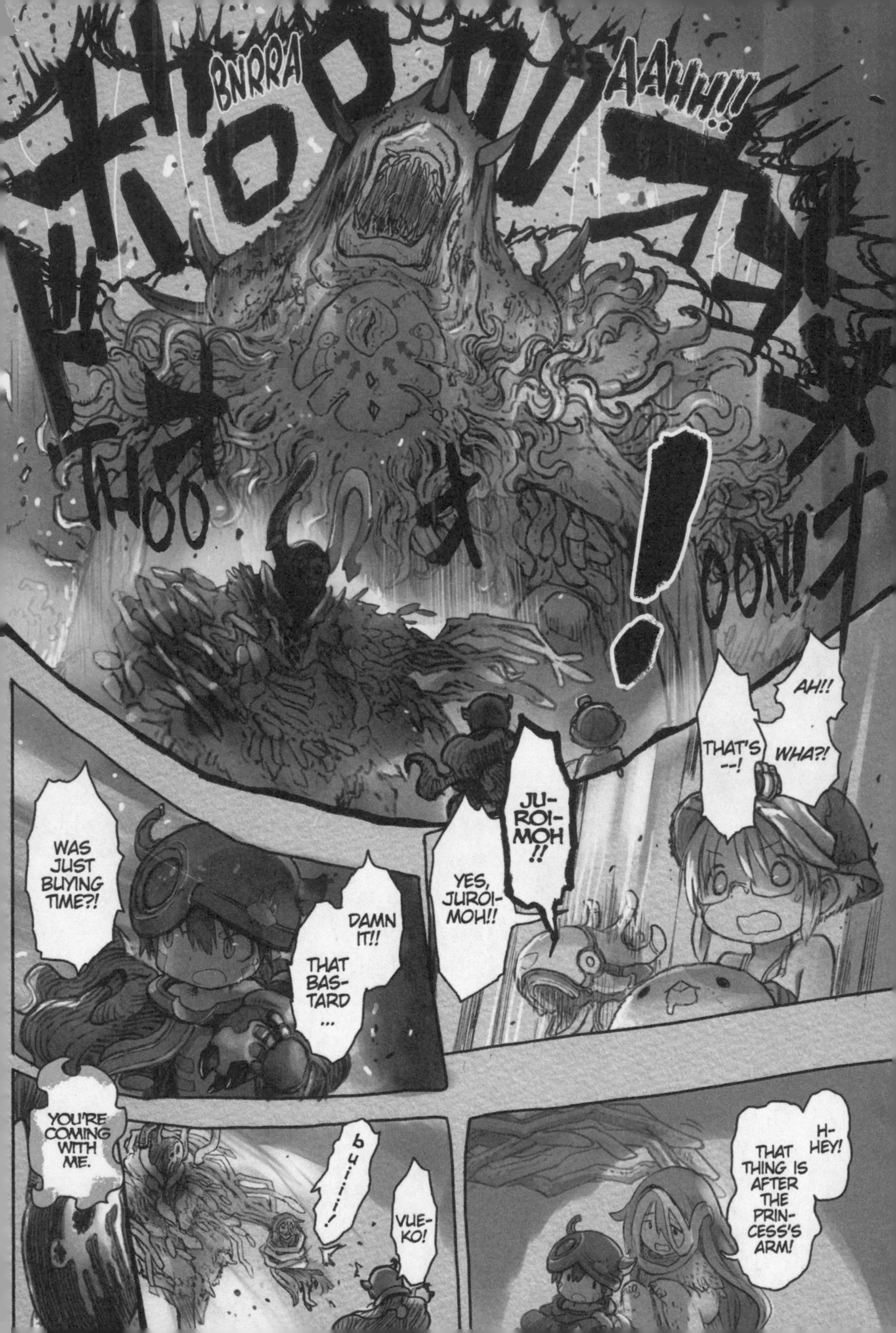

AAHH!!
BNRRA
OON!
THOO
AH!!
WHA?!
THAT'S --!
JUROI-MOH!!
YES, JUROI-MOH!!
DAMN IT!!
THAT BASTARD ...
WAS JUST BUYING TIME?!
H-HEY!
THAT THING IS AFTER THE PRINCESS'S ARM!
VUEKO!
YOU'RE COMING WITH ME.

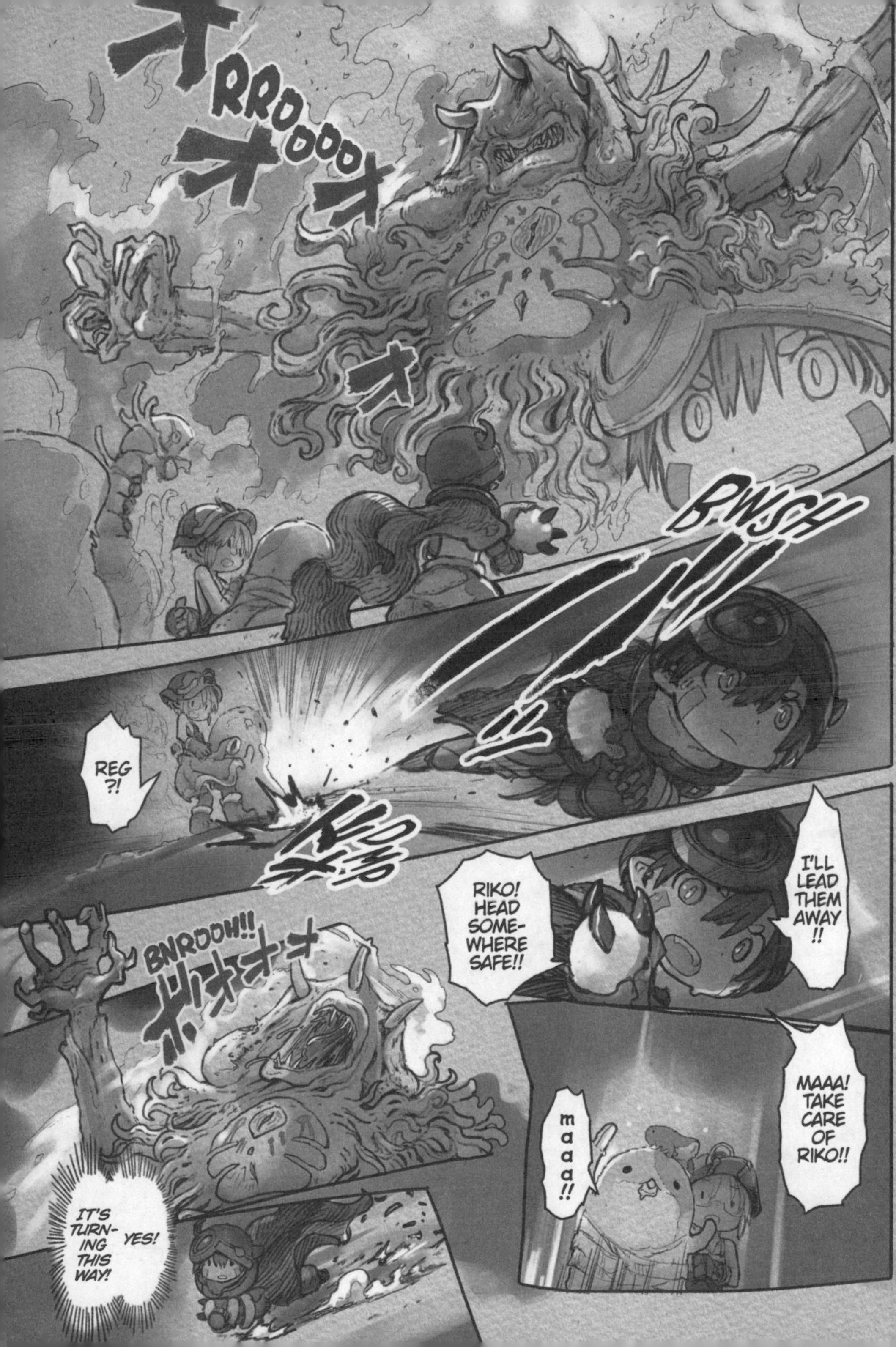
RROOOO
BWSH
REG ?!
I'LL LEAD THEM AWAY!!
RIKO! HEAD SOMEWHERE SAFE!!
BNROOH!!
MAAA! TAKE CARE OF RIKO!!
maaa!!
YES!
IT'S TURNING THIS WAY!

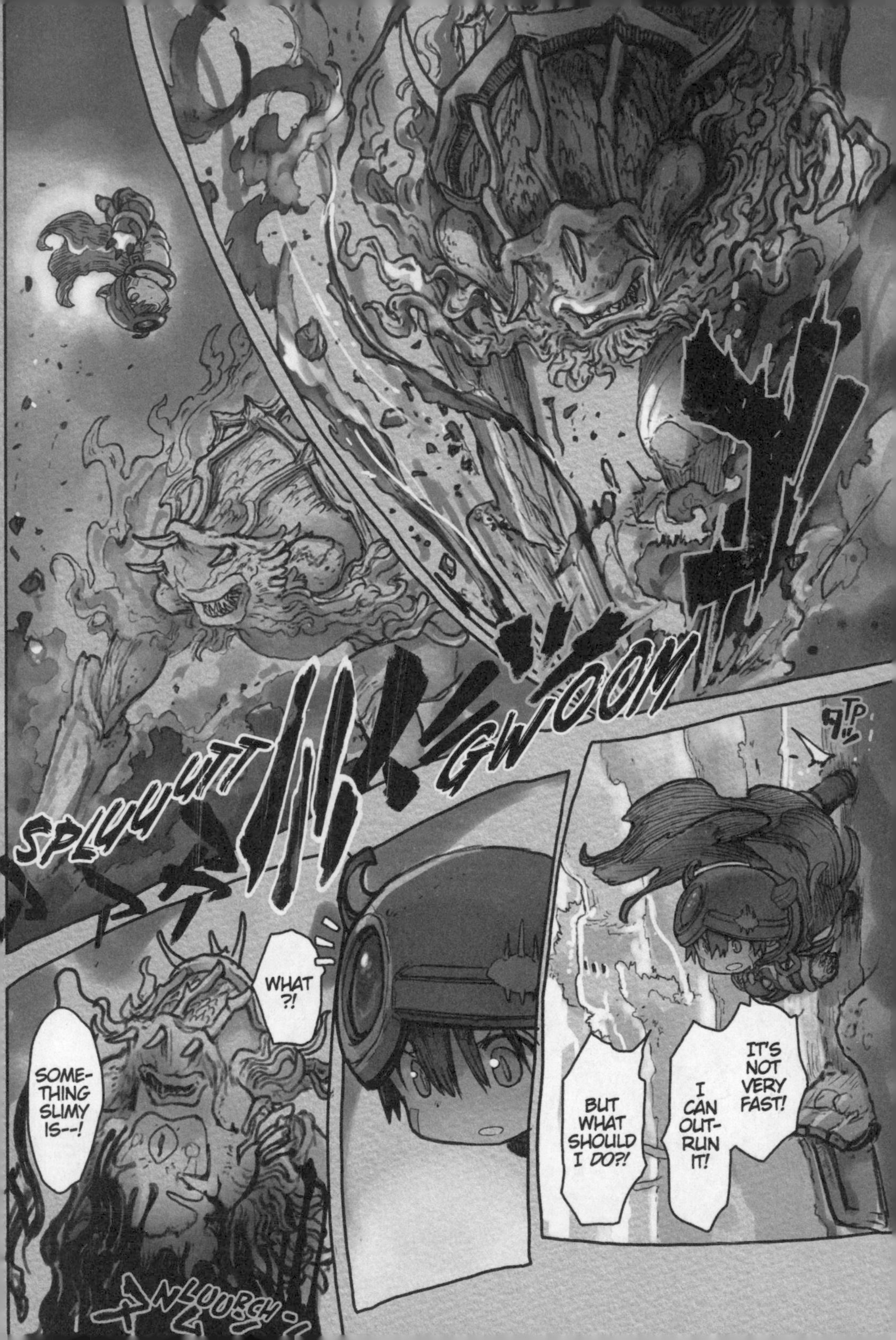
GWOOM
SPLUUUTT
TP
IT'S NOT VERY FAST!
I CAN OUT-RUN IT!
BUT WHAT SHOULD I DO?!
WHAT ?!
SOME-THING SLIMY IS--!

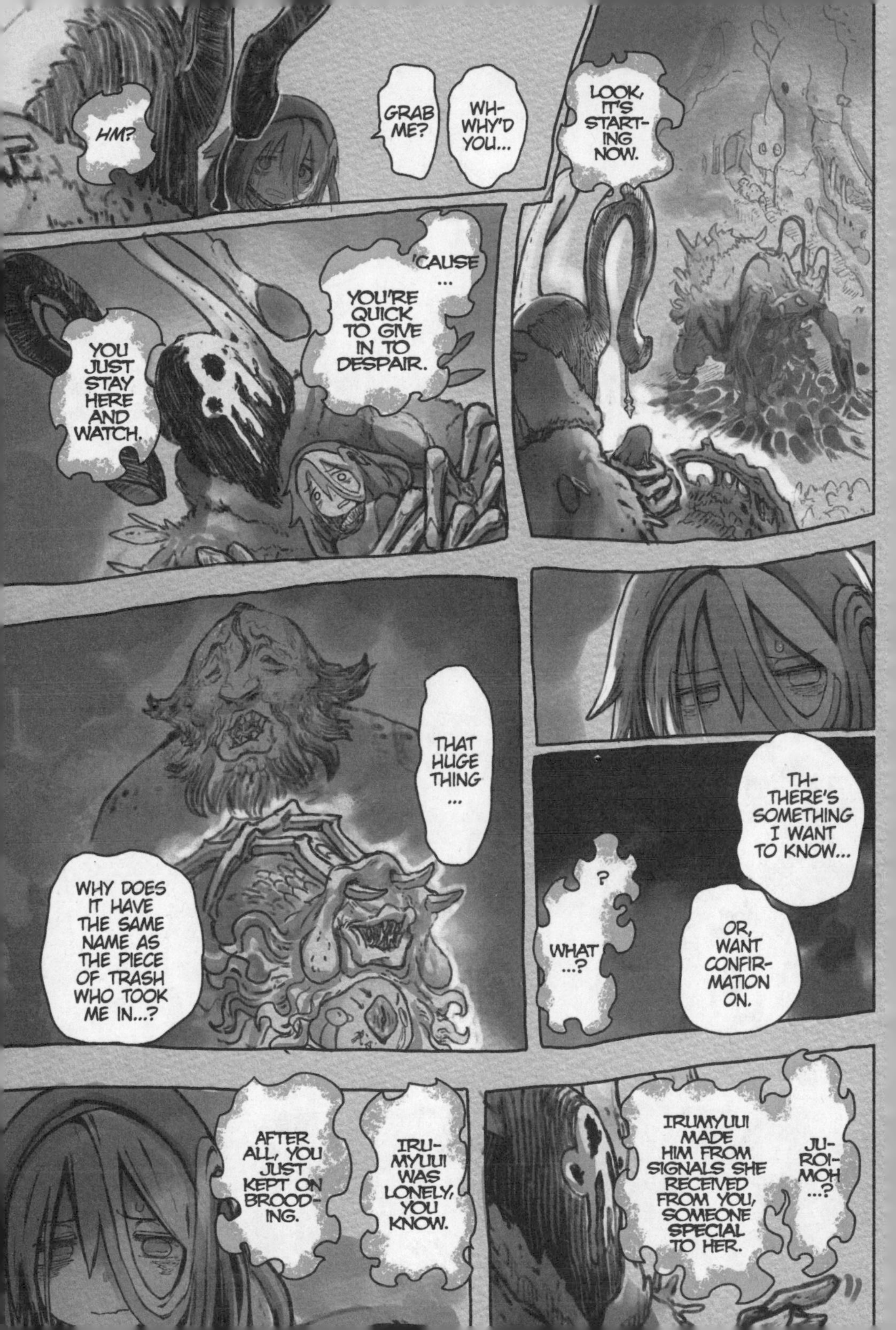
LOOK, IT'S STARTING NOW.
WH-WHY'D YOU...
GRAB ME?
HM?
'CAUSE...
YOU'RE QUICK TO GIVE IN TO DESPAIR.
YOU JUST STAY HERE AND WATCH.
TH-THERE'S SOMETHING I WANT TO KNOW...
OR, WANT CONFIRMATION ON.
?
WHAT...?
THAT HUGE THING...
WHY DOES IT HAVE THE SAME NAME AS THE PIECE OF TRASH WHO TOOK ME IN...?
JU-ROI-MOH...?
IRUMYUUI MADE HIM FROM SIGNALS SHE RECEIVED FROM YOU, SOMEONE SPECIAL TO HER.
IRU-MYUUI WAS LONELY, YOU KNOW.
AFTER ALL, YOU JUST KEPT ON BROODING.

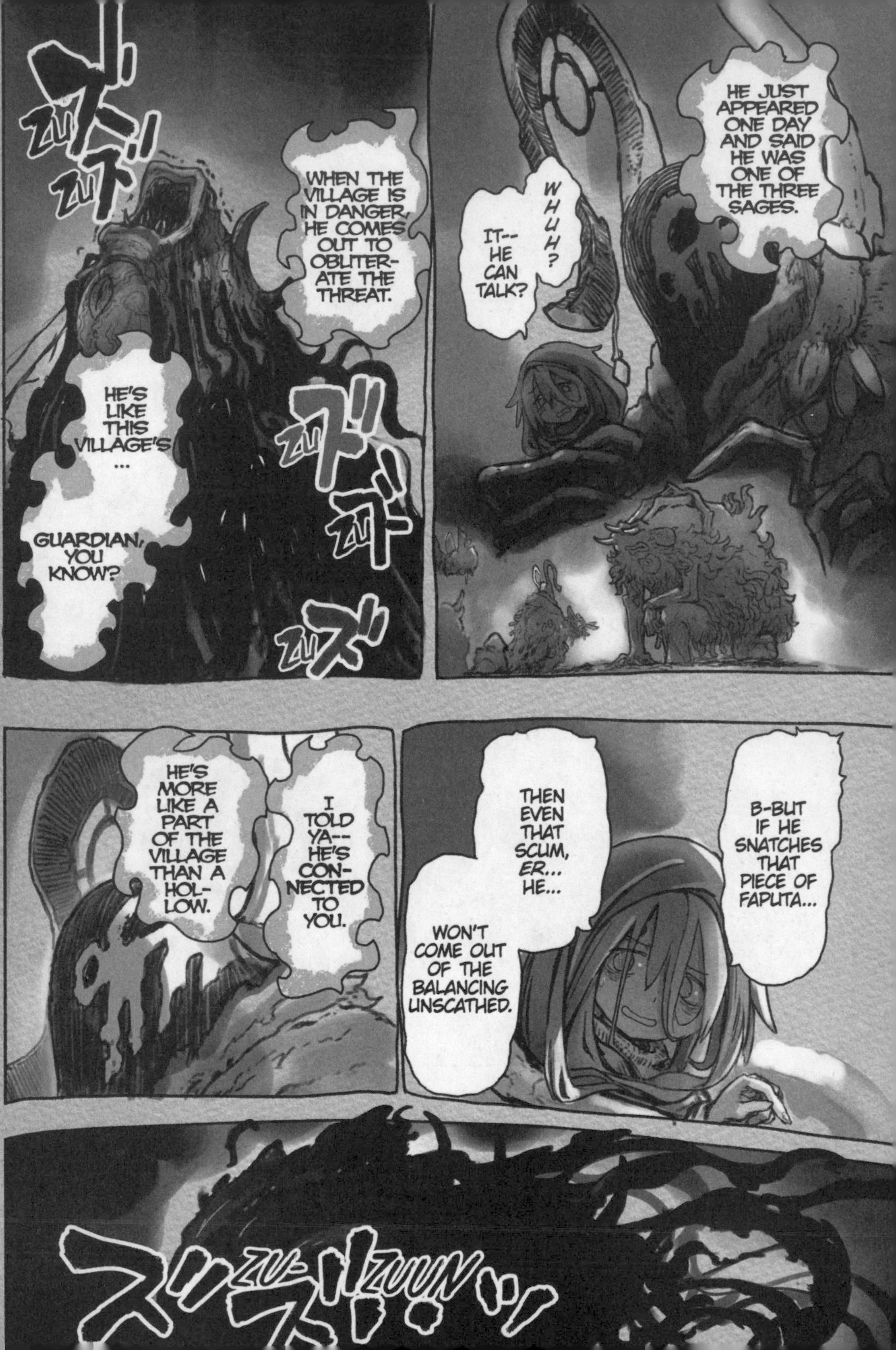
HE JUST APPEARED ONE DAY AND SAID HE WAS ONE OF THE THREE SAGES.
WHUH?
IT-- HE CAN TALK?
ZU ZU
WHEN THE VILLAGE IS IN DANGER, HE COMES OUT TO OBLITERATE THE THREAT.
HE'S LIKE THIS VILLAGE'S ...
GUARDIAN, YOU KNOW?
ZU ZU ZU
B-BUT IF HE SNATCHES THAT PIECE OF FAPUTA...
THEN EVEN THAT SCUM, ER... HE...
WON'T COME OUT OF THE BALANCING UNSCATHED.
I TOLD YA-- HE'S CONNECTED TO YOU.
HE'S MORE LIKE A PART OF THE VILLAGE THAN A HOL-LOW.
ZU-ZUUN

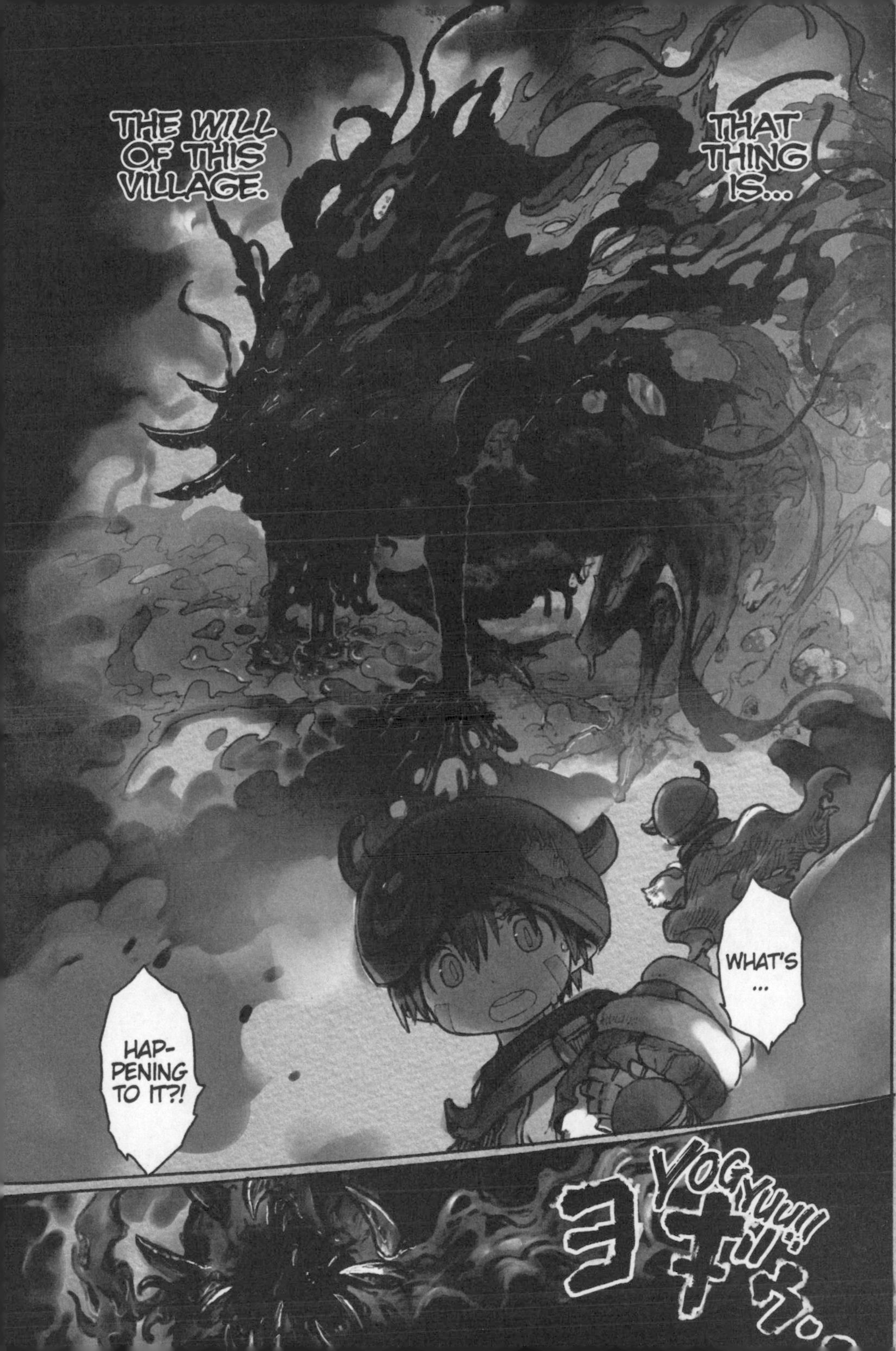
THAT THING IS...
THE WILL OF THIS VILLAGE.
WHAT'S ...
HAP-PENING TO IT?!
YOGYUU!!
ヨギュ...

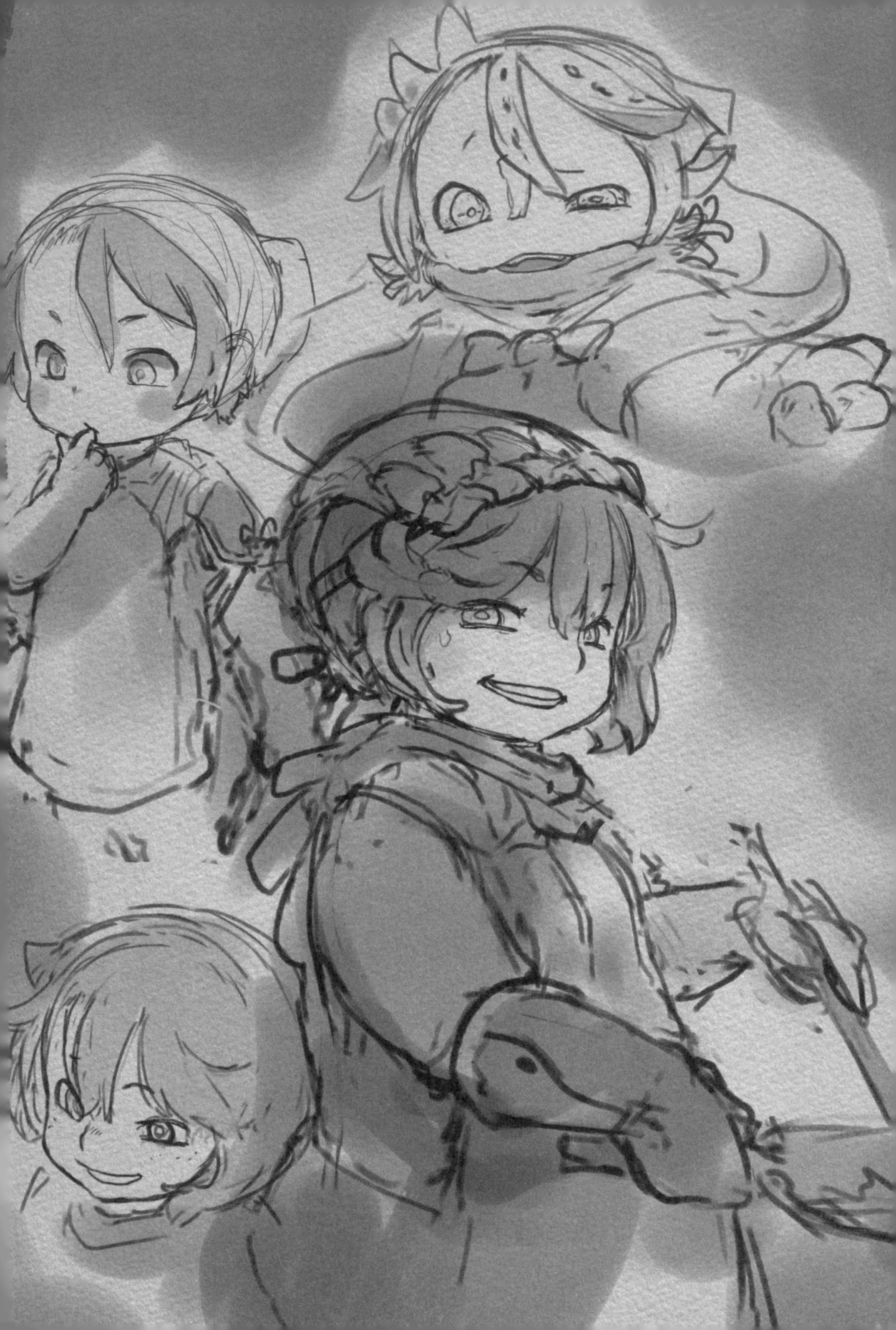

MADE IN ABYSS

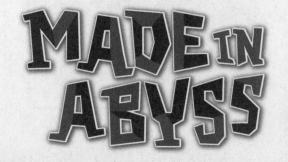

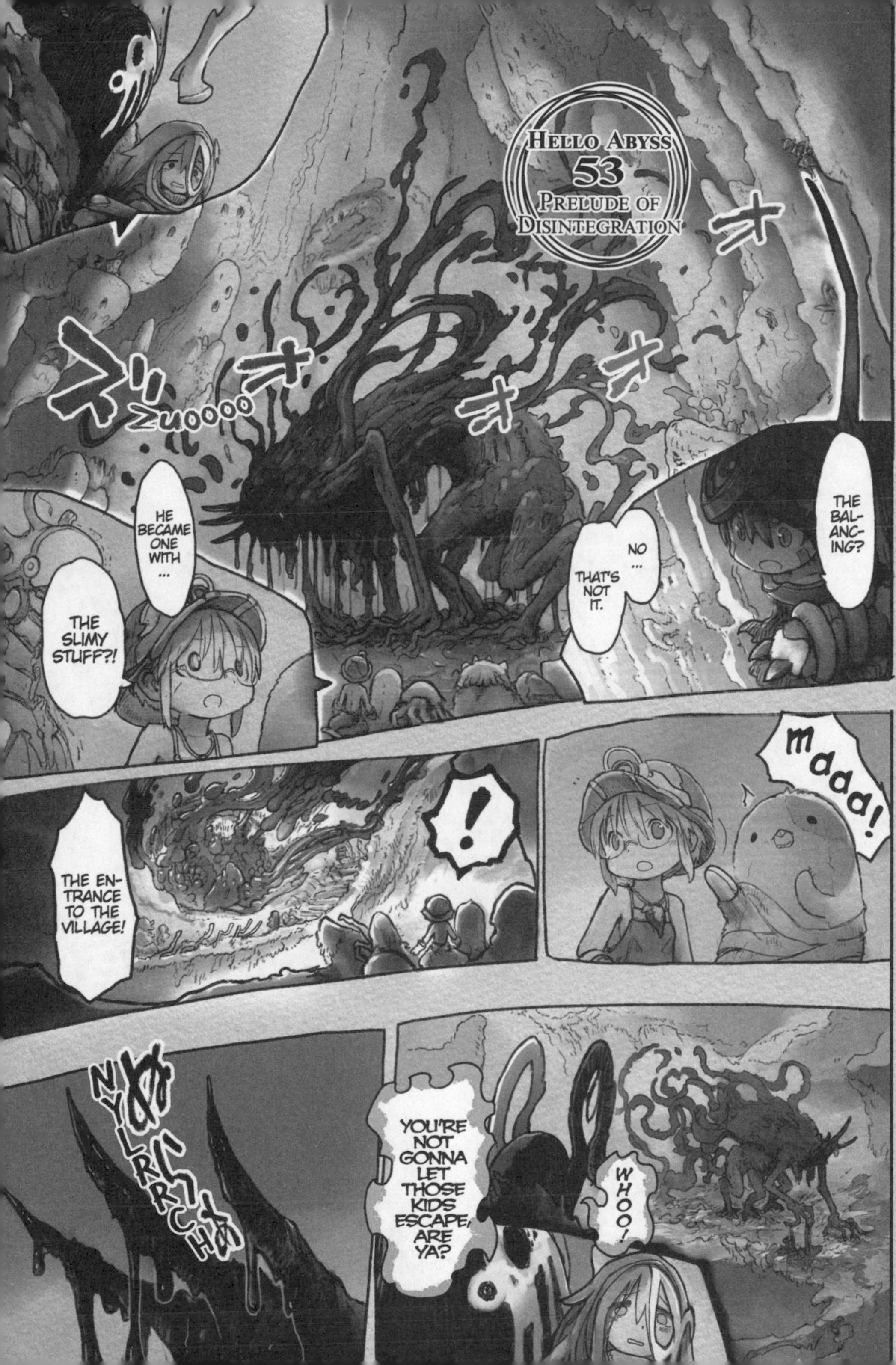
HELLO ABYSS
53
PRELUDE OF DISINTEGRATION
ZUOOOO
THE BALANCING?
NO ... THAT'S NOT IT.
HE BECAME ONE WITH ...
THE SLIMY STUFF?!
maaa!
!
THE ENTRANCE TO THE VILLAGE!
WHOO!
YOU'RE NOT GONNA LET THOSE KIDS ESCAPE, ARE YA?
NYLRRRCH

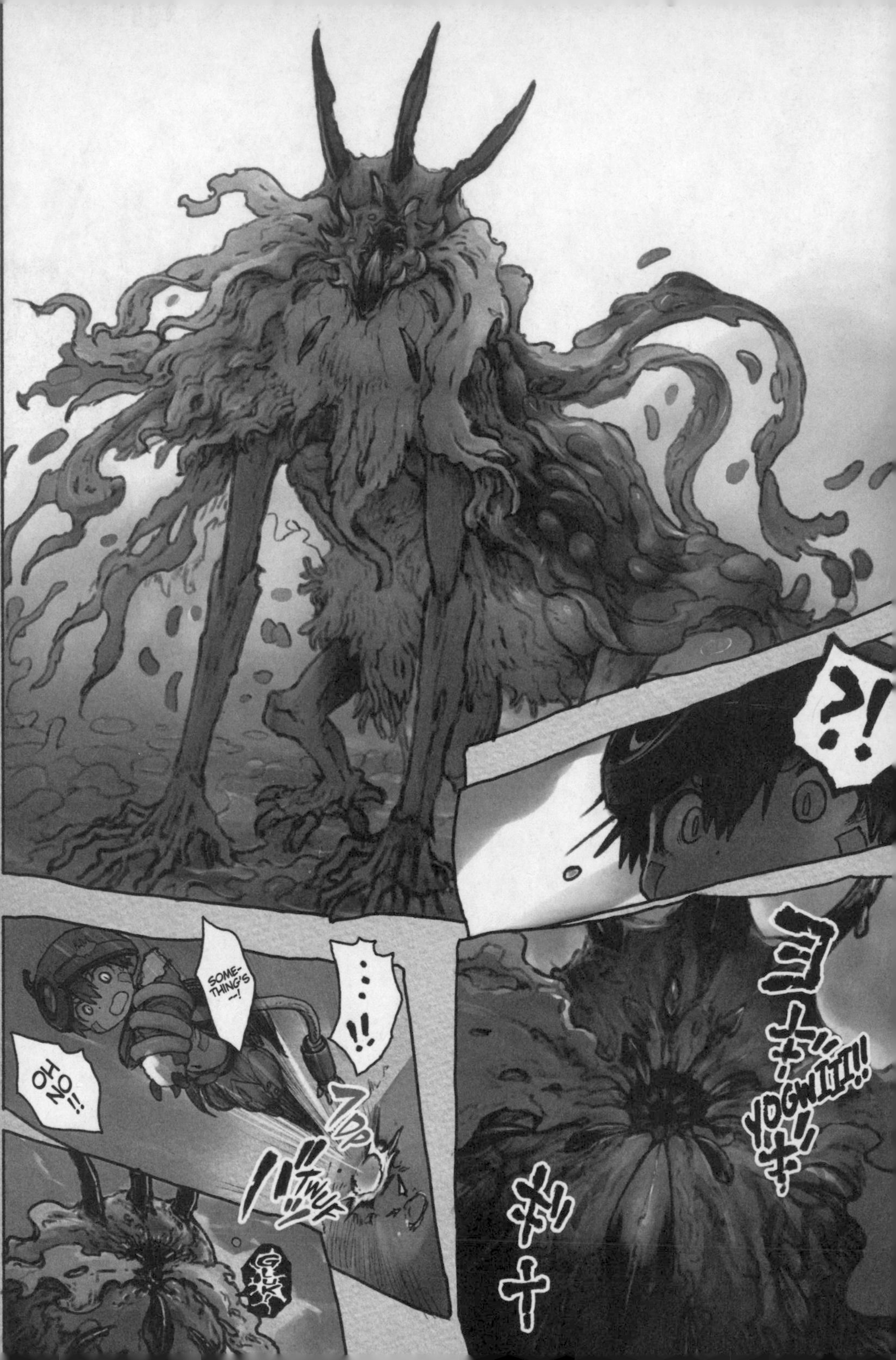

?!
YOGWIIII!!
...!!
SOME-THING'S --!
OH NO!!
ZOOP
THWUP
GLK

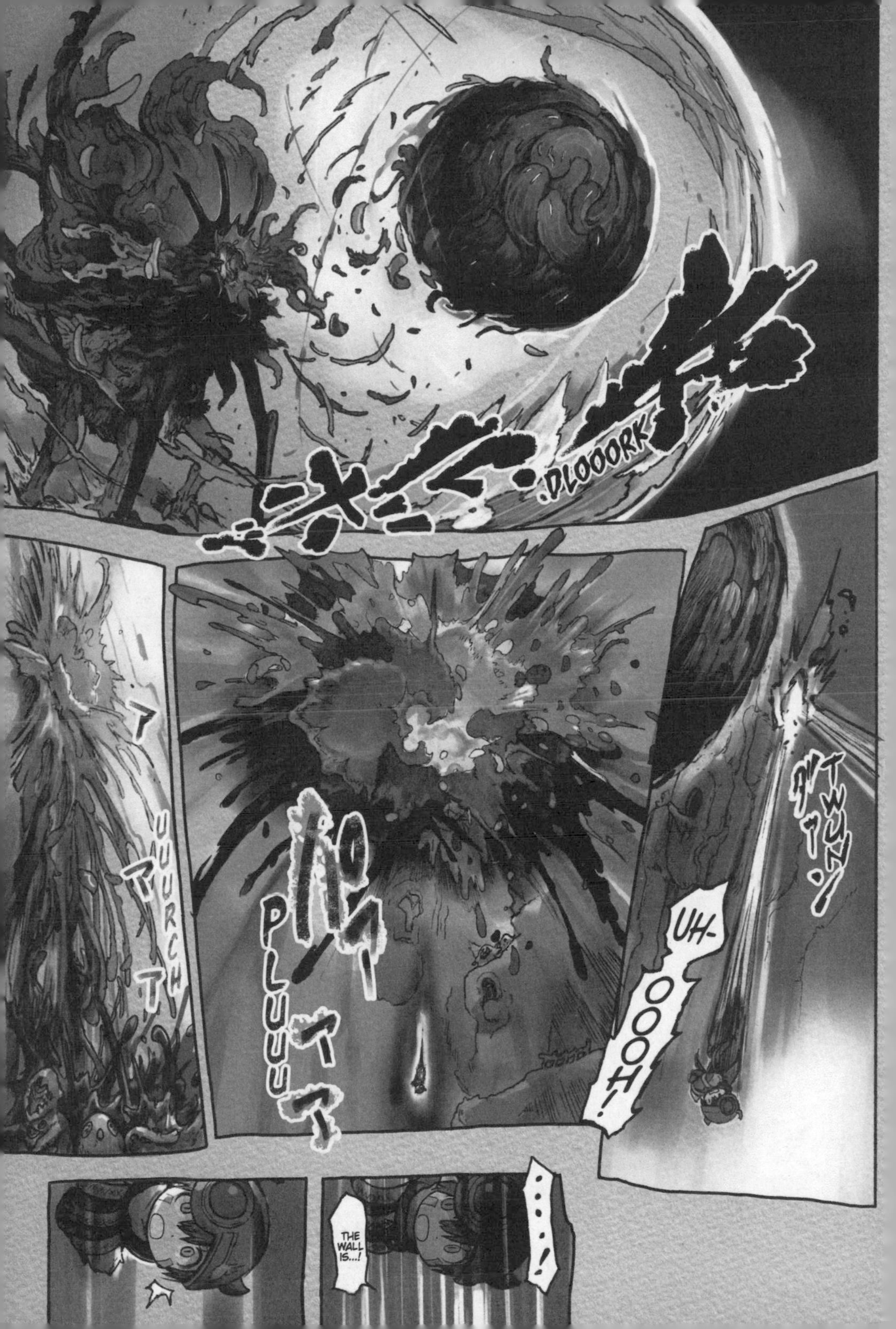

DLOOORK
TWUNK!
UH-OOOOH!
UUURCH
PLUUUU
...!
THE WALL IS...!

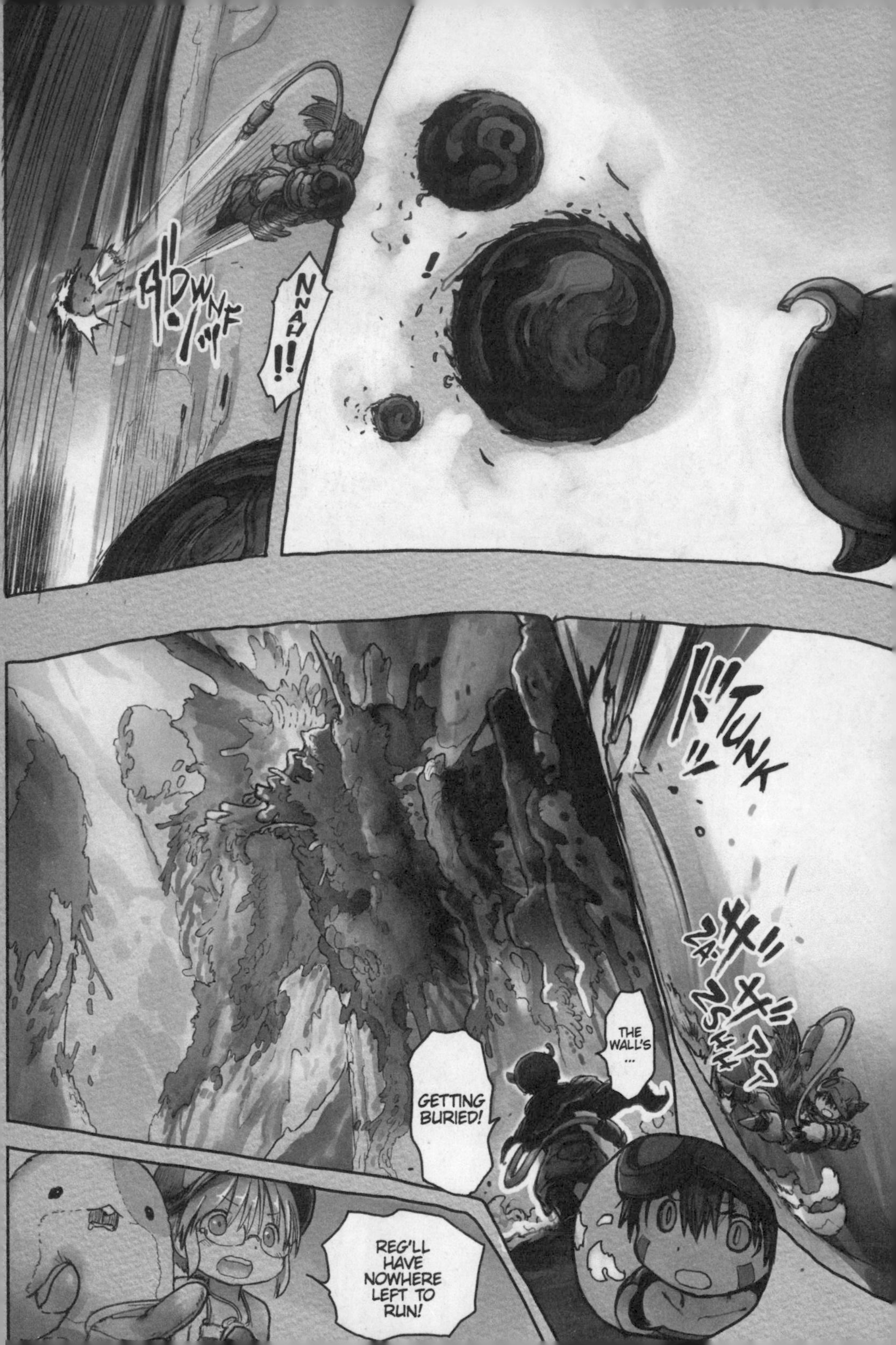
!
NNAH!!
DWNF
TUNK
ZSHHT
THE WALL'S...
GETTING BURIED!
REG'LL HAVE NOWHERE LEFT TO RUN!

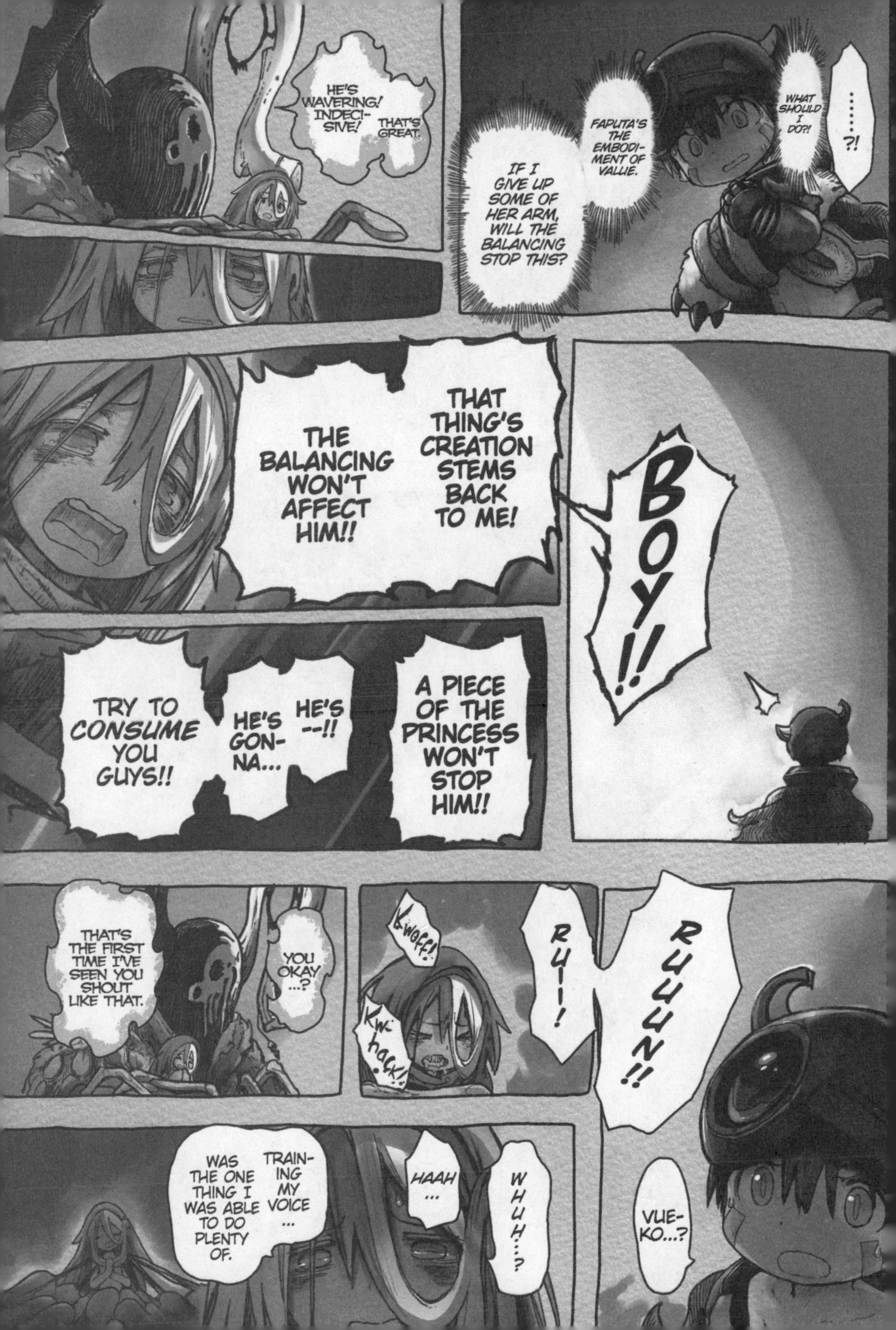

......?!
WHAT SHOULD I DO?!
FAPUTA'S THE EMBODIMENT OF VALUE.
IF I GIVE UP SOME OF HER ARM, WILL THE BALANCING STOP THIS?
HE'S WAVERING! INDECISIVE! THAT'S GREAT.
BOY!!
THAT THING'S CREATION STEMS BACK TO ME!
THE BALANCING WON'T AFFECT HIM!!
A PIECE OF THE PRINCESS WON'T STOP HIM!!
HE'S --!!
HE'S GONNA...
TRY TO CONSUME YOU GUYS!!
RUUUN!!
RU--!
Kwoff!
Kwhack!
YOU OKAY...?
THAT'S THE FIRST TIME I'VE SEEN YOU SHOUT LIKE THAT.
VUEKO...?
WHUH...?
HAAH...
TRAINING MY VOICE...
WAS THE ONE THING I WAS ABLE TO DO PLENTY OF.

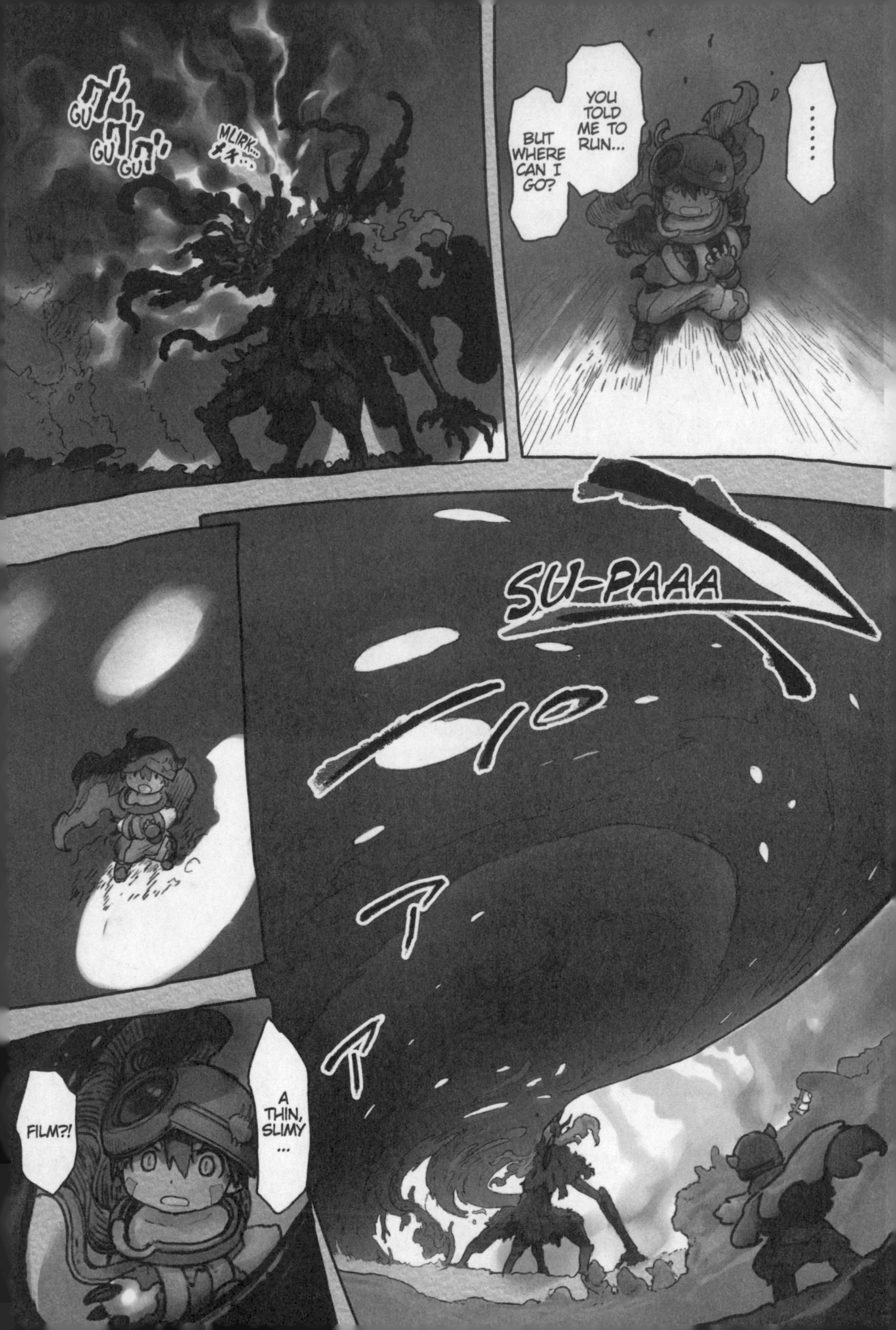
......
YOU TOLD ME TO RUN...
BUT WHERE CAN I GO?
GU GU GU GU
MLIRK...
SU-PAAA
A THIN, SLIMY ...
FILM?!

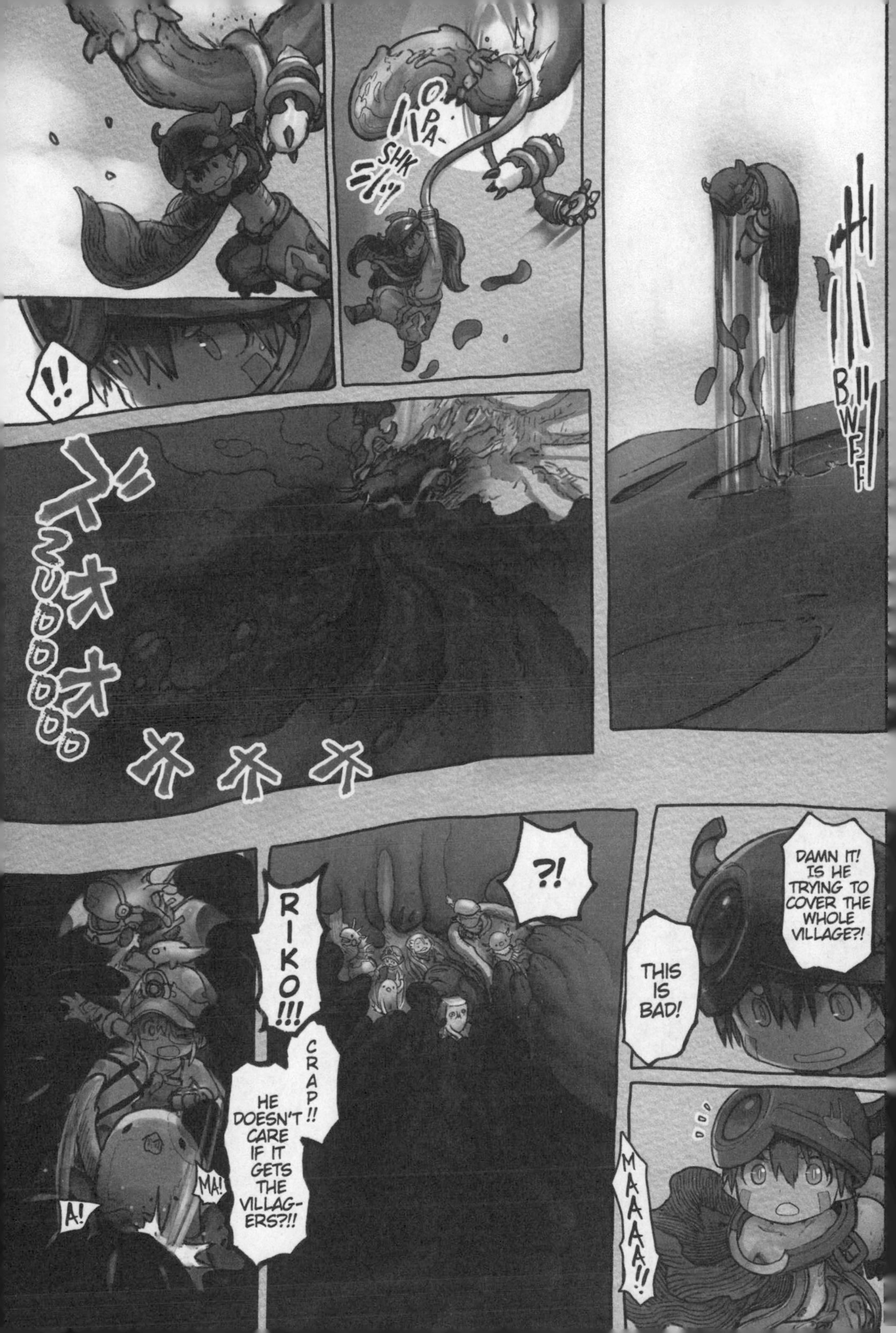
BWFF
PA-SHK
!!
ZUDOOOOOOO
DAMN IT! IS HE TRYING TO COVER THE WHOLE VILLAGE?!
THIS IS BAD!
MAAAA!!
?!
RIKO!!!
CRAP!!
HE DOESN'T CARE IF IT GETS THE VILLAGERS?!!
MA!
A!

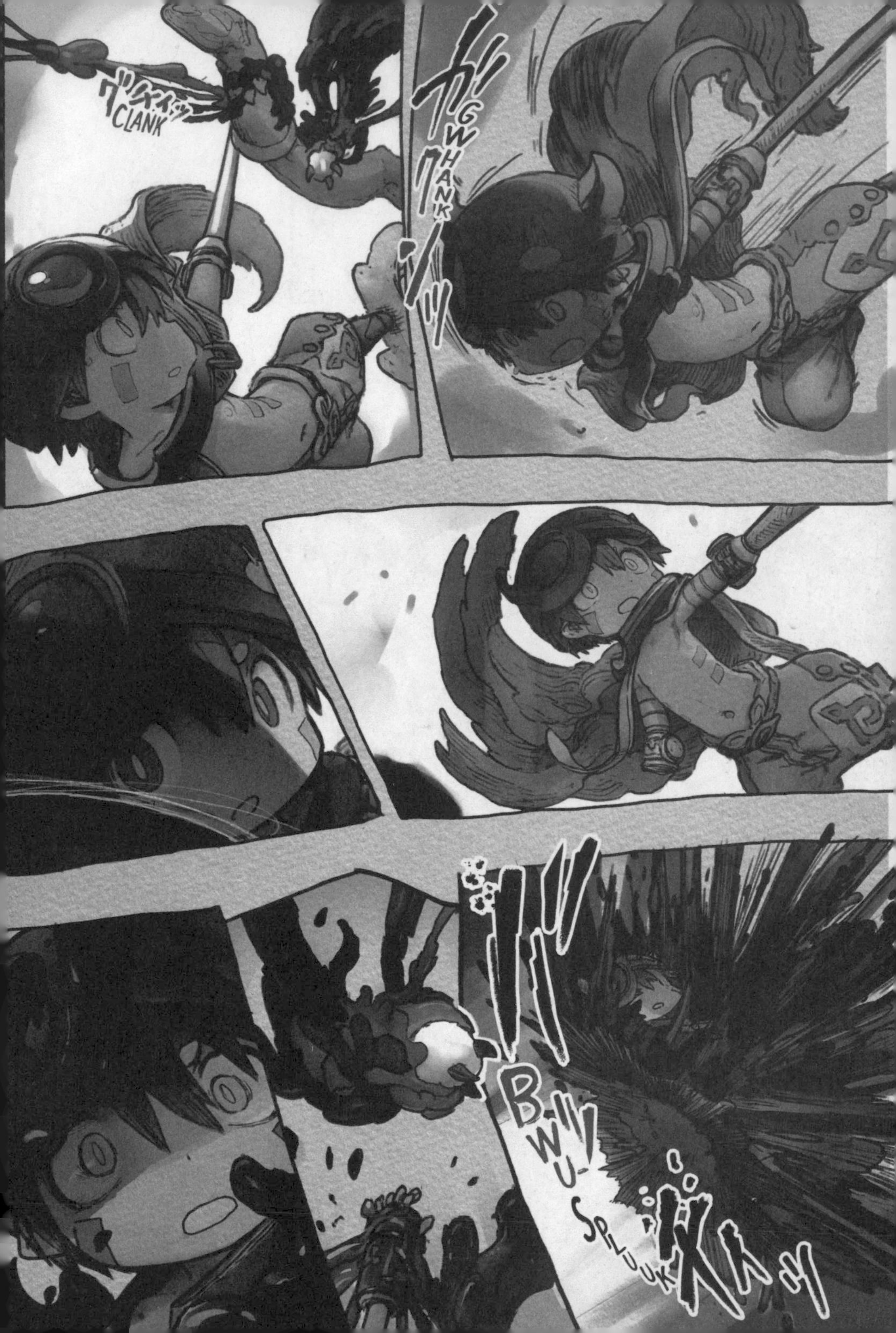
GWHANK
CLANK
BWU-
SPLUUK

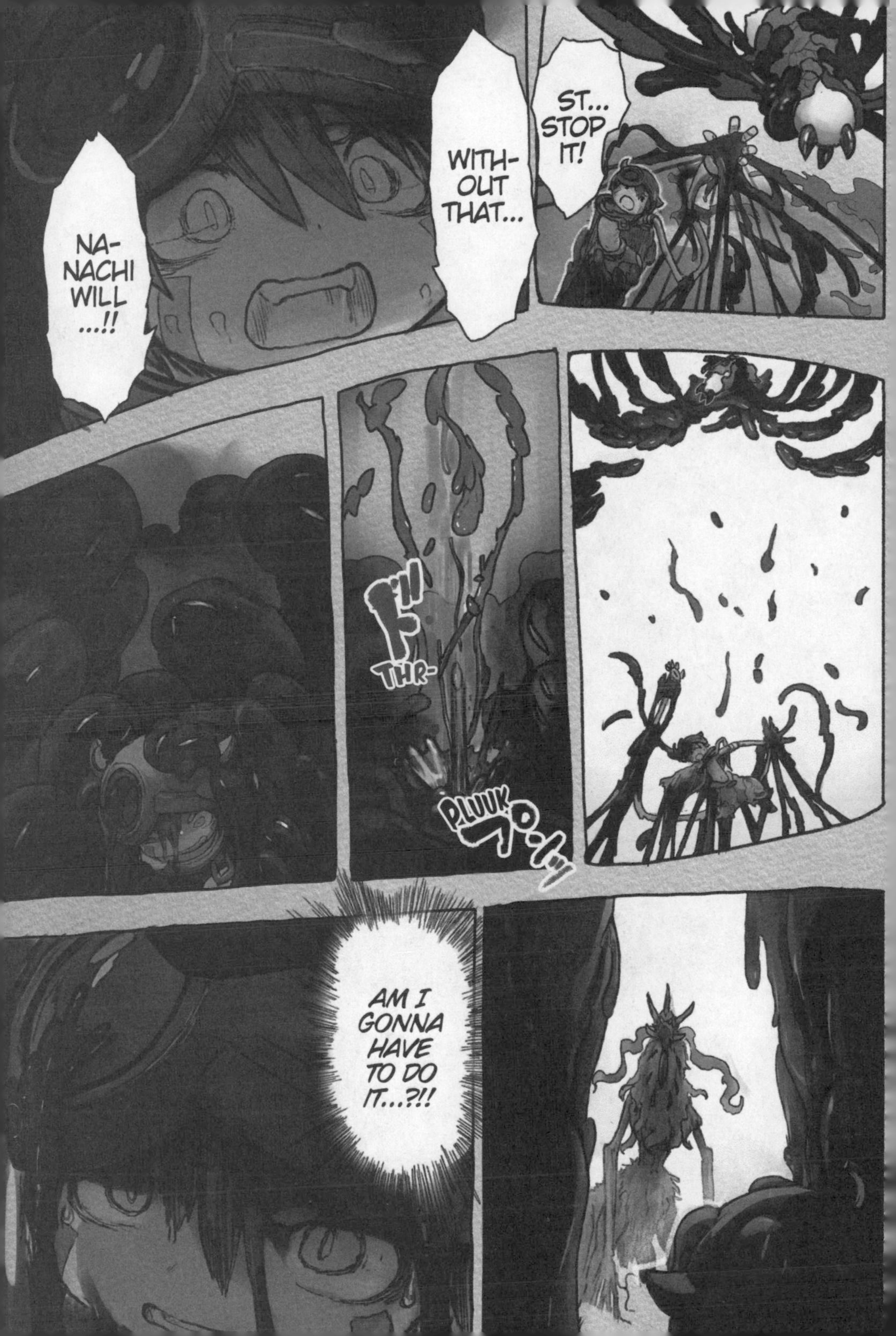
ST... STOP IT!
WITH-OUT THAT...
NA-NACHI WILL ...!!
THR-
PLUUK
AM I GONNA HAVE TO DO IT...?!!

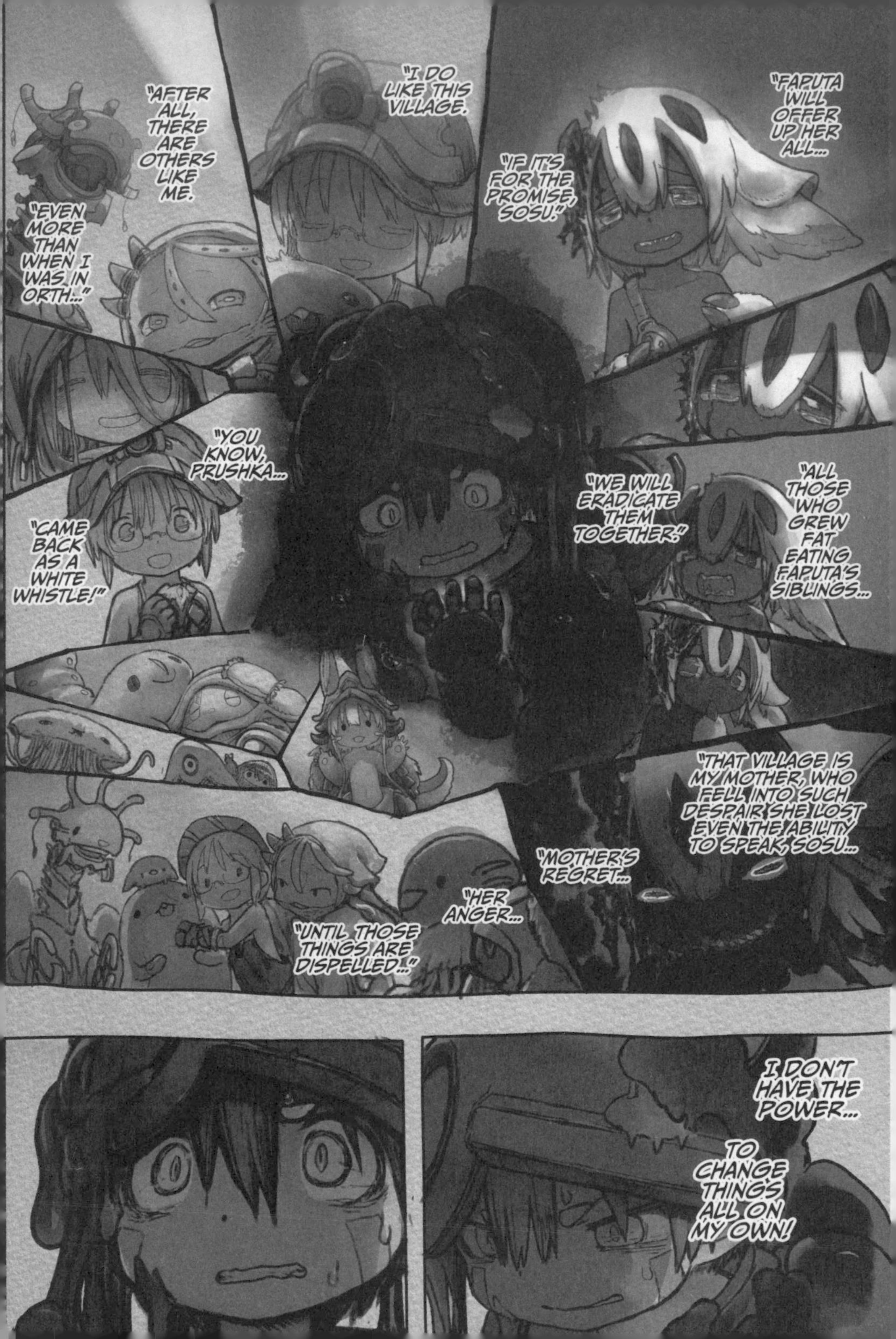
"FAPUTA WILL OFFER UP HER ALL...
"IF IT'S FOR THE PROMISE, SOSU."
"I DO LIKE THIS VILLAGE.
"AFTER ALL, THERE ARE OTHERS LIKE ME.
"EVEN MORE THAN WHEN I WAS IN ORTH..."
"ALL THOSE WHO GREW FAT EATING FAPUTA'S SIBLINGS...
"WE WILL ERADICATE THEM TOGETHER."
"YOU KNOW, PRUSHKA...
"CAME BACK AS A WHITE WHISTLE!"
"THAT VILLAGE IS MY MOTHER, WHO FELL INTO SUCH DESPAIR SHE LOST EVEN THE ABILITY TO SPEAK, SOSU...
"MOTHER'S REGRET...
"HER ANGER...
"UNTIL THOSE THINGS ARE DISPELLED..."
I DON'T HAVE THE POWER...
TO CHANGE THINGS ALL ON MY OWN!

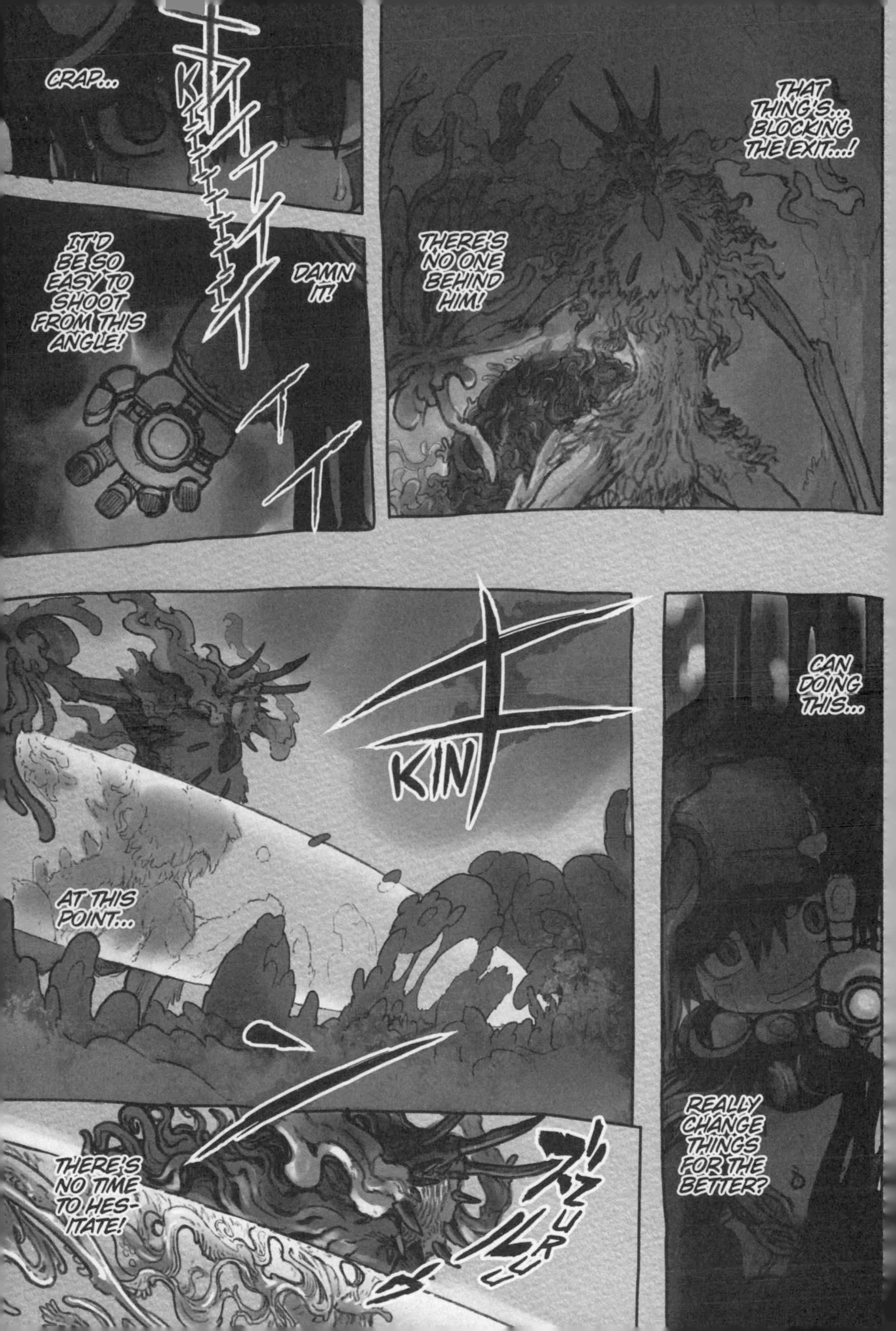
THAT THING'S... BLOCKING THE EXIT...!
THERE'S NO ONE BEHIND HIM!
CRAP...
KIIIIII
IT'D BE SO EASY TO SHOOT FROM THIS ANGLE!
DAMN IT!
CAN DOING THIS...
REALLY CHANGE THINGS FOR THE BETTER?
KIN
AT THIS POINT...
ZURU
THERE'S NO TIME TO HES-ITATE!

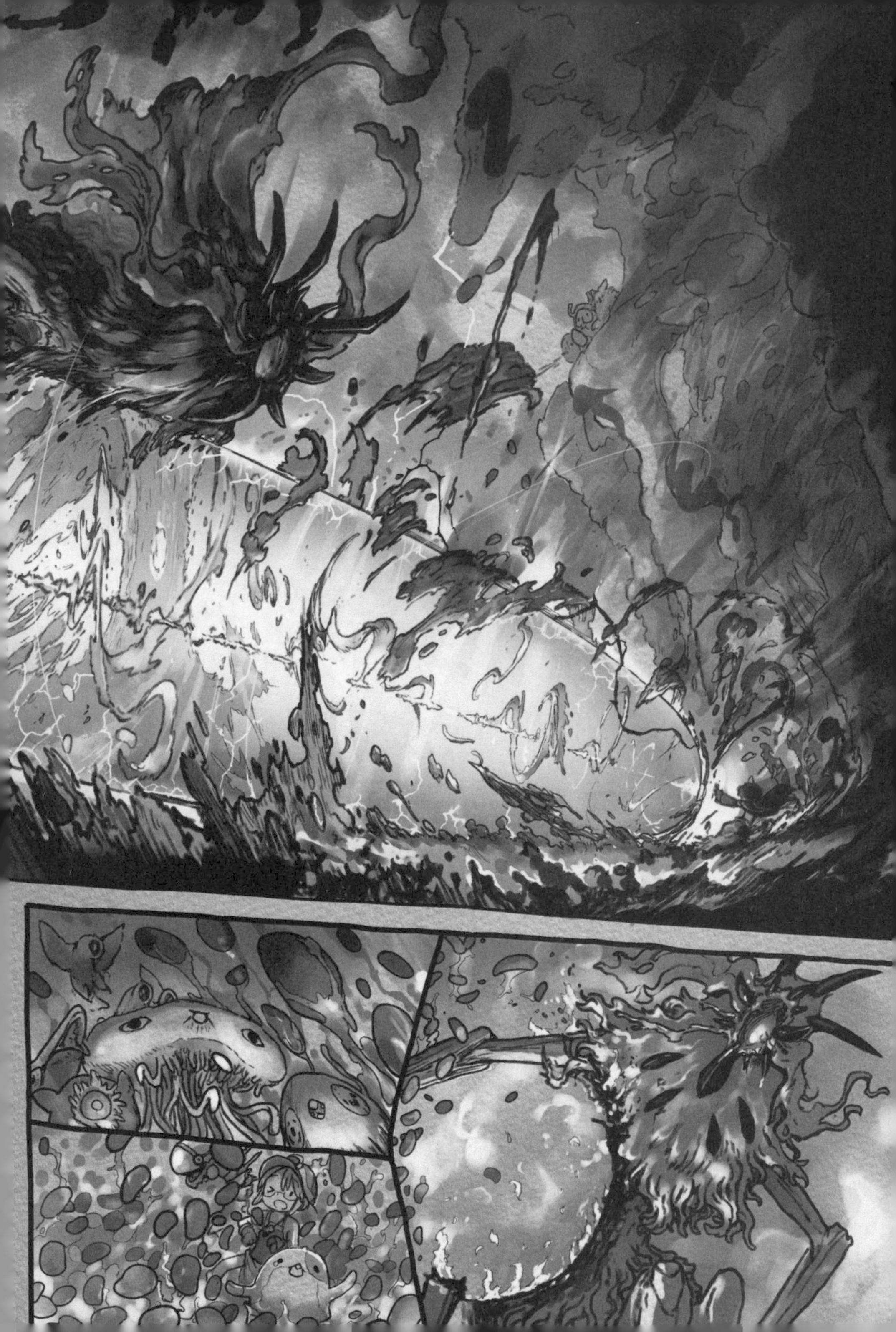

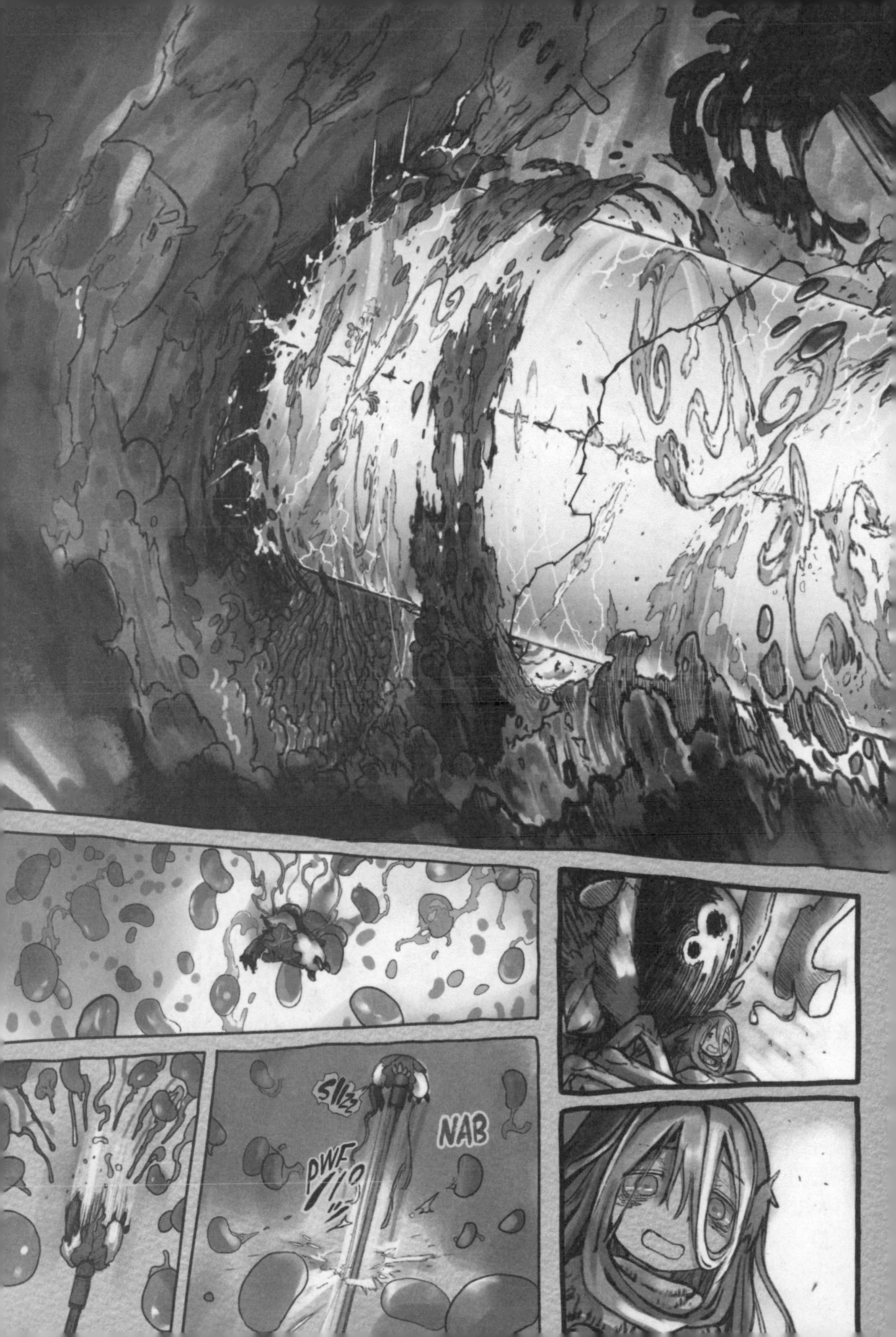
SIZZ
NAB
PWF

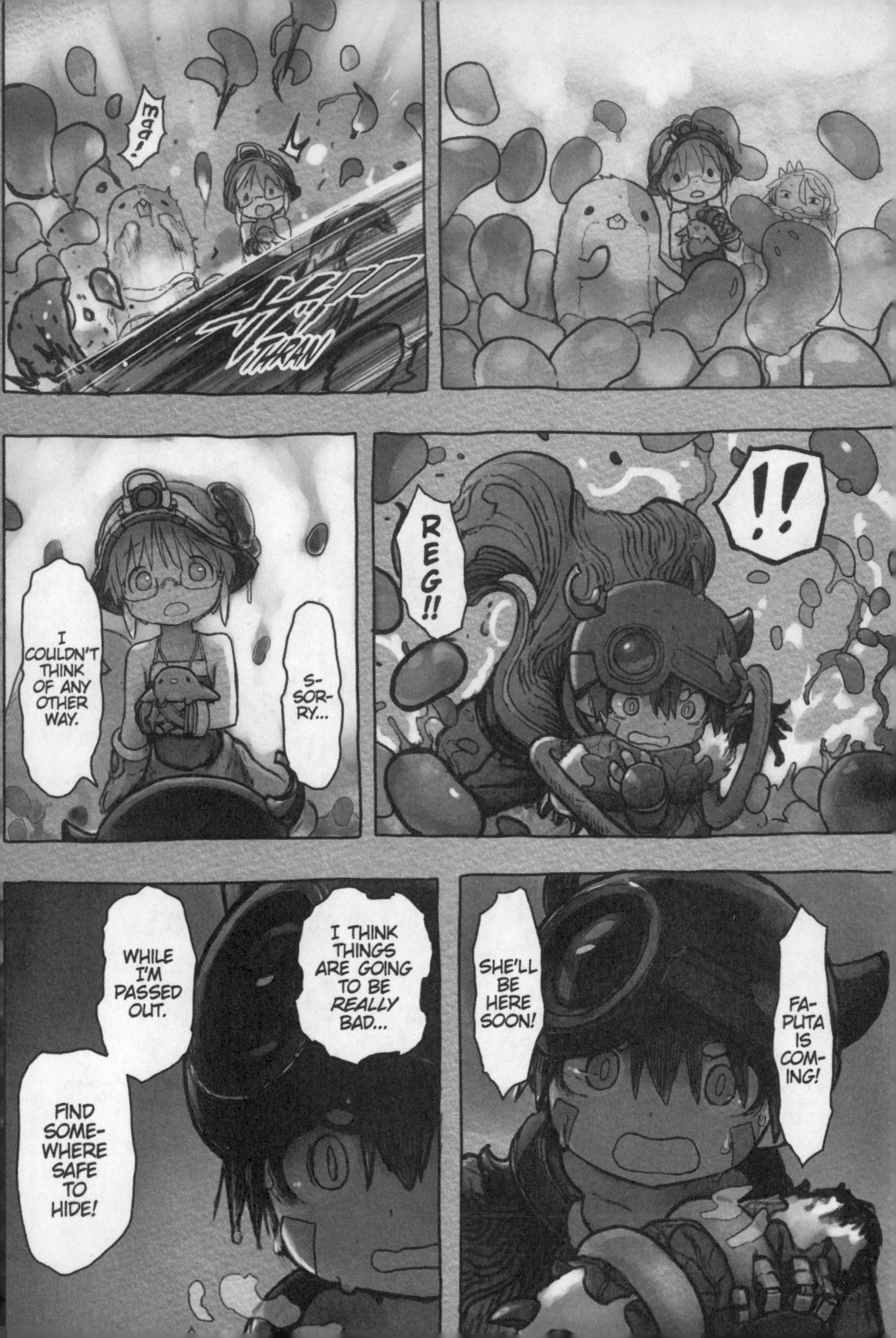
maa!
THRAN
!!
REG!!
S-SORRY...
I COULDN'T THINK OF ANY OTHER WAY.
FAPUTA IS COMING!
SHE'LL BE HERE SOON!
I THINK THINGS ARE GOING TO BE *REALLY* BAD...
WHILE I'M PASSED OUT.
FIND SOMEWHERE SAFE TO HIDE!

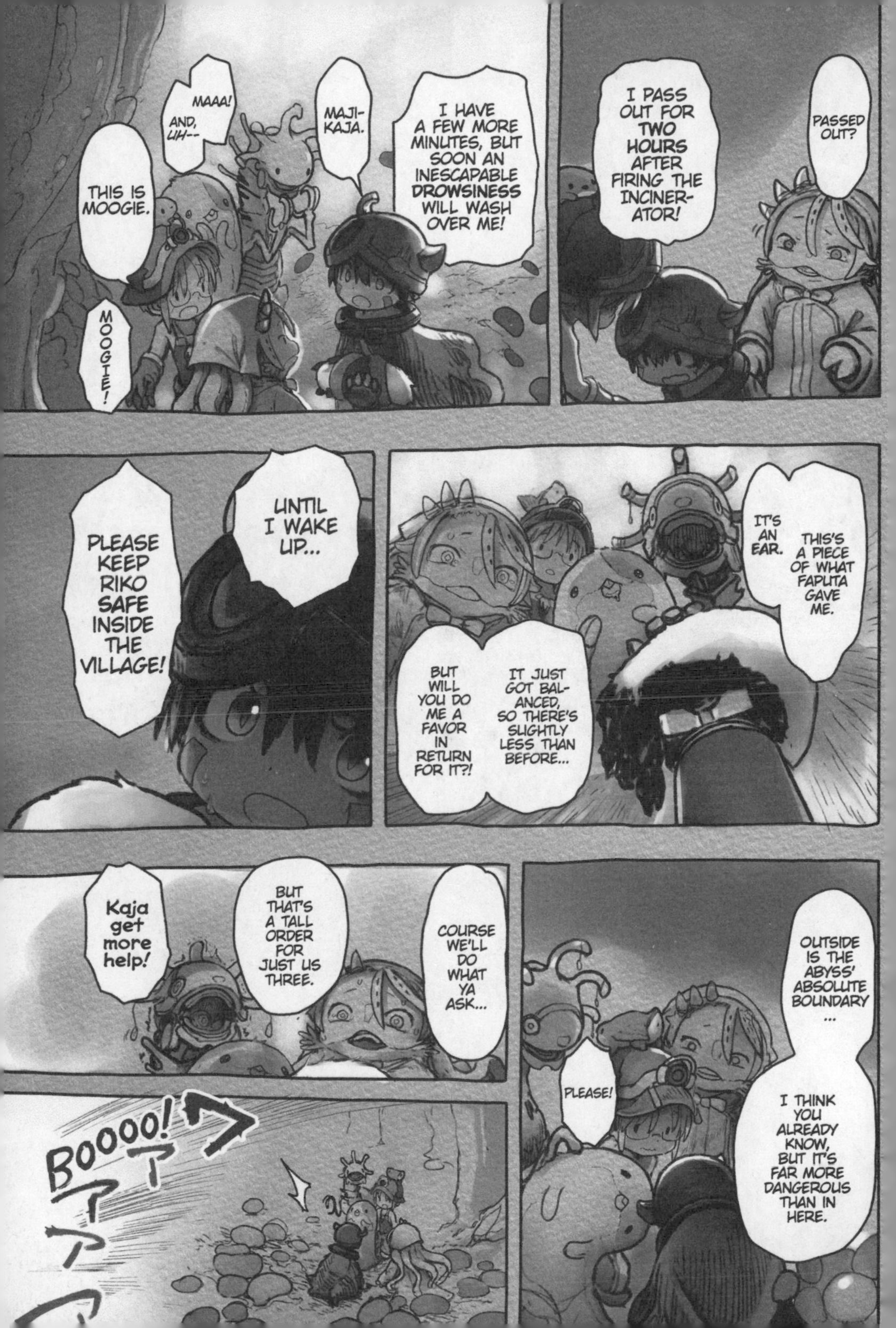
PASSED OUT?
I PASS OUT FOR **TWO HOURS** AFTER FIRING THE INCINERATOR!
I HAVE A FEW MORE MINUTES, BUT SOON AN INESCAPABLE **DROWSINESS** WILL WASH OVER ME!
MAJI-KAJA.
MAAA!
AND, UH--
THIS IS MOOGIE.
MOOGIE!
THIS'S A PIECE OF WHAT FAPUTA GAVE ME.
IT'S AN EAR.
IT JUST GOT BALANCED, SO THERE'S SLIGHTLY LESS THAN BEFORE...
BUT WILL YOU DO ME A FAVOR IN RETURN FOR IT?!
UNTIL I WAKE UP...
PLEASE KEEP RIKO SAFE INSIDE THE VILLAGE!
OUTSIDE IS THE ABYSS' ABSOLUTE BOUNDARY...
I THINK YOU ALREADY KNOW, BUT IT'S FAR MORE DANGEROUS THAN IN HERE.
PLEASE!
COURSE WE'LL DO WHAT YA ASK...
BUT THAT'S A TALL ORDER FOR JUST US THREE.
Kaja get more help!
BOOOO!

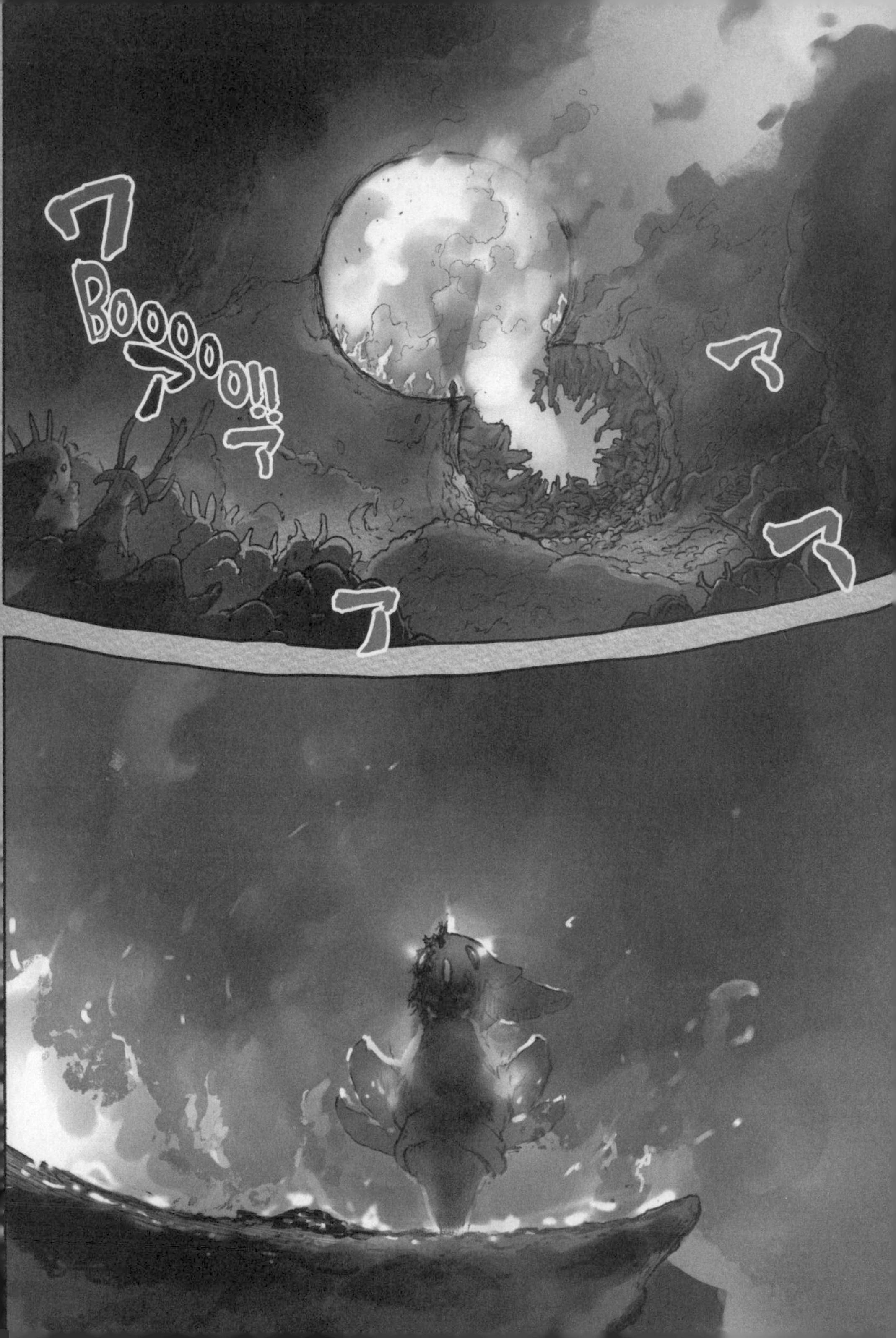
BOOOOOO!!

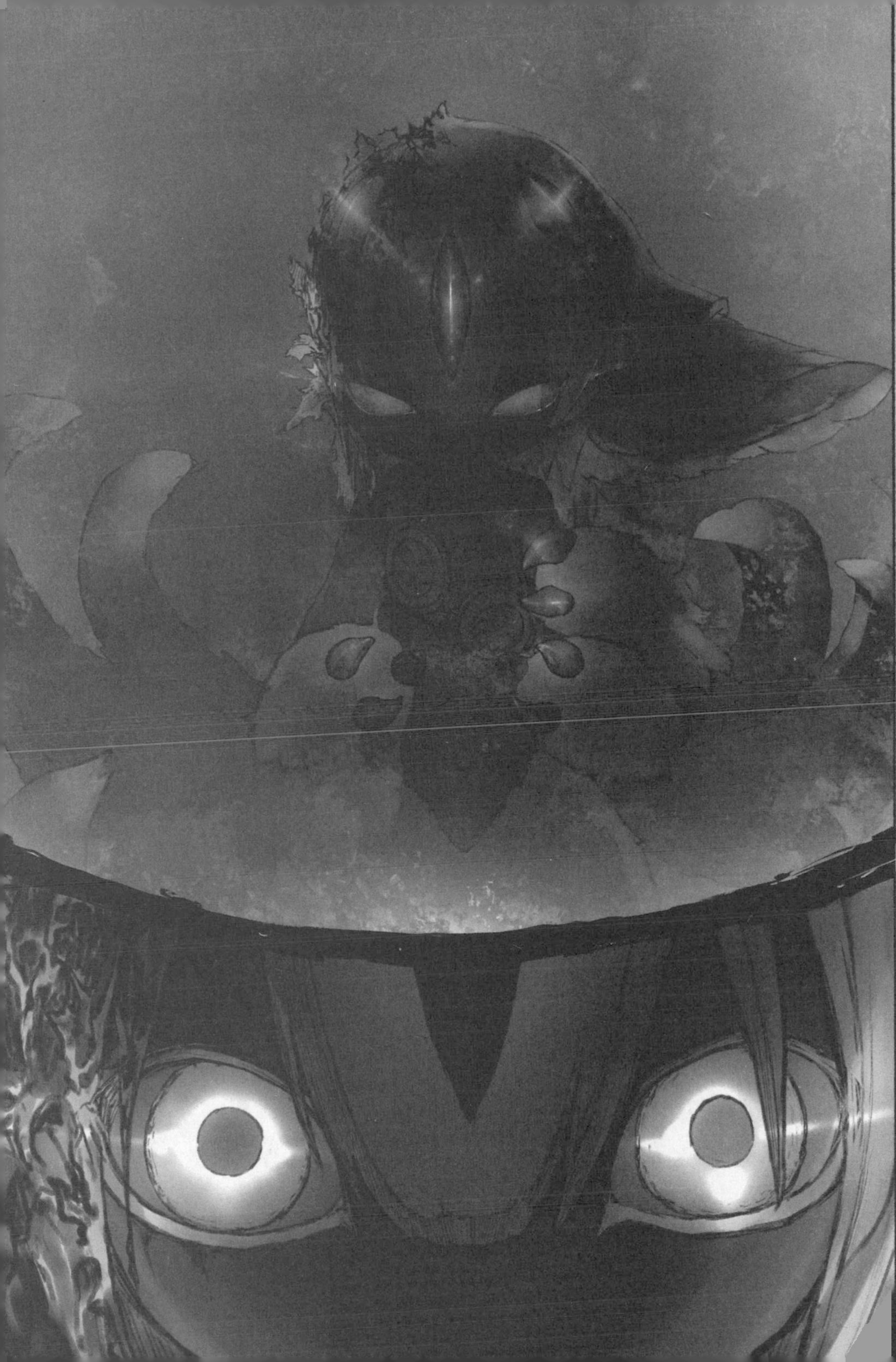

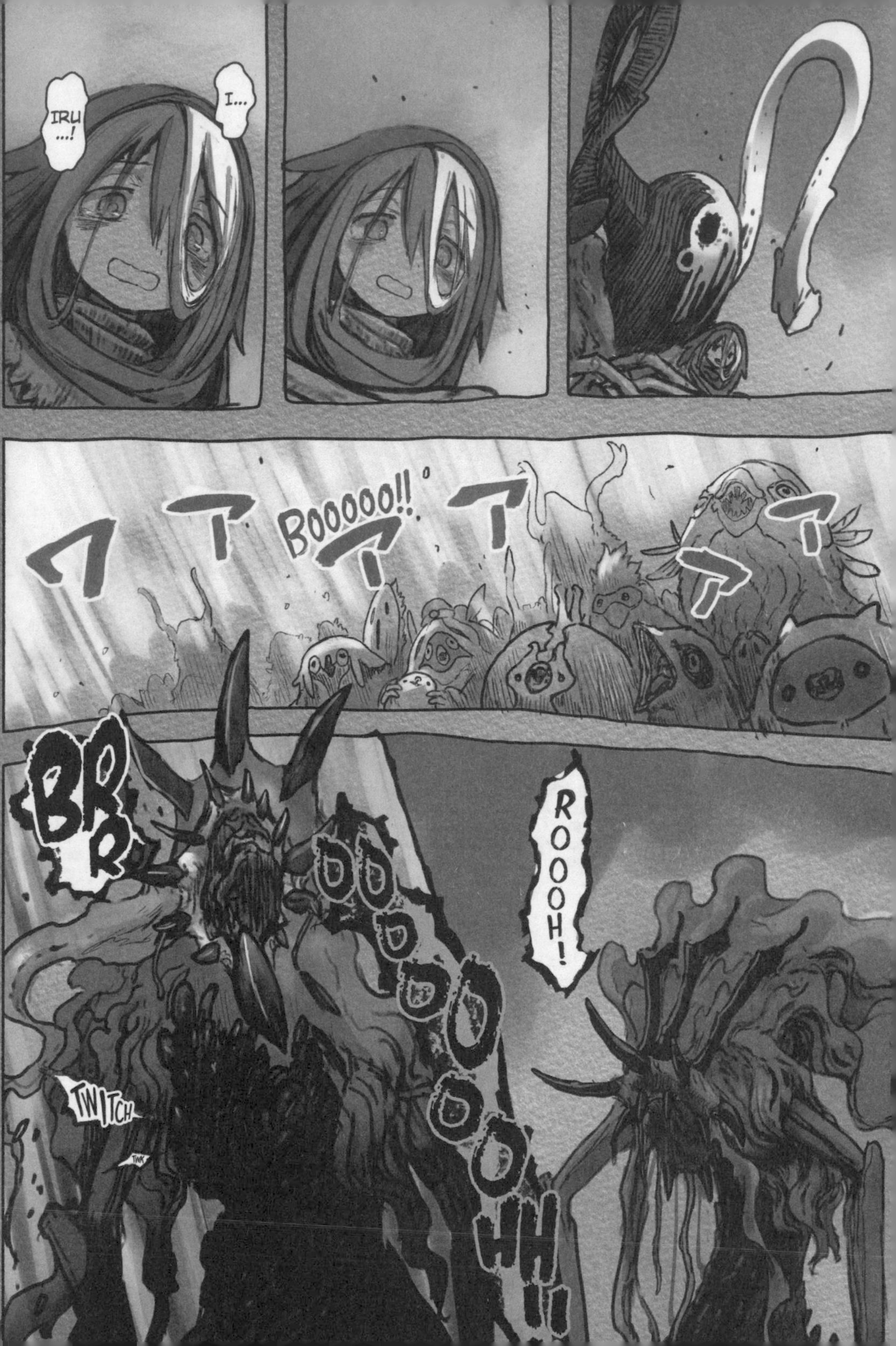

I...
IRU ...!
ア ア ア ア ア ア
BOOOOO!!
ROOOH!
DDDDDDOOOOOOHH!!!
BRR
TWITCH
TWK

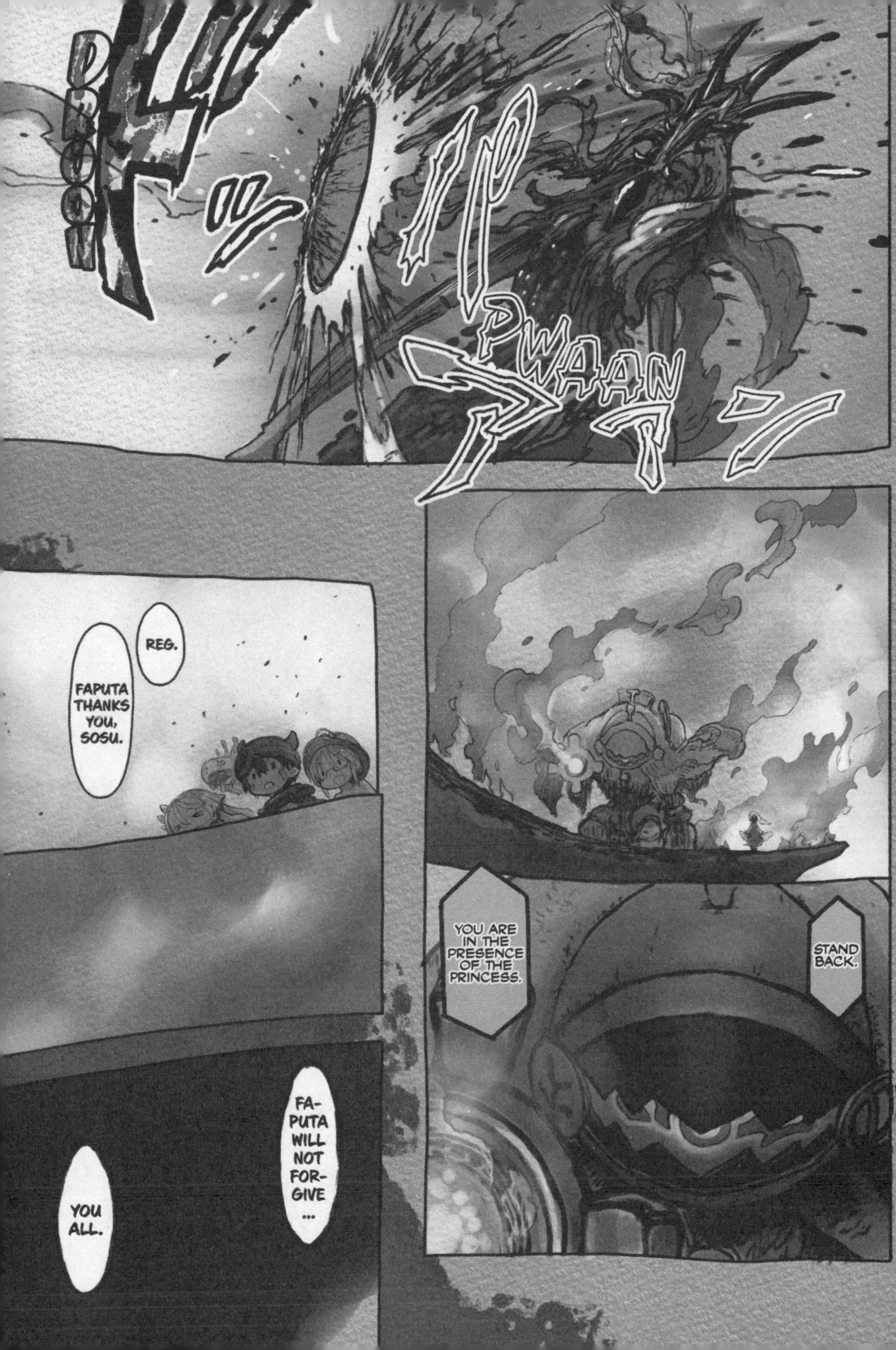
PWAAN
STAND BACK.
YOU ARE IN THE PRESENCE OF THE PRINCESS.
REG.
FAPUTA THANKS YOU, SOSU.
FA-PUTA WILL NOT FOR-GIVE ...
YOU ALL.

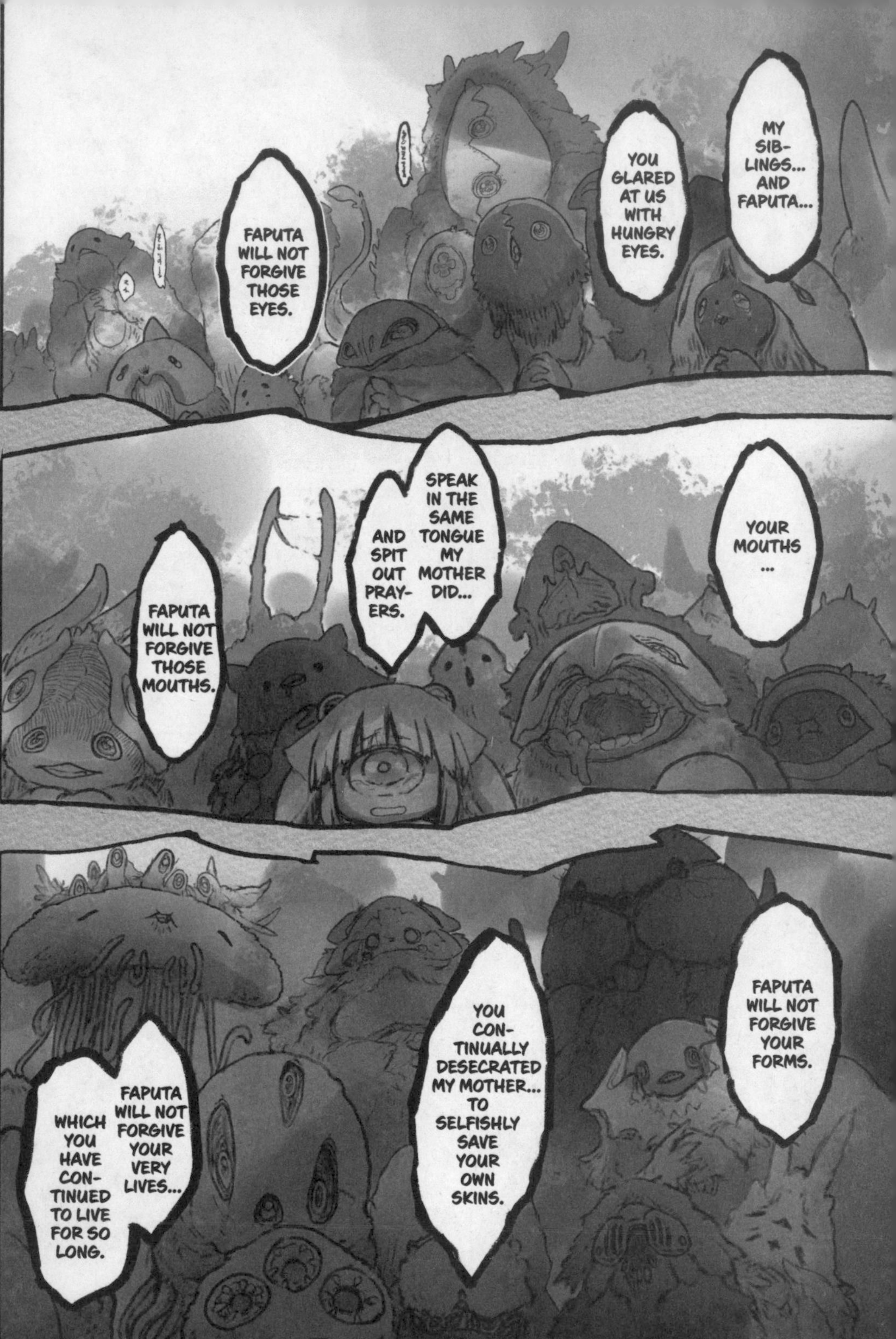
MY SIBLINGS... AND FAPUTA...
YOU GLARED AT US WITH HUNGRY EYES.
FAPUTA WILL NOT FORGIVE THOSE EYES.
YOUR MOUTHS...
SPEAK IN THE SAME TONGUE MY MOTHER DID...
AND SPIT OUT PRAYERS.
FAPUTA WILL NOT FORGIVE THOSE MOUTHS.
FAPUTA WILL NOT FORGIVE YOUR FORMS.
YOU CONTINUALLY DESECRATED MY MOTHER... TO SELFISHLY SAVE YOUR OWN SKINS.
FAPUTA WILL NOT FORGIVE YOUR VERY LIVES...
WHICH YOU HAVE CONTINUED TO LIVE FOR SO LONG.

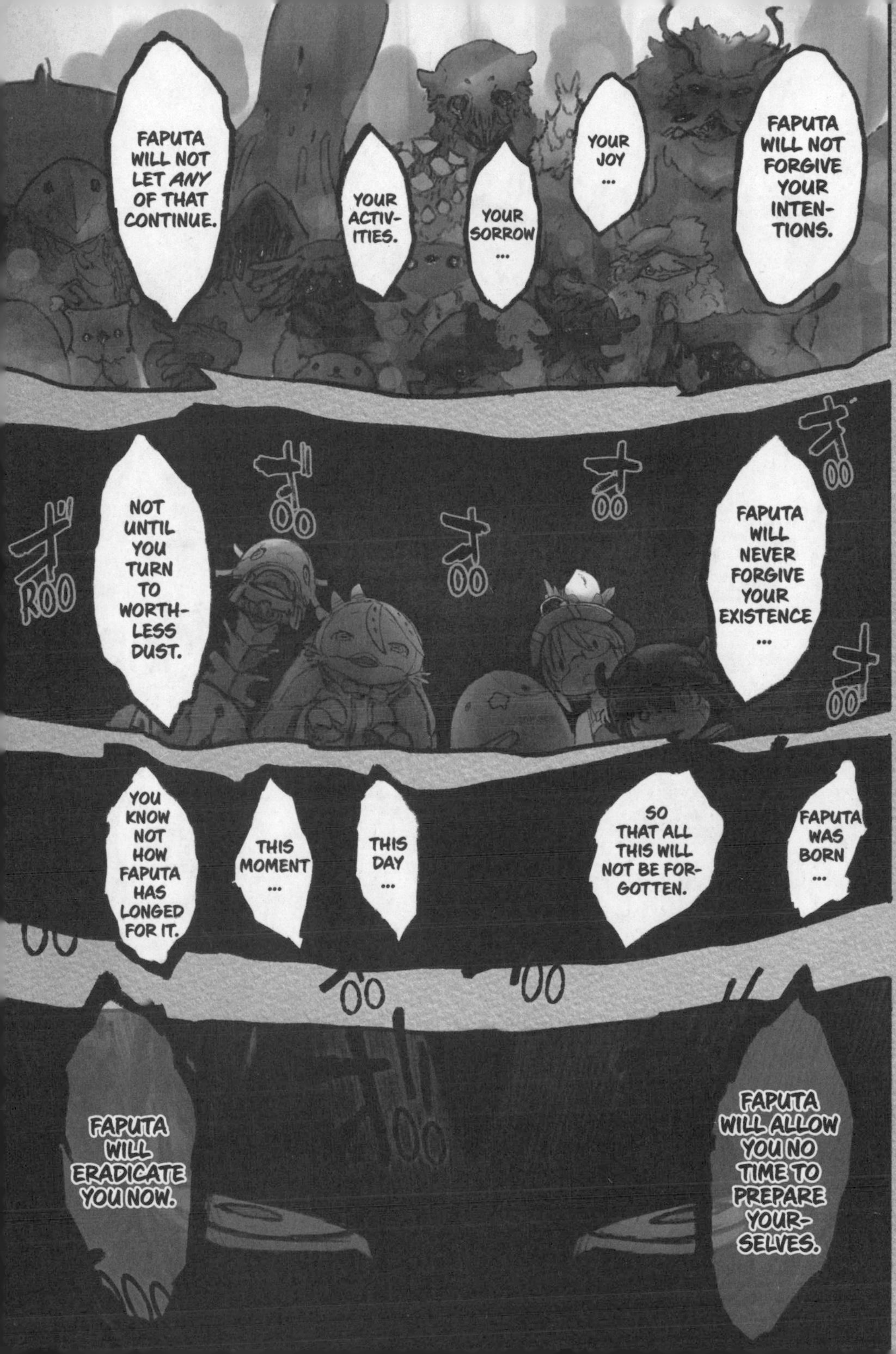
FAPUTA WILL NOT FORGIVE YOUR INTENTIONS.
YOUR JOY ...
YOUR SORROW ...
YOUR ACTIVITIES.
FAPUTA WILL NOT LET *ANY* OF THAT CONTINUE.
FAPUTA WILL NEVER FORGIVE YOUR EXISTENCE ...
NOT UNTIL YOU TURN TO WORTHLESS DUST.
ROO
FAPUTA WAS BORN ...
SO THAT ALL THIS WILL NOT BE FORGOTTEN.
THIS DAY ...
THIS MOMENT ...
YOU KNOW NOT HOW FAPUTA HAS LONGED FOR IT.
FAPUTA WILL ALLOW YOU NO TIME TO PREPARE YOURSELVES.
FAPUTA WILL ERADICATE YOU NOW.

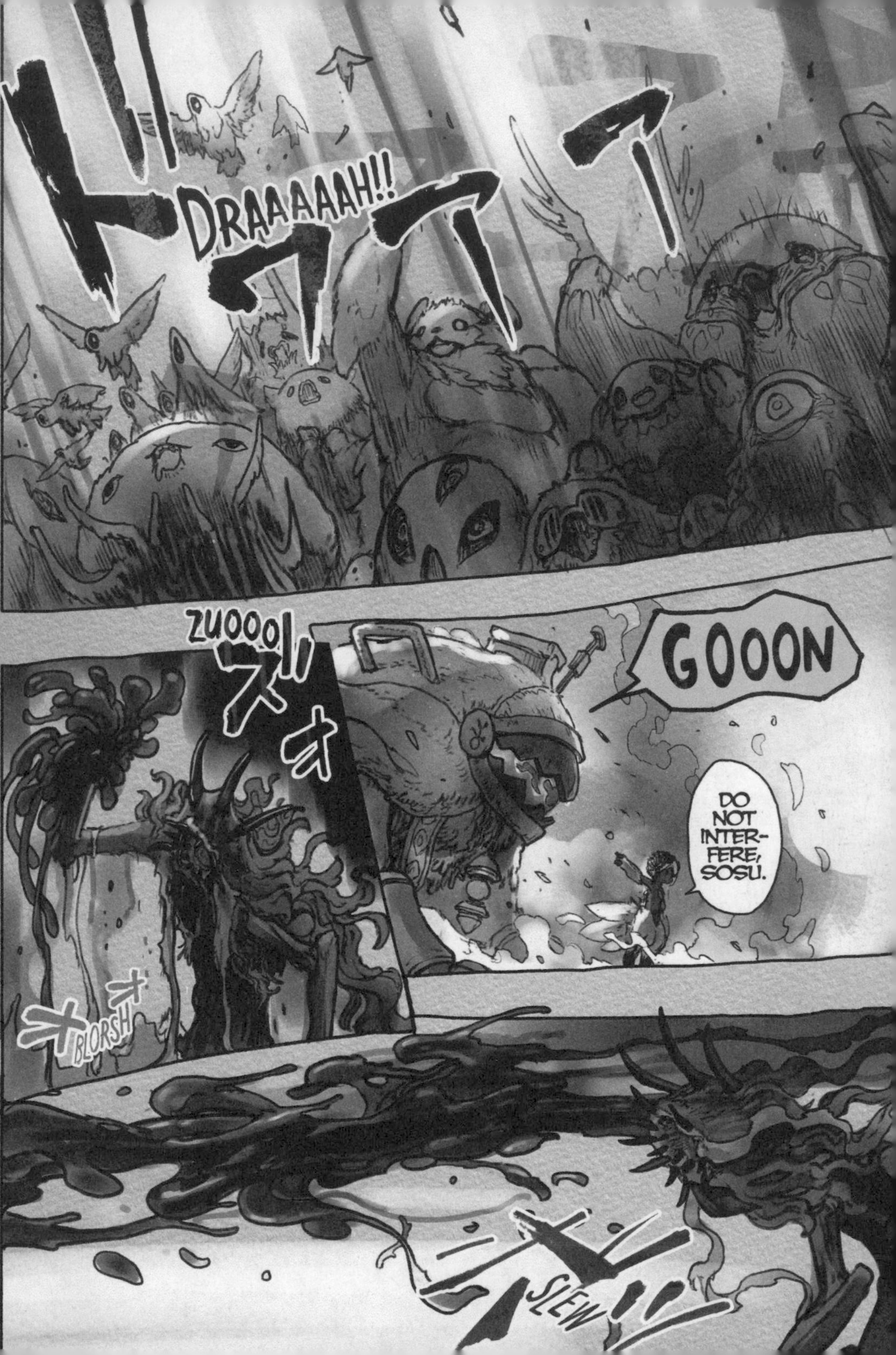
DRAAAAAH!!
GOOON
DO NOT INTERFERE, SOSU.
ZUOOO
BLORSH
SLEW!!

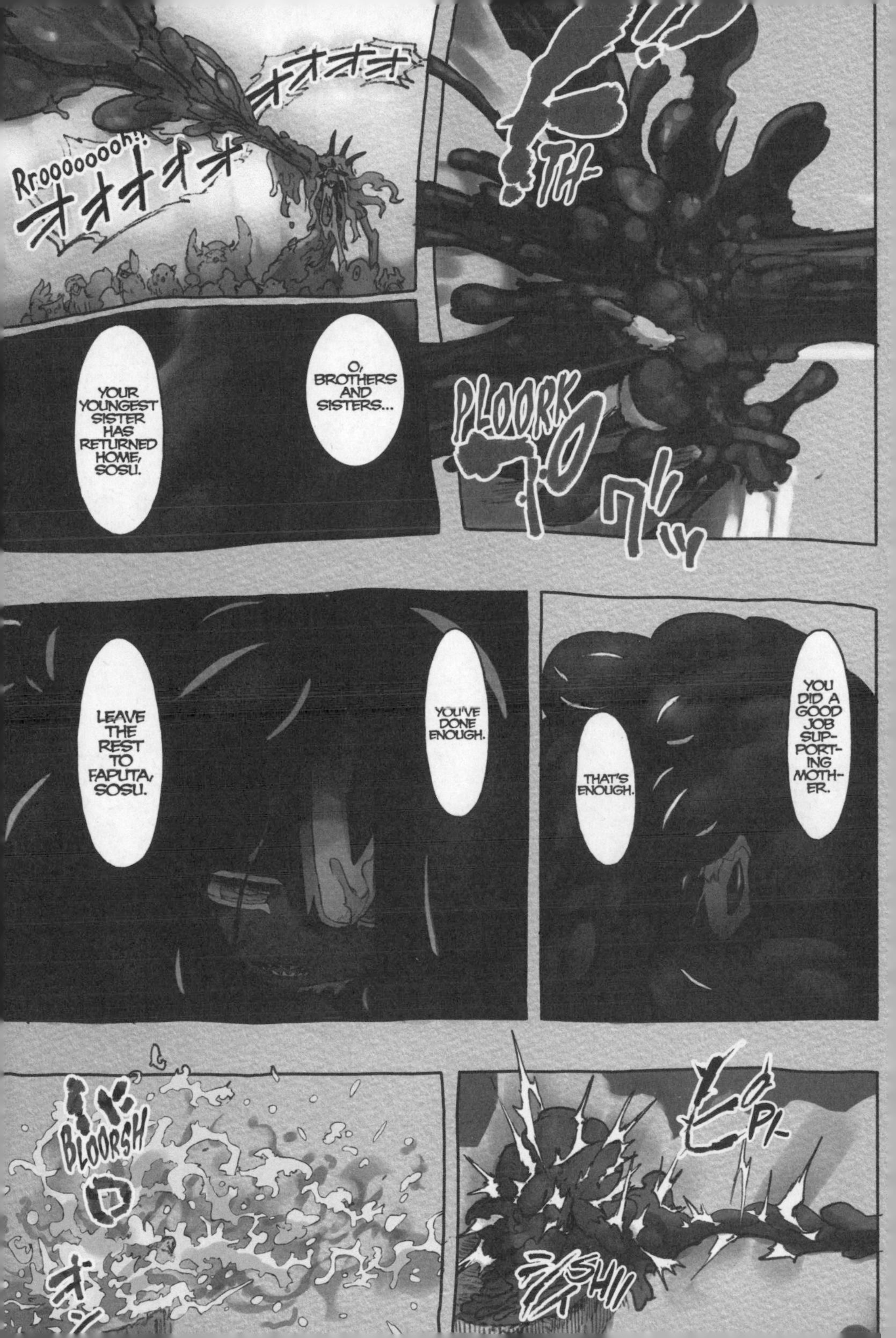
TH-
PLOORK
グッ
Rrooooooh!!
オオオオ
オオオオオ
O, BROTHERS AND SISTERS...
YOUR YOUNGEST SISTER HAS RETURNED HOME, SOSU.
YOU DID A GOOD JOB SUP-PORT-ING MOTH-ER.
THAT'S ENOUGH.
YOU'VE DONE ENOUGH.
LEAVE THE REST TO FAPUTA, SOSU.
PI-
SHII
BLOORSH

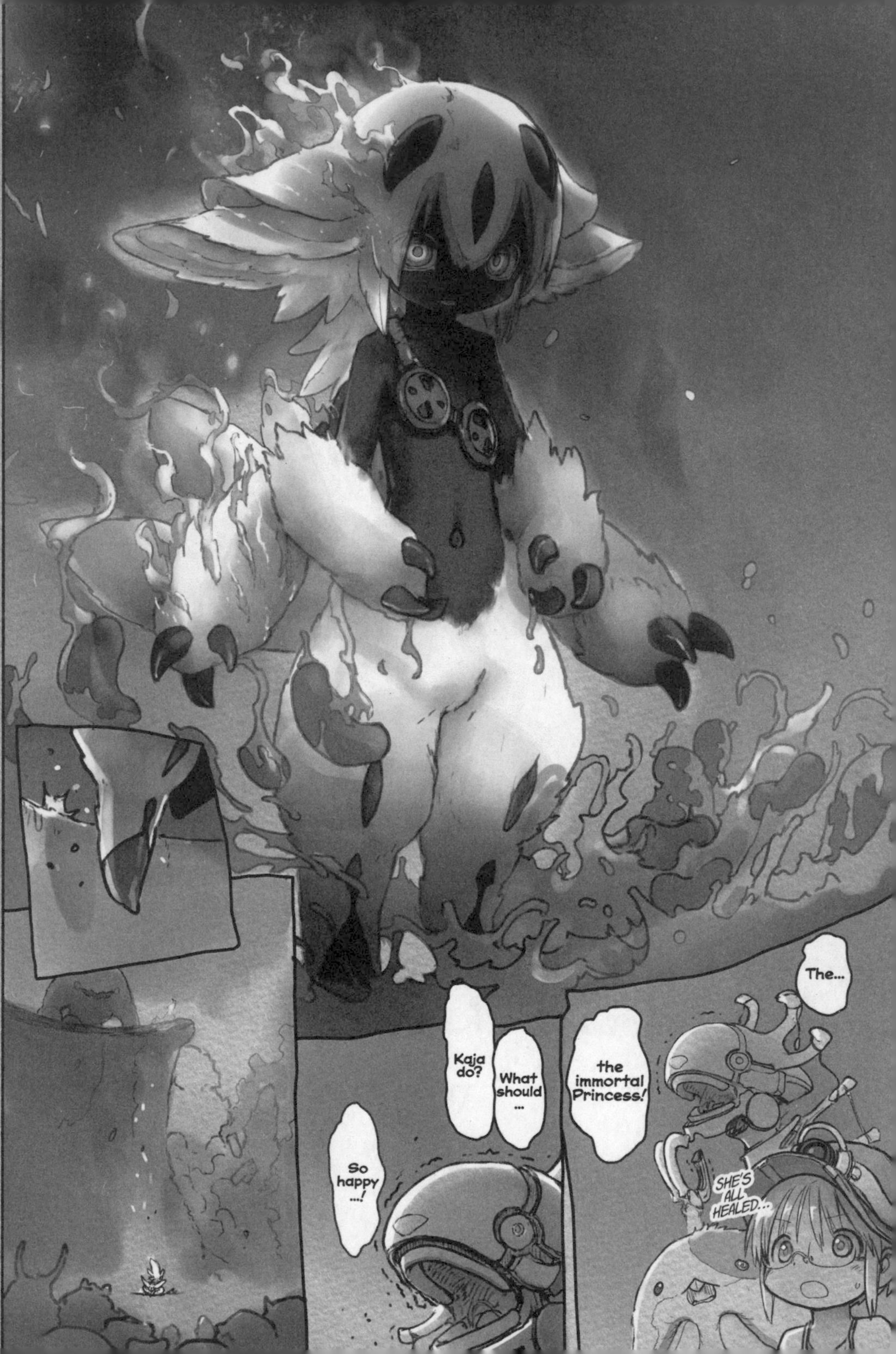
The...
the immortal Princess!
SHE'S ALL HEALED...
What should ...
Kaja do?
So happy ...!

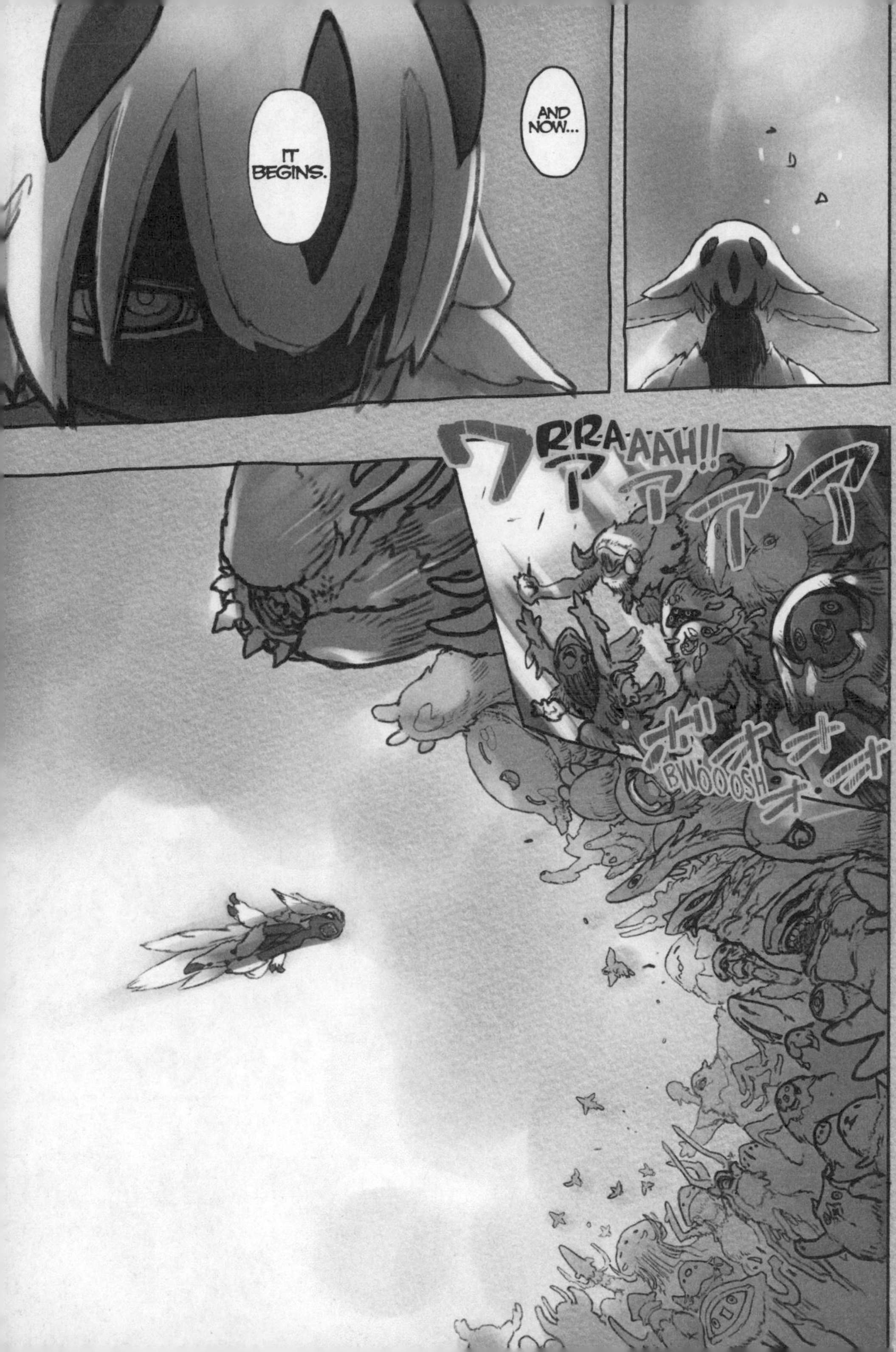

AND NOW...
IT BEGINS.
RRA-AAAH!!
BWOOOOSH

ZUUUUNNN...
CRUMBLE
CRUMBLE
FAMUTUU—IBII.
HEMUTIII—JAA—GYU.
SHIITSUE.
MUTUU—IBI.
GYU.
NNAA...
A SONG ...?
PUU—
......
PUKO.
MITTY ...
I...
WAS DREAMING.
THERE WAS A GUY...
WHO I WAS SUPER DEPENDENT ON.

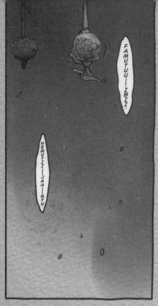

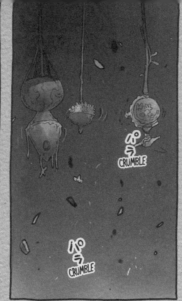

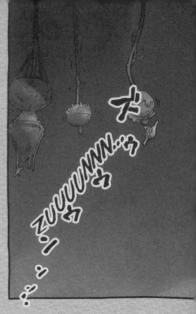

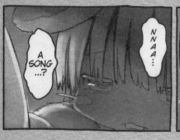

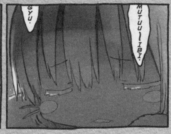

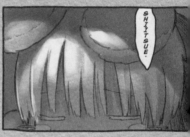

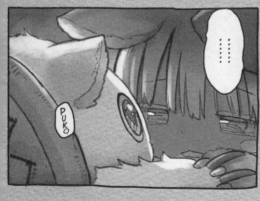

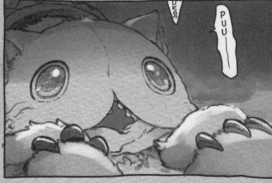

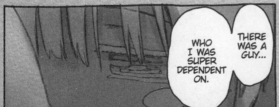

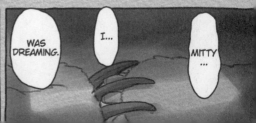

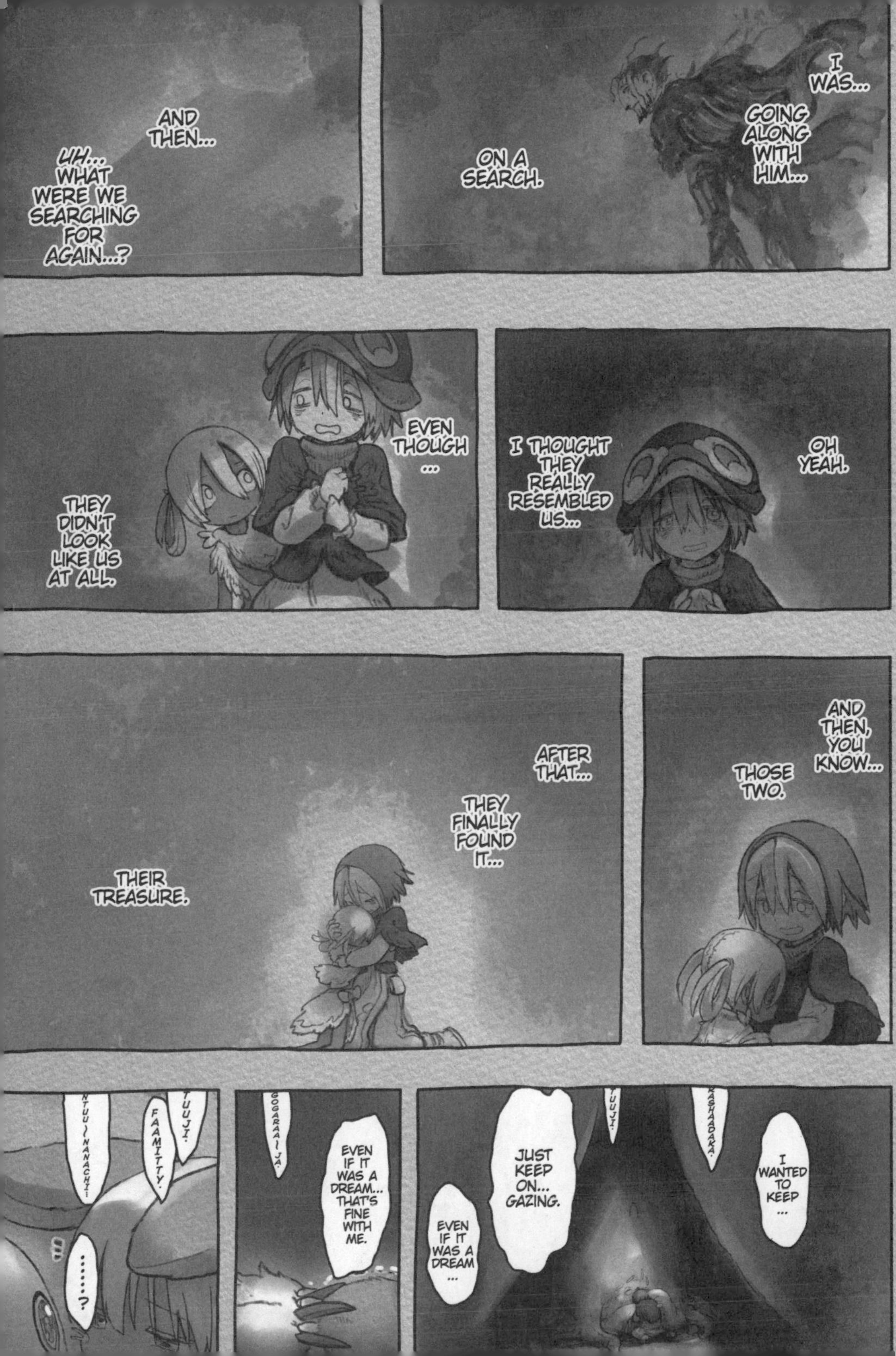
I WAS...
GOING ALONG WITH HIM...
ON A SEARCH.
AND THEN...
UH... WHAT WERE WE SEARCHING FOR AGAIN...?
OH YEAH.
I THOUGHT THEY REALLY RESEMBLED US...
EVEN THOUGH ...
THEY DIDN'T LOOK LIKE US AT ALL.
AND THEN, YOU KNOW...
THOSE TWO.
AFTER THAT...
THEY FINALLY FOUND IT...
THEIR TREASURE.
RASHAADAKA.
TUUJI.
I WANTED TO KEEP ...
JUST KEEP ON... GAZING.
EVEN IF IT WAS A DREAM ...
GOGARAA~JA.
EVEN IF IT WAS A DREAM... THAT'S FINE WITH ME.
TUUJI.
FAAMITTY.
NTUU~NANACHI!
......?

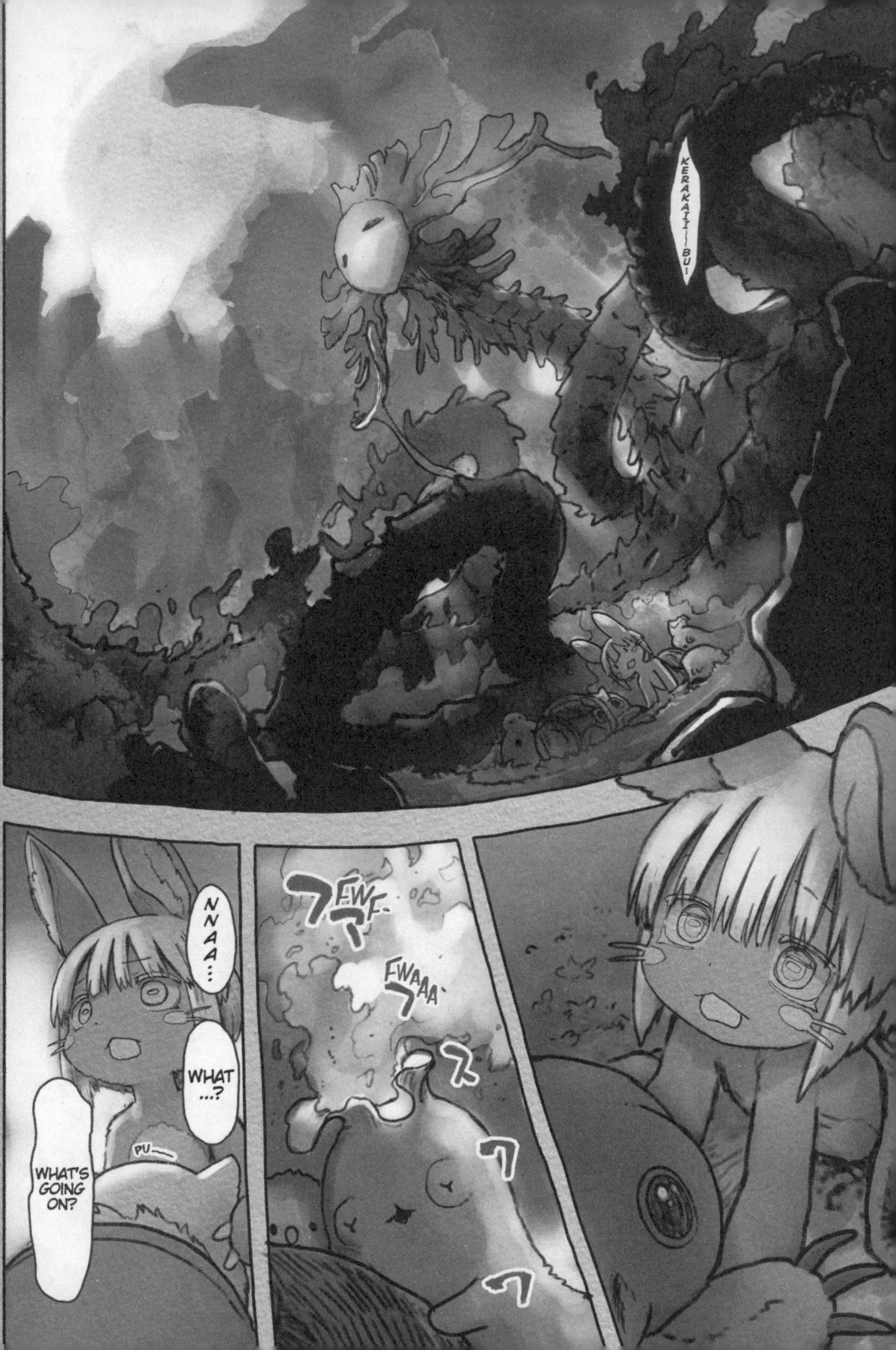
KERAKAII—BU…
FWF
FWAAA
NNAAA…
WHAT…?
PU—
WHAT'S GOING ON?

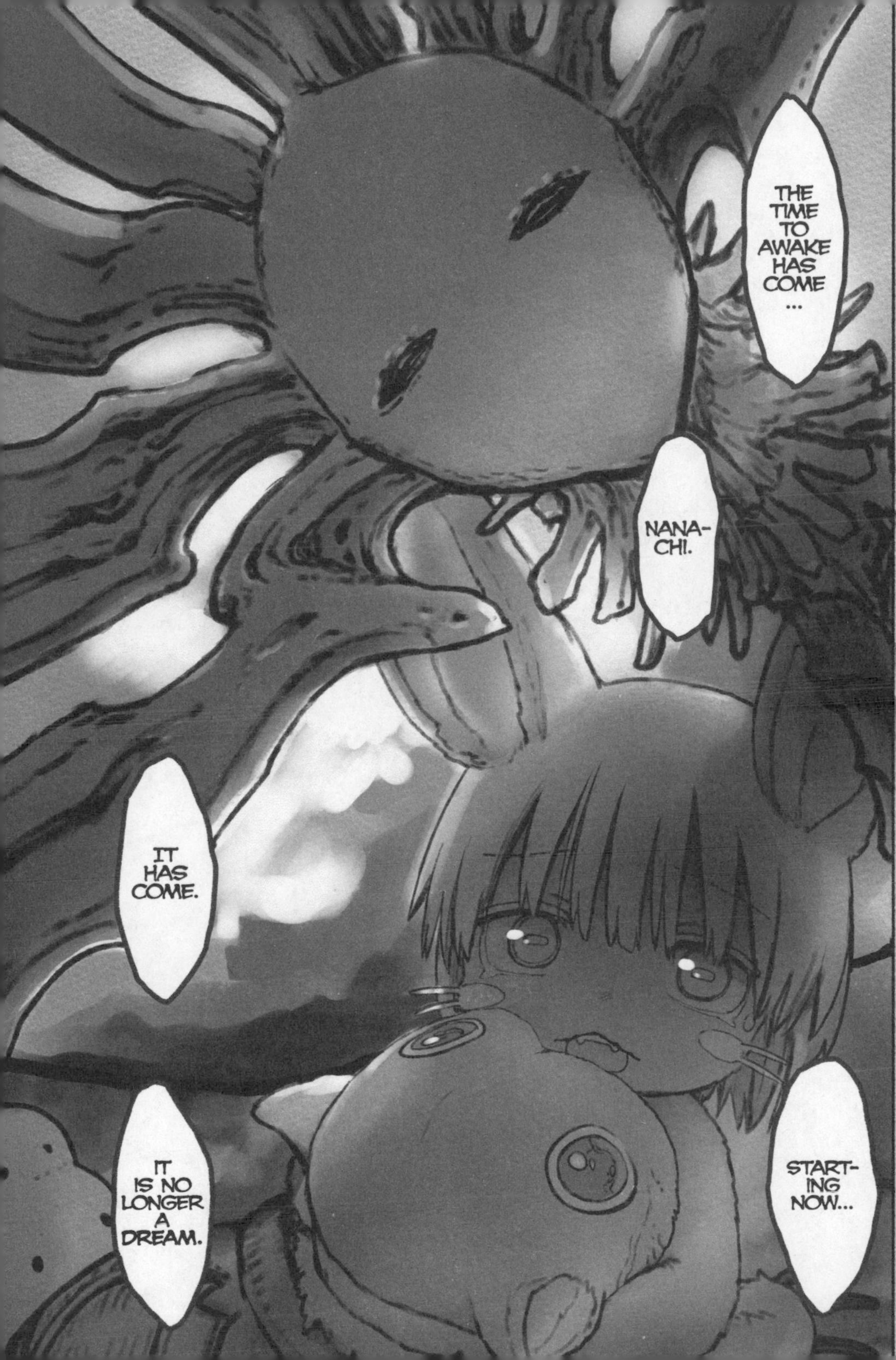
THE TIME TO AWAKE HAS COME...
NANA-CHI.
IT HAS COME.
STARTING NOW...
IT IS NO LONGER A DREAM.

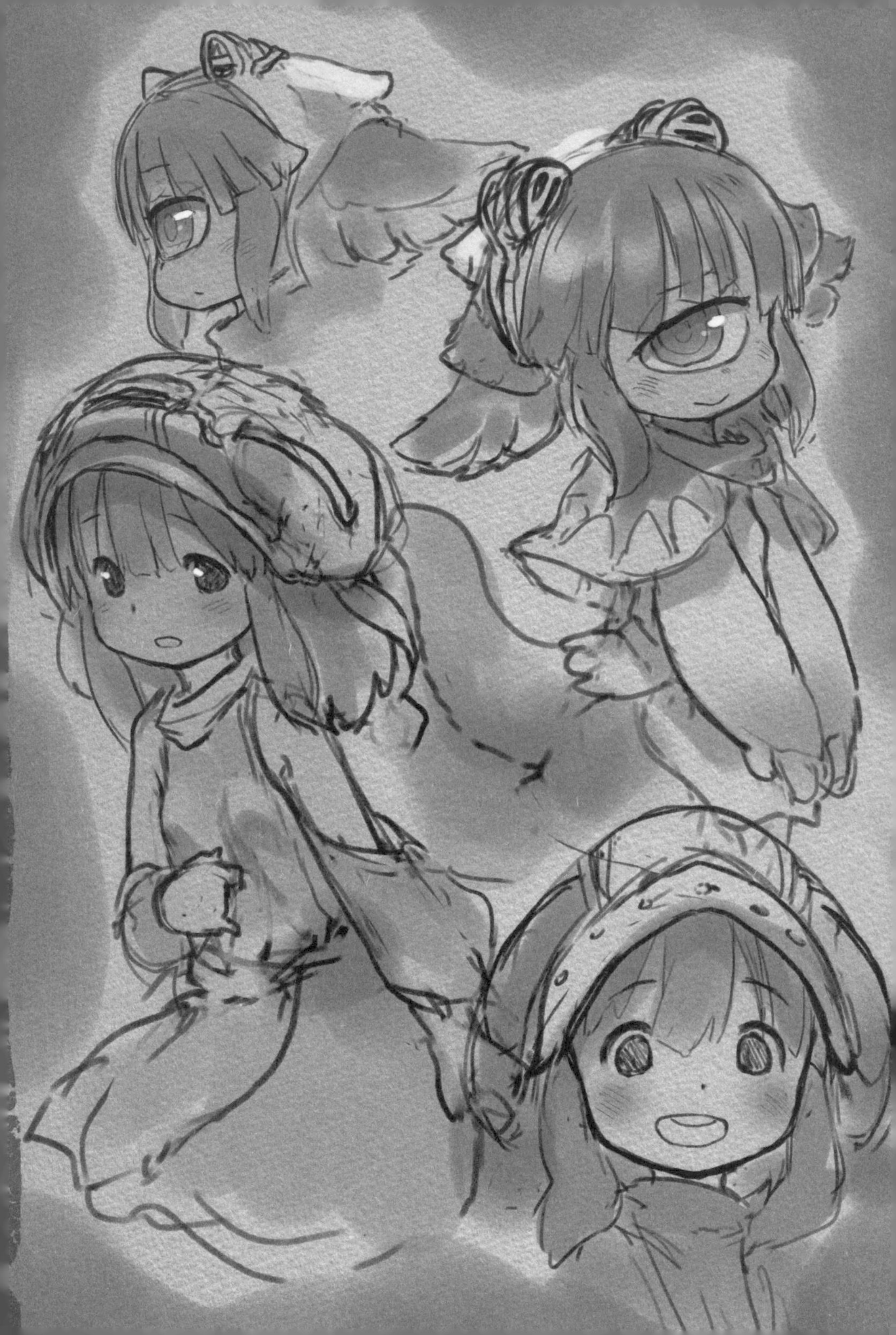

MADE IN ABYSS

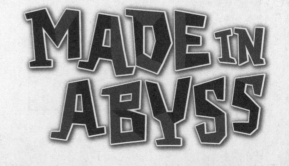

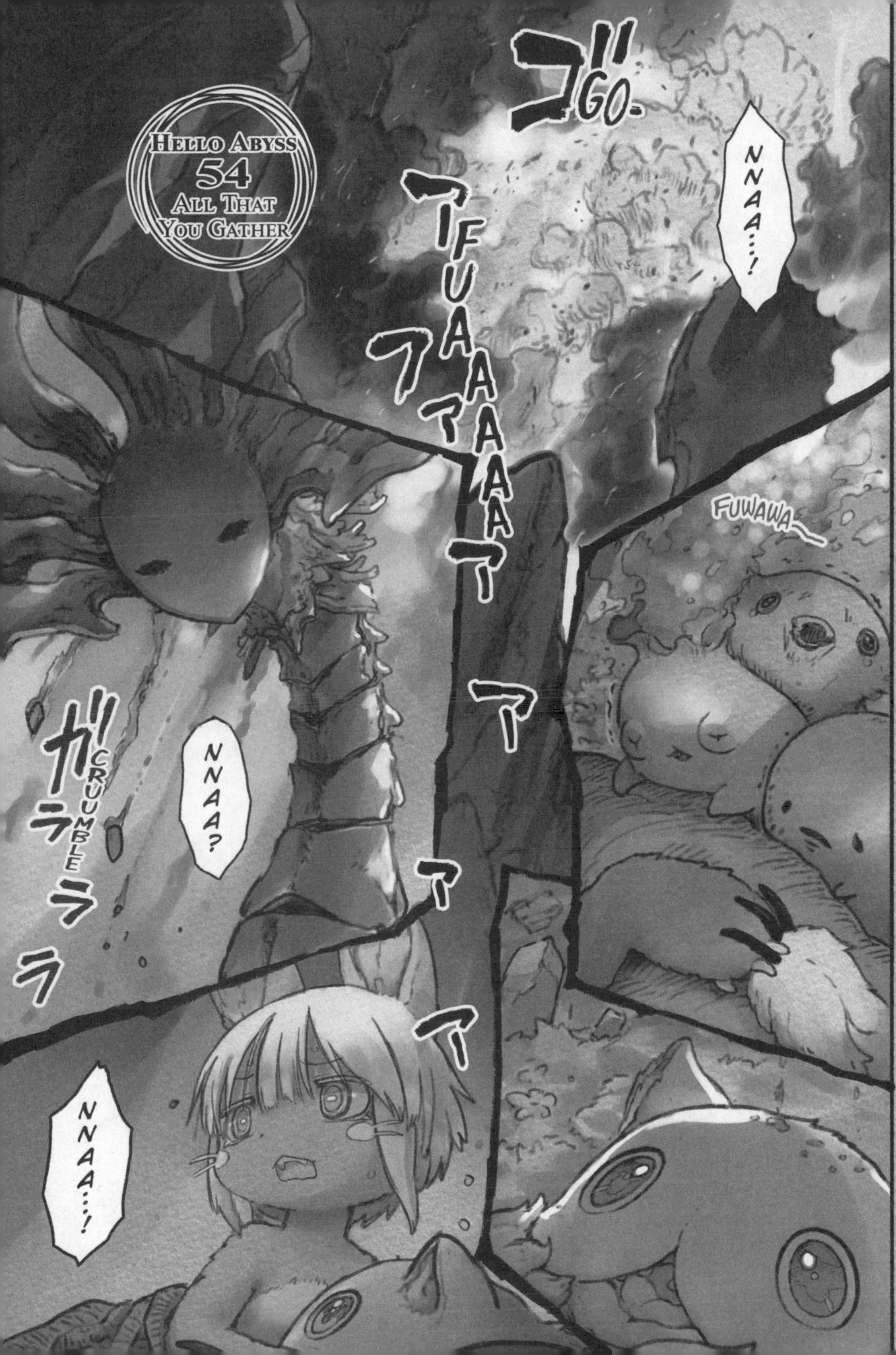

HELLO ABYSS
54
ALL THAT YOU GATHER
GO-
NNAA...!
FUAAAAAAA
FUWAWA~
NNAA?
CRUUMBLE
NNAA...!

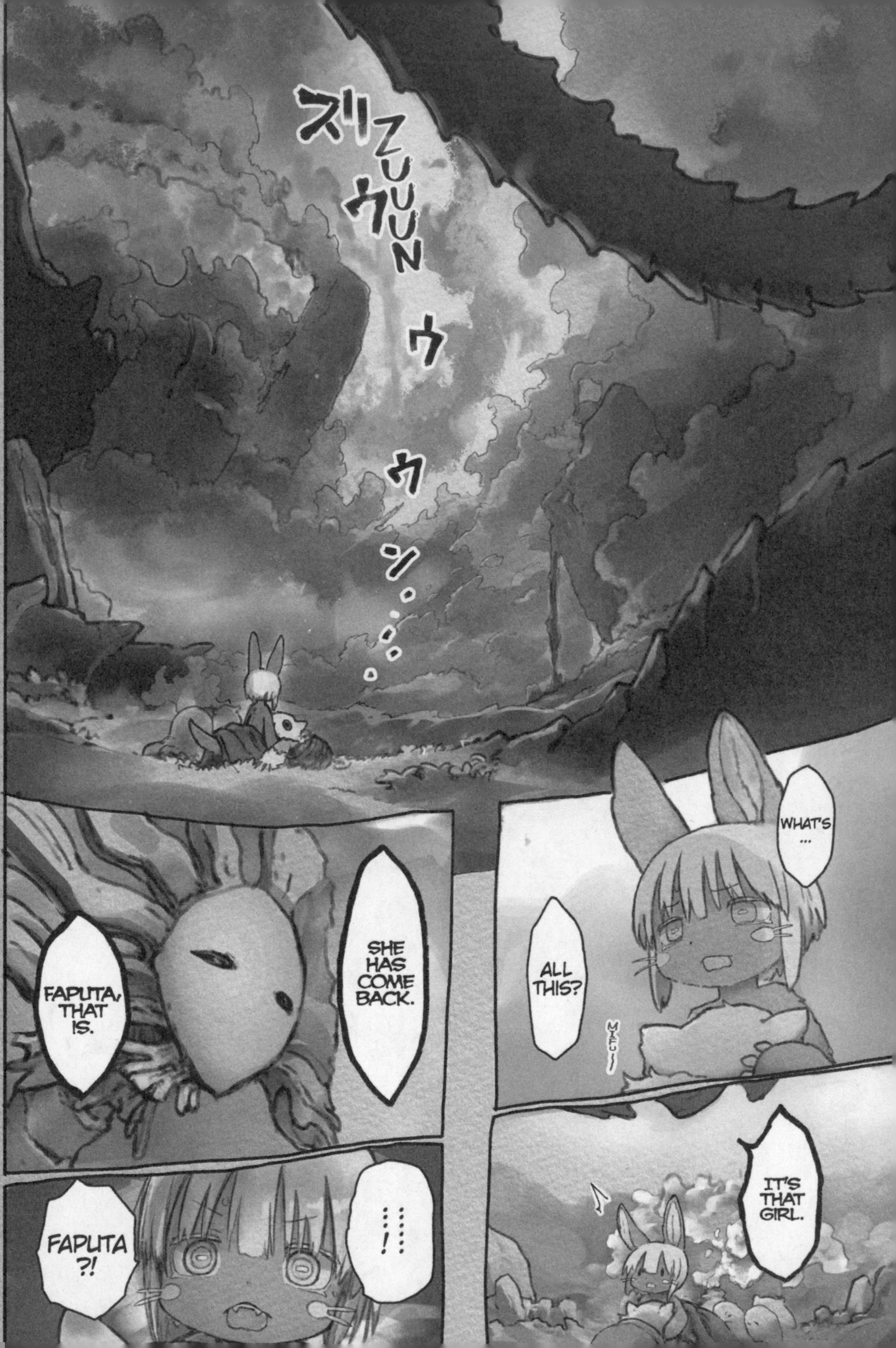
ズ ZUUUN ウ ウ ウ ン...
WHAT'S ...
ALL THIS?
MIFU~
SHE HAS COME BACK.
FAPUTA, THAT IS.
IT'S THAT GIRL.
......!
FAPUTA ?!

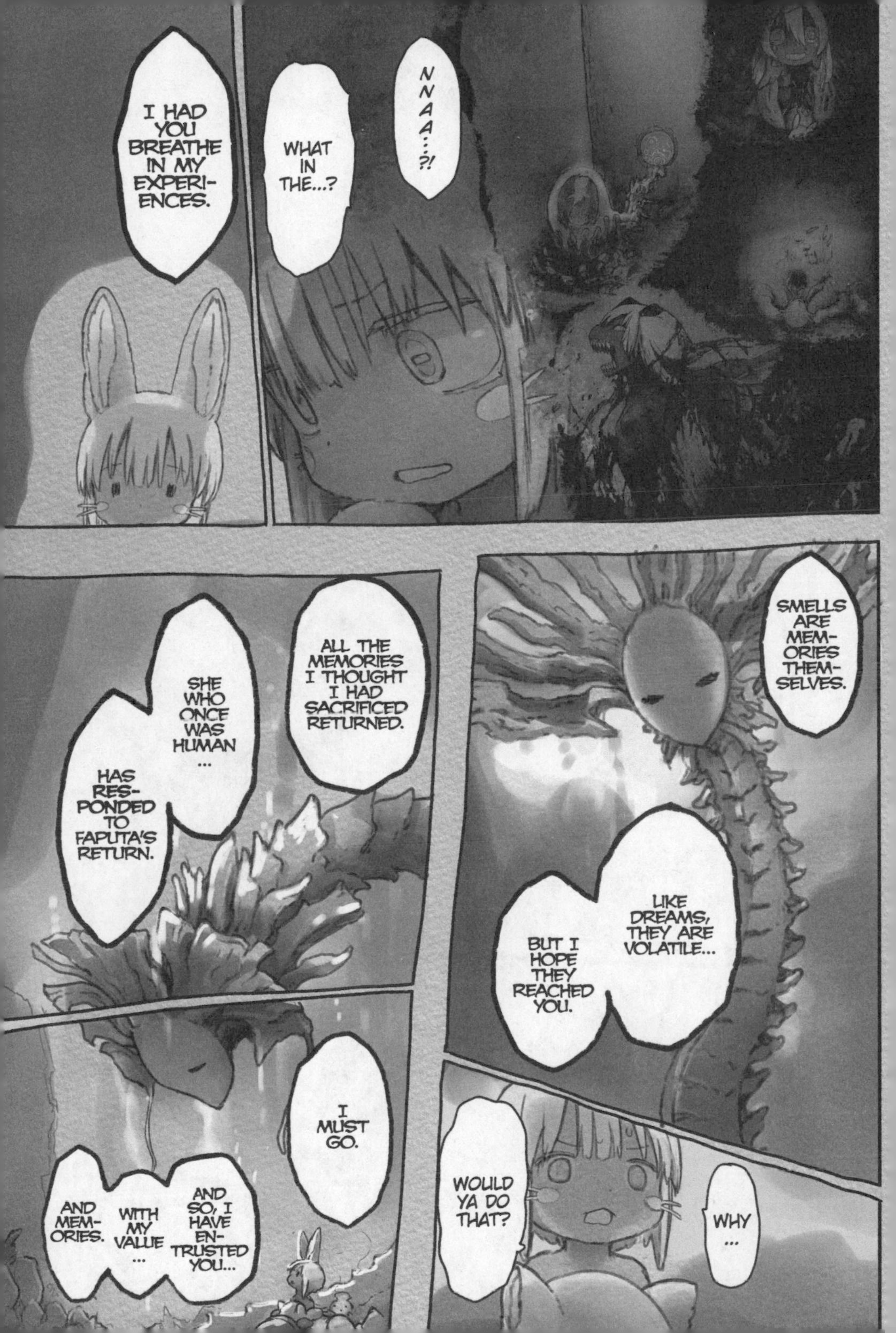
NNAA...?!
WHAT IN THE...?
I HAD YOU BREATHE IN MY EXPERIENCES.
SMELLS ARE MEMORIES THEMSELVES.
LIKE DREAMS, THEY ARE VOLATILE...
BUT I HOPE THEY REACHED YOU.
ALL THE MEMORIES I THOUGHT I HAD SACRIFICED RETURNED.
SHE WHO ONCE WAS HUMAN ...
HAS RESPONDED TO FAPUTA'S RETURN.
I MUST GO.
AND SO, I HAVE ENTRUSTED YOU...
WITH MY VALUE ...
AND MEMORIES.
WHY ...
WOULD YA DO THAT?

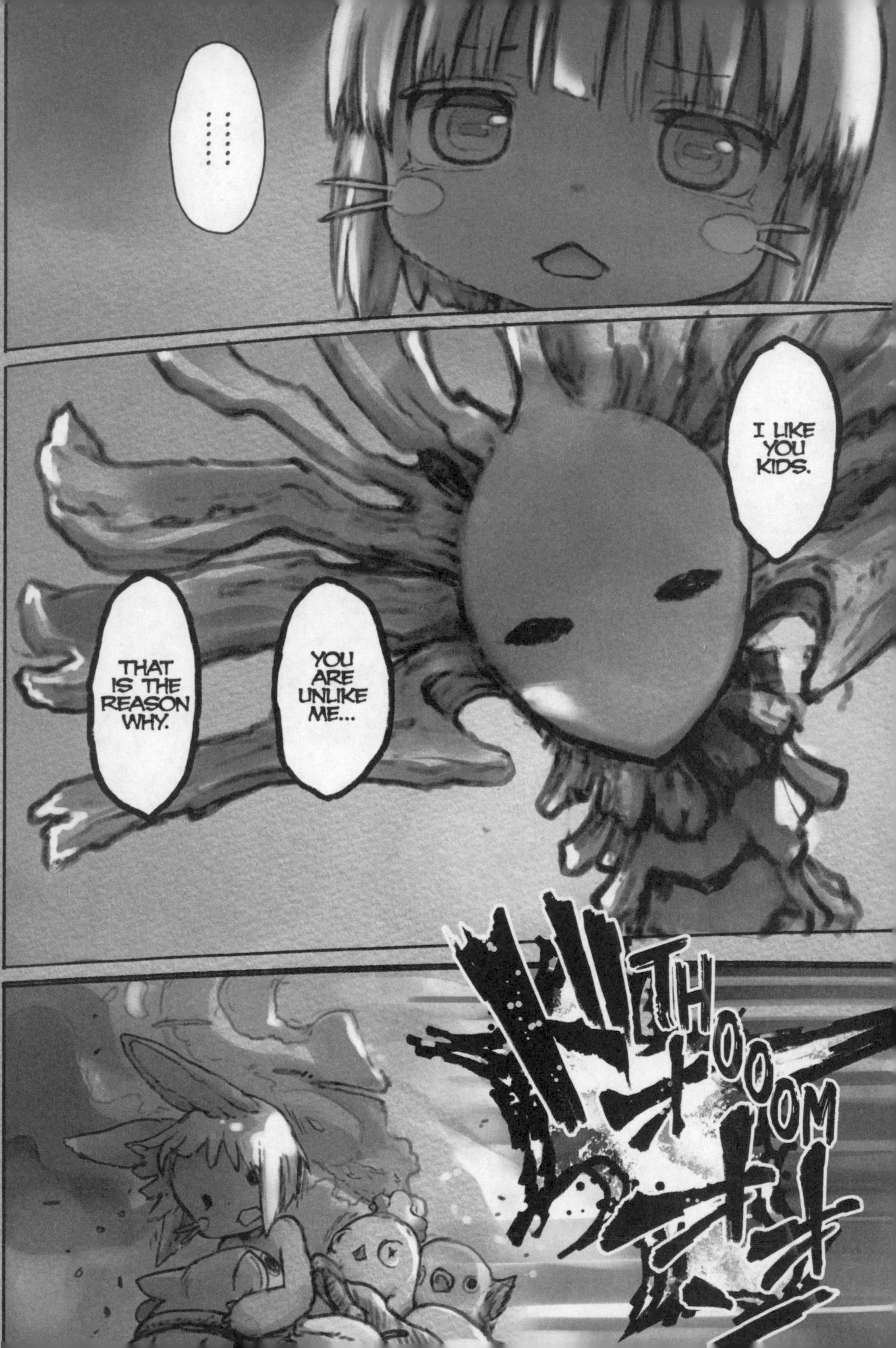
......
I LIKE YOU KIDS.
YOU ARE UNLIKE ME...
THAT IS THE REASON WHY.
THOOOM

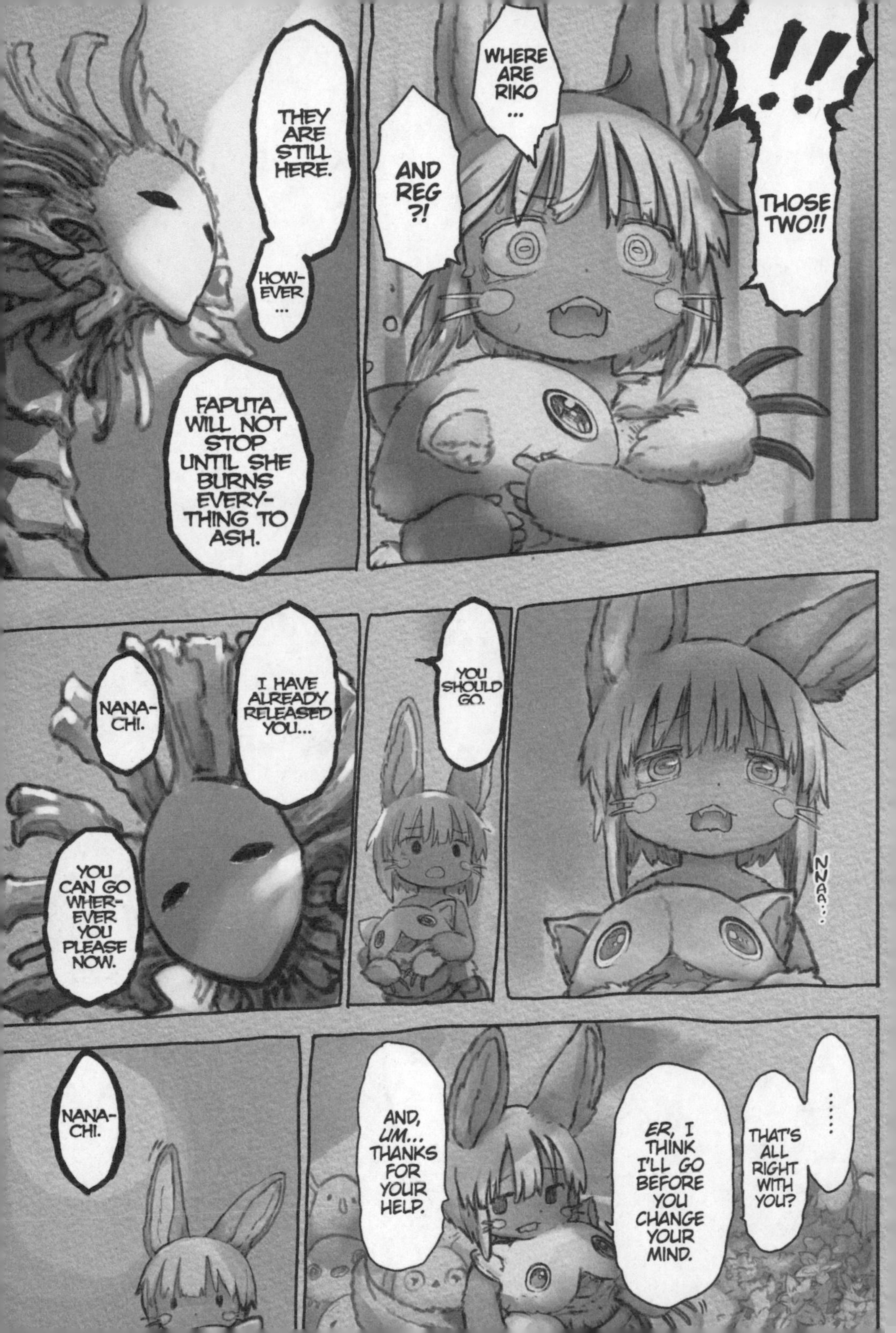
!!
THOSE TWO!!
WHERE ARE RIKO ...
AND REG ?!
THEY ARE STILL HERE.
HOWEVER ...
FAPUTA WILL NOT STOP UNTIL SHE BURNS EVERYTHING TO ASH.
NNAA...
YOU SHOULD GO.
I HAVE ALREADY RELEASED YOU...
NANA-CHI.
YOU CAN GO WHEREVER YOU PLEASE NOW.
......
THAT'S ALL RIGHT WITH YOU?
ER, I THINK I'LL GO BEFORE YOU CHANGE YOUR MIND.
AND, *UM*... THANKS FOR YOUR HELP.
NANA-CHI.

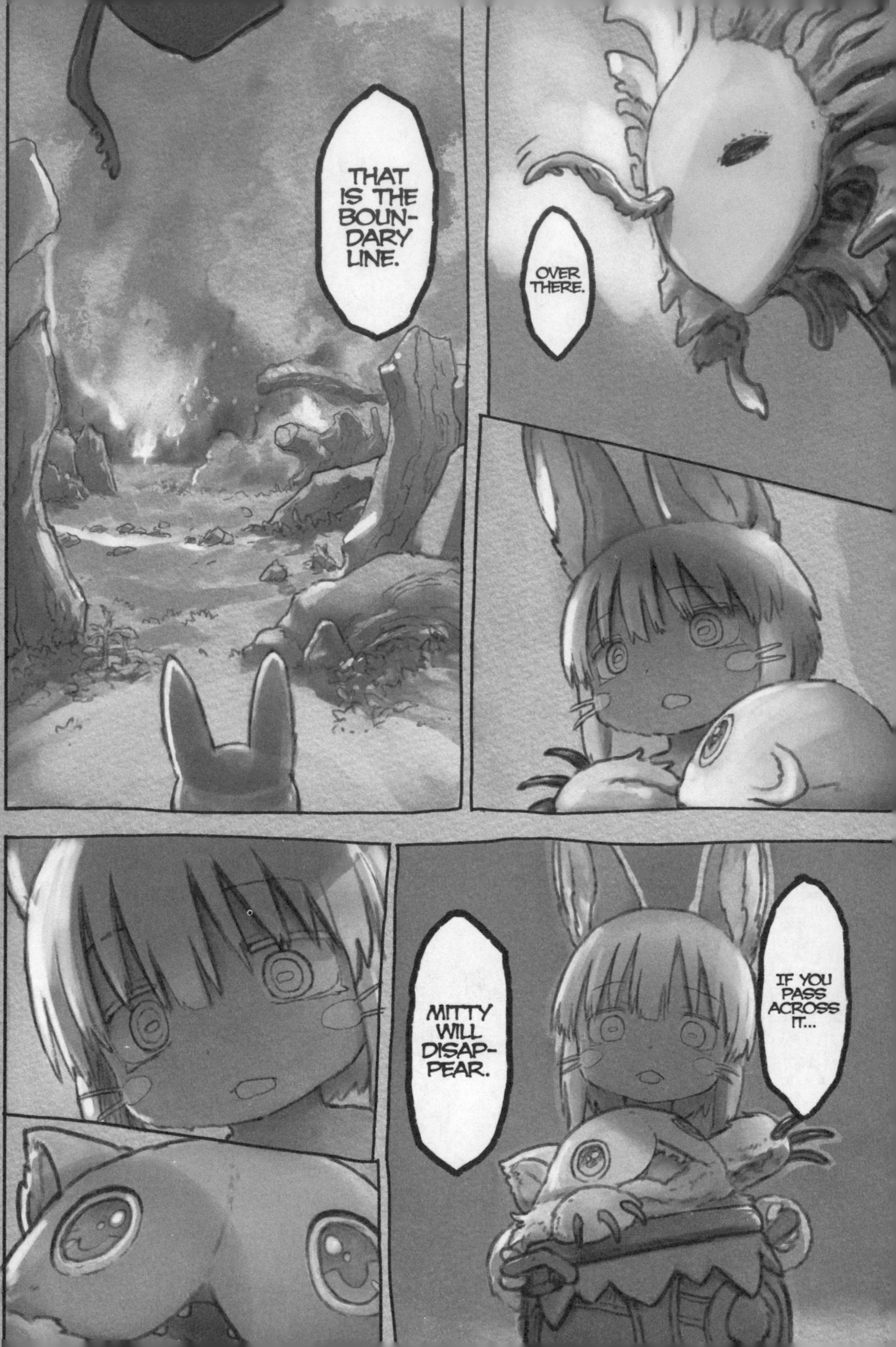
OVER THERE.
THAT IS THE BOUNDARY LINE.
IF YOU PASS ACROSS IT...
MITTY WILL DISAPPEAR.

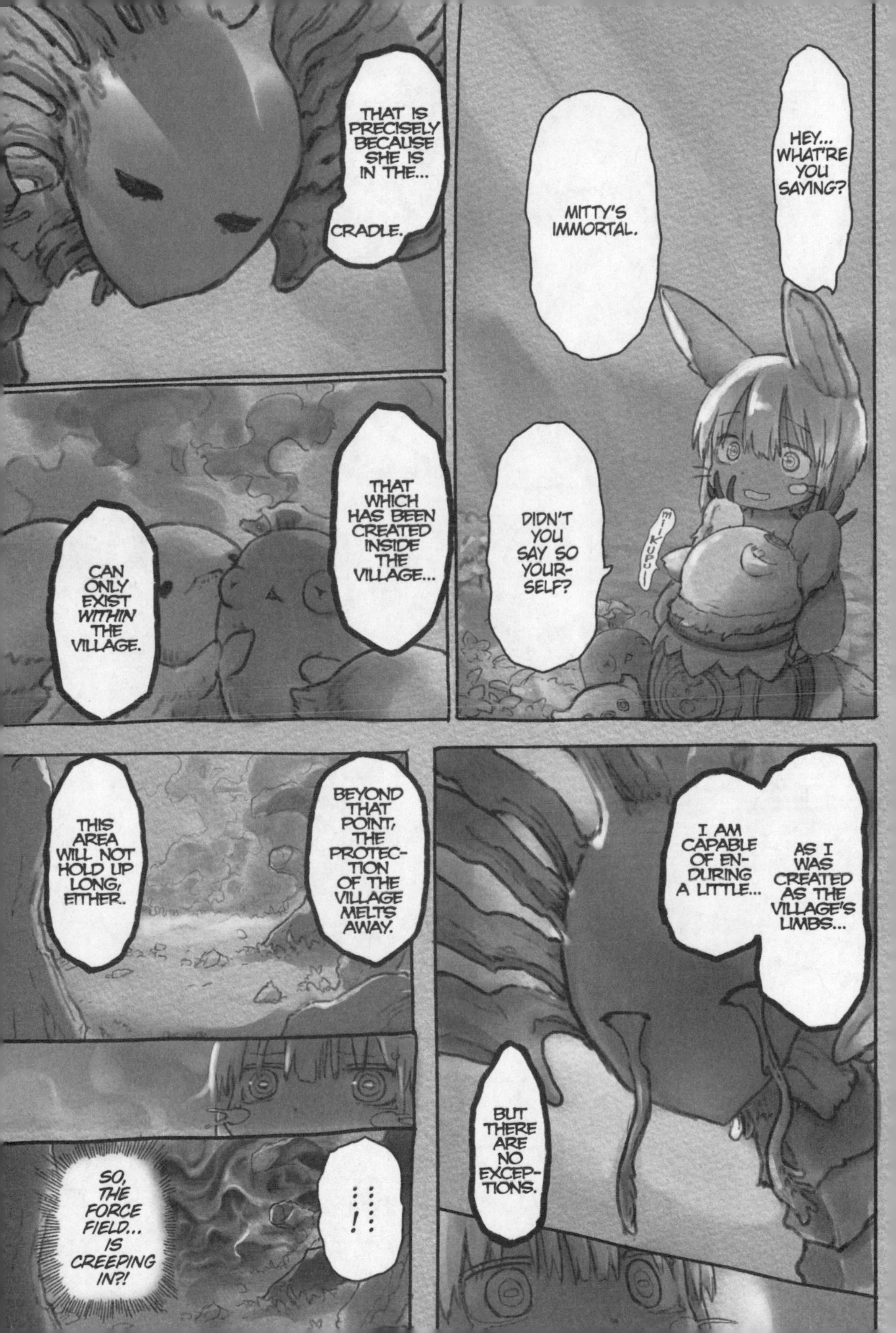
HEY... WHAT'RE YOU SAYING?
MITTY'S IMMORTAL.
DIDN'T YOU SAY SO YOURSELF?
MIKUPU!
THAT IS PRECISELY BECAUSE SHE IS IN THE...
CRADLE.
THAT WHICH HAS BEEN CREATED INSIDE THE VILLAGE...
CAN ONLY EXIST *WITHIN* THE VILLAGE.
AS I WAS CREATED AS THE VILLAGE'S LIMBS...
I AM CAPABLE OF ENDURING A LITTLE...
BUT THERE ARE NO EXCEPTIONS.
BEYOND THAT POINT, THE PROTECTION OF THE VILLAGE MELTS AWAY.
THIS AREA WILL NOT HOLD UP LONG, EITHER.
......!
SO, THE FORCE FIELD... IS CREEPING IN?!

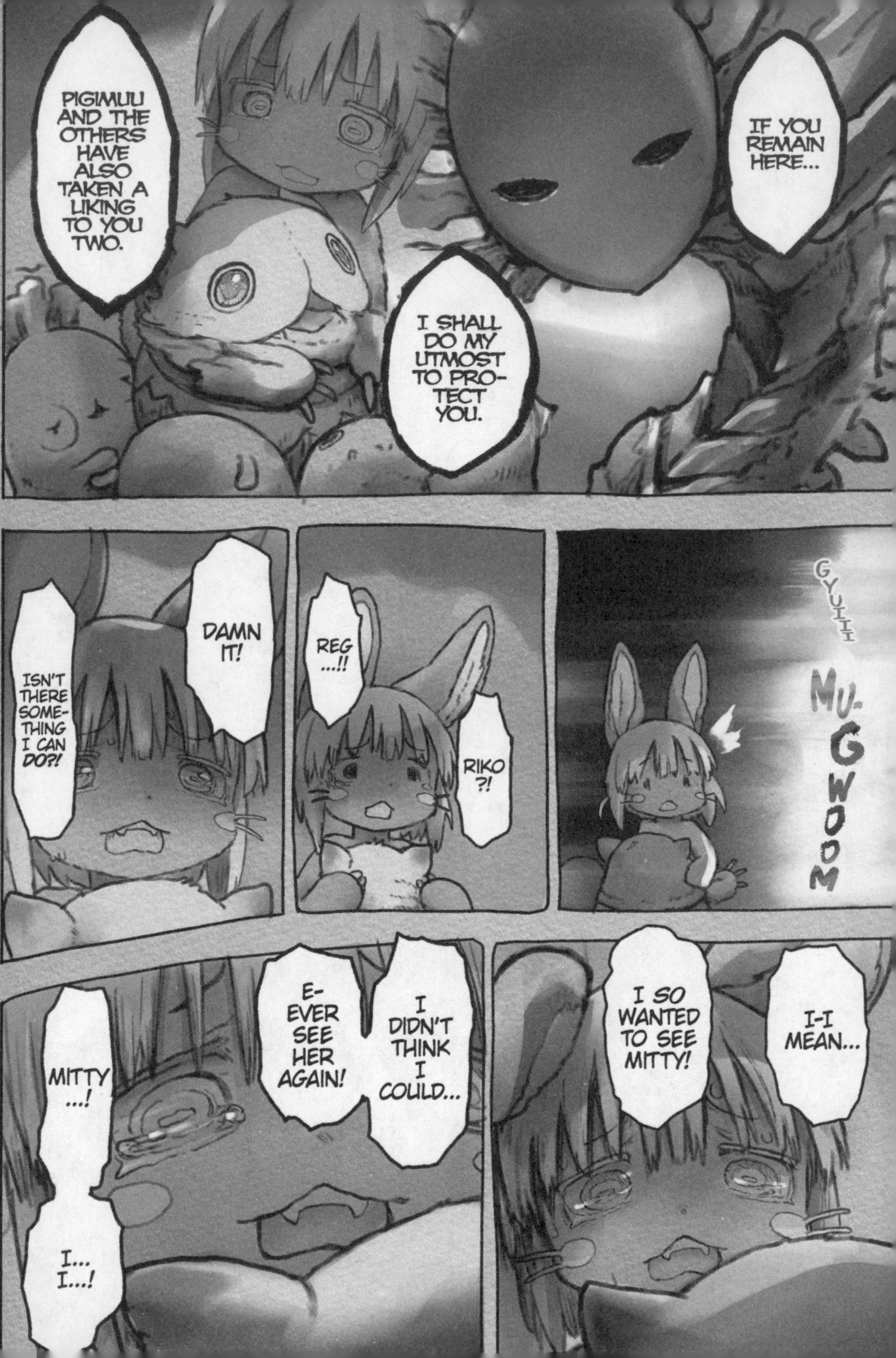
IF YOU REMAIN HERE...
I SHALL DO MY UTMOST TO PROTECT YOU.
PIGIMUU AND THE OTHERS HAVE ALSO TAKEN A LIKING TO YOU TWO.
GYUIII
MU-GWOOM
RIKO?!
REG...!!
DAMN IT!
ISN'T THERE SOMETHING I CAN DO?!
I-I MEAN...
I SO WANTED TO SEE MITTY!
I DIDN'T THINK I COULD...
E-EVER SEE HER AGAIN!
MITTY...!
I... I...!

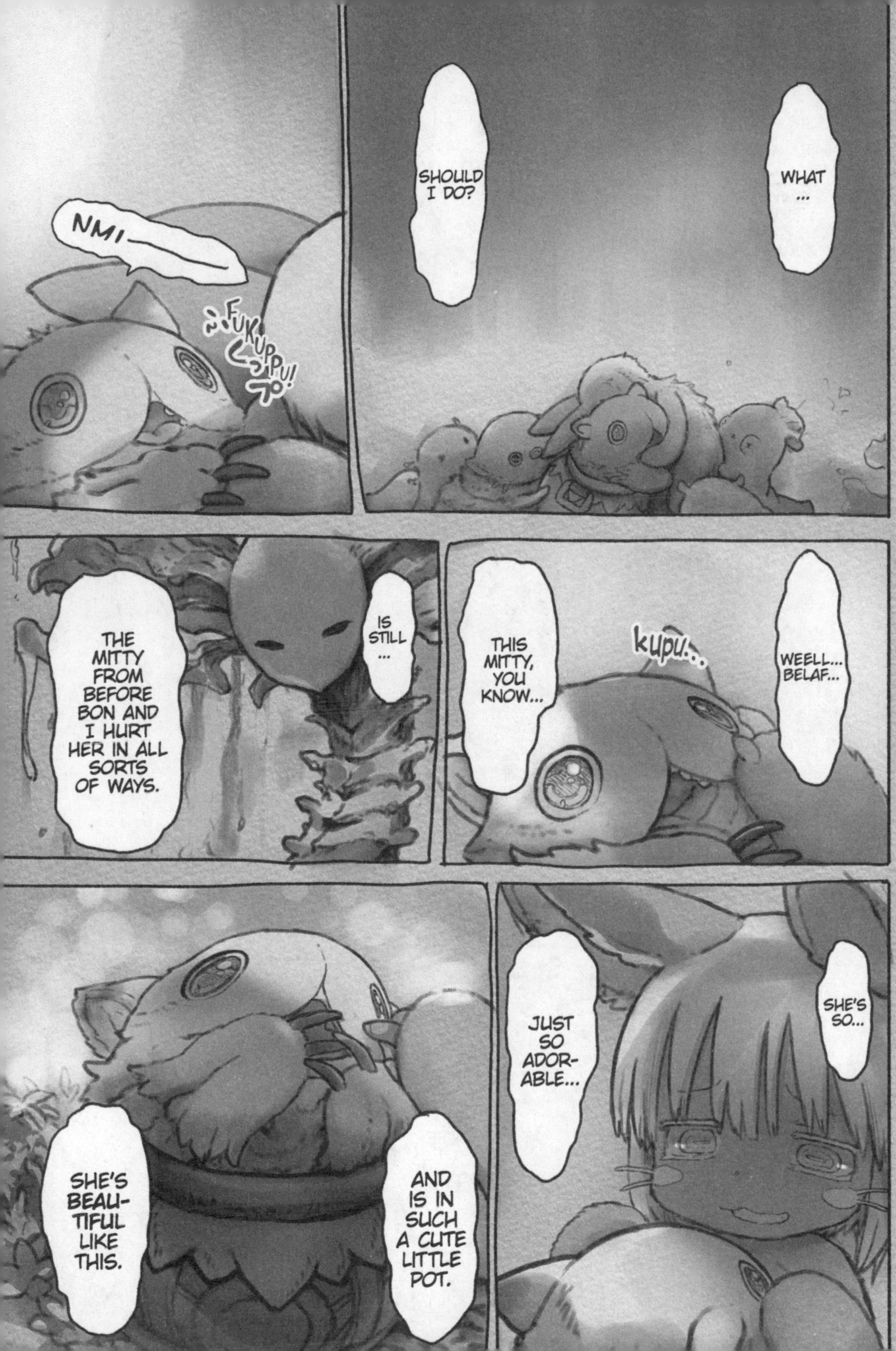
WHAT ...
SHOULD I DO?
NMI—
FUKUPPU!
WEELL... BELAF...
kupu...
THIS MITTY, YOU KNOW...
IS STILL ...
THE MITTY FROM BEFORE BON AND I HURT HER IN ALL SORTS OF WAYS.
SHE'S SO...
JUST SO ADORABLE...
AND IS IN SUCH A CUTE LITTLE POT.
SHE'S BEAUTIFUL LIKE THIS.

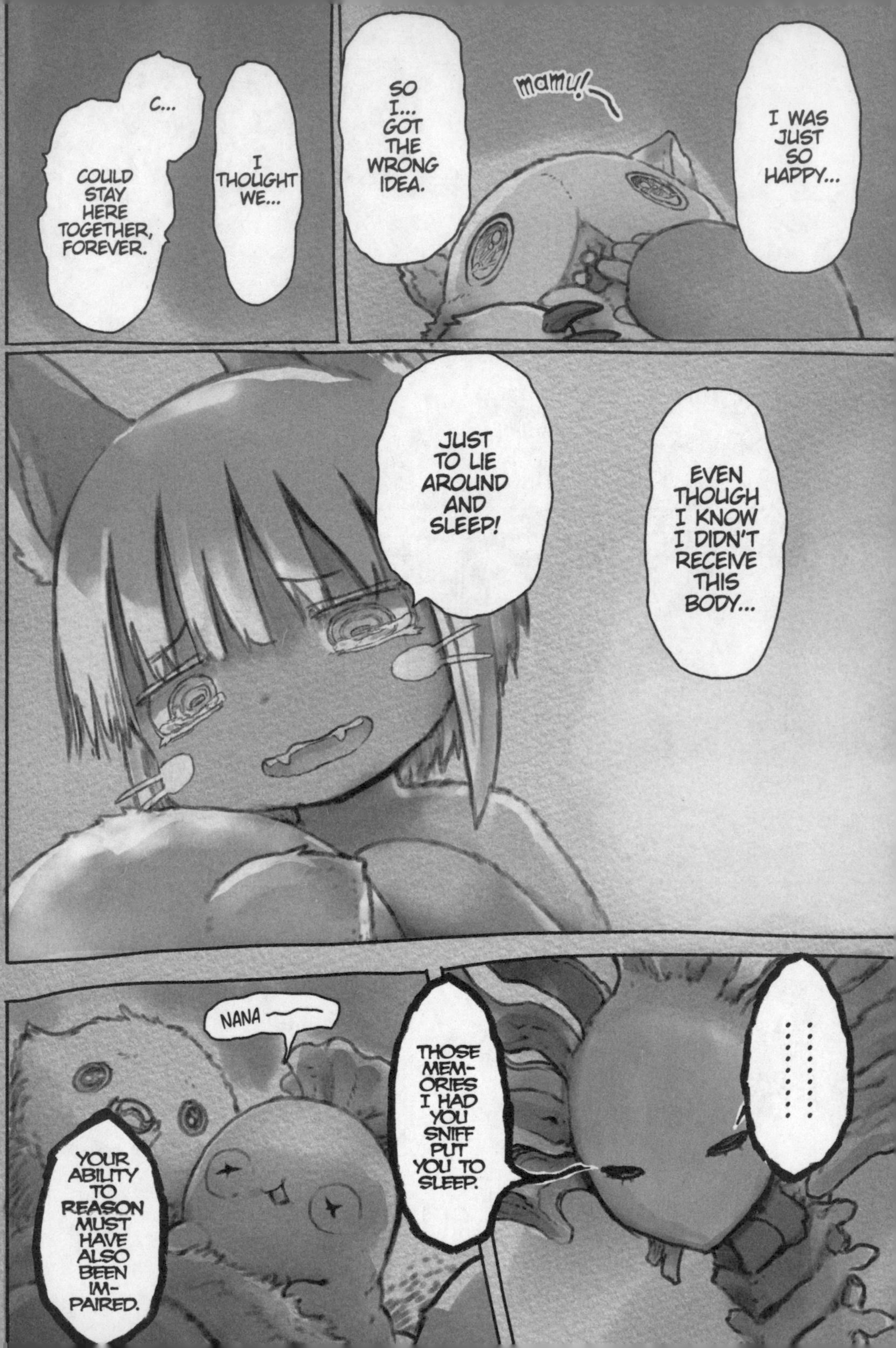
I WAS JUST SO HAPPY...
mamu!~
SO I... GOT THE WRONG IDEA.
I THOUGHT WE...
C...
COULD STAY HERE TOGETHER, FOREVER.
EVEN THOUGH I KNOW I DIDN'T RECEIVE THIS BODY...
JUST TO LIE AROUND AND SLEEP!
......
THOSE MEMORIES I HAD YOU SNIFF PUT YOU TO SLEEP.
NANA ~~
YOUR ABILITY TO REASON MUST HAVE ALSO BEEN IMPAIRED.

EITHER WAY, I WOULD'VE CHOSEN TO STAY BY MITTY'S SIDE.

THAT'S THE WAY I AM.

I KNOW THAT ABOUT MYSELF.

THAT'S OKAY.

PUIE.

NA!~

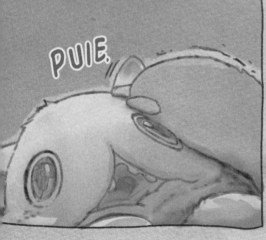

BE GOING NOW.

I'LL...

H....

HEY, BELAF ...?

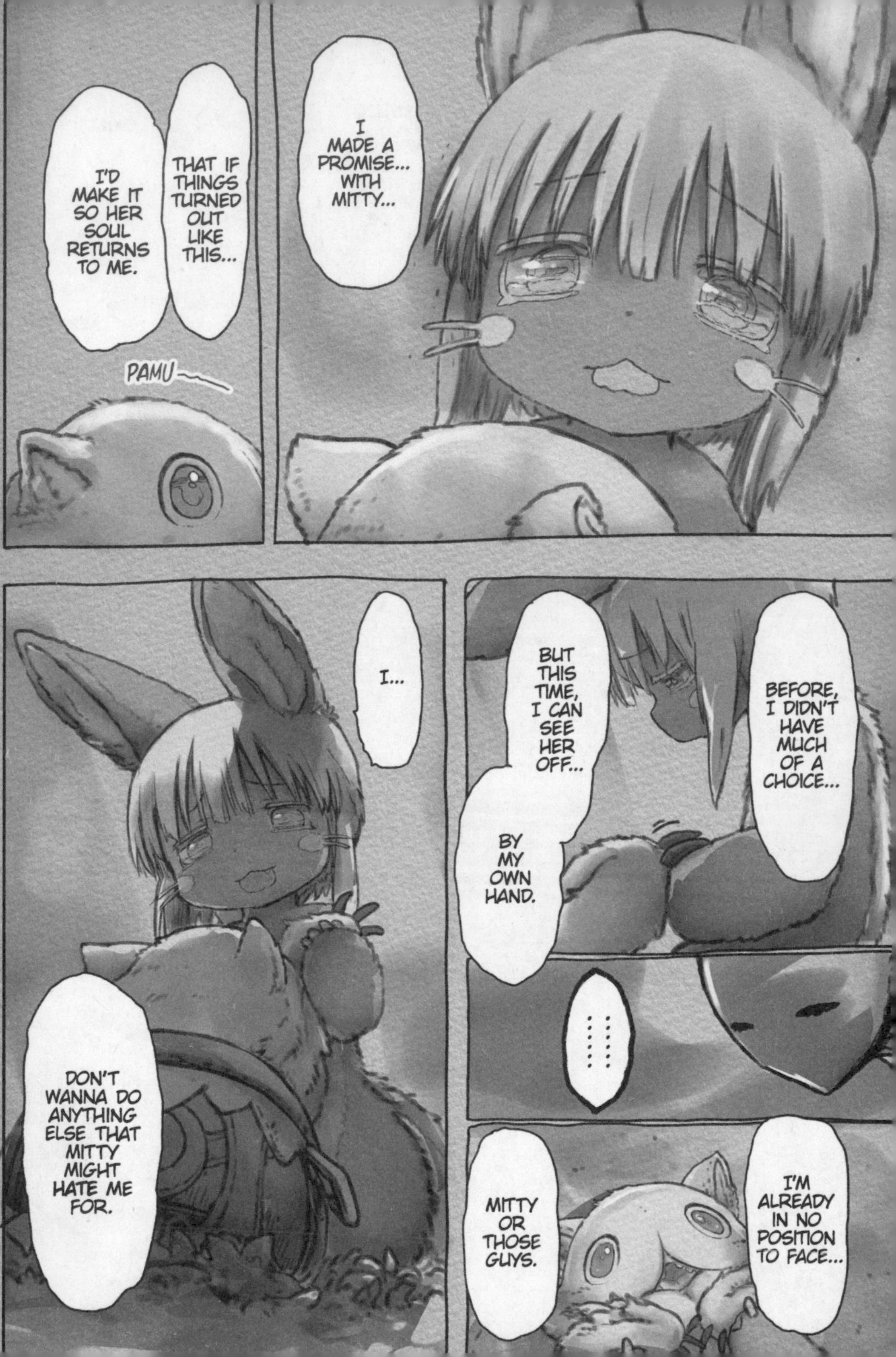
I MADE A PROMISE... WITH MITTY...
THAT IF THINGS TURNED OUT LIKE THIS...
I'D MAKE IT SO HER SOUL RETURNS TO ME.
PAMU~
BEFORE, I DIDN'T HAVE MUCH OF A CHOICE...
BUT THIS TIME, I CAN SEE HER OFF...
BY MY OWN HAND.
......
I'M ALREADY IN NO POSITION TO FACE...
MITTY OR THOSE GUYS.
I...
DON'T WANNA DO ANYTHING ELSE THAT MITTY MIGHT HATE ME FOR.

TAKING A LIKING TO MITTY.

THANKS FOR...

SEE YA, BELAF.

WEELL...

FU

RAFU

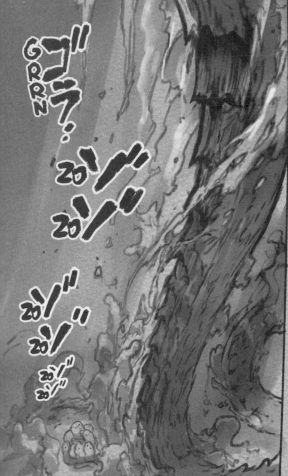

GRRRN

ZO

ZO

ZO

ZO

ZO

ZO

ZU

ZO

ZO

PI=
CRMBL

BEKYA

KISI

KI PU PU PU.

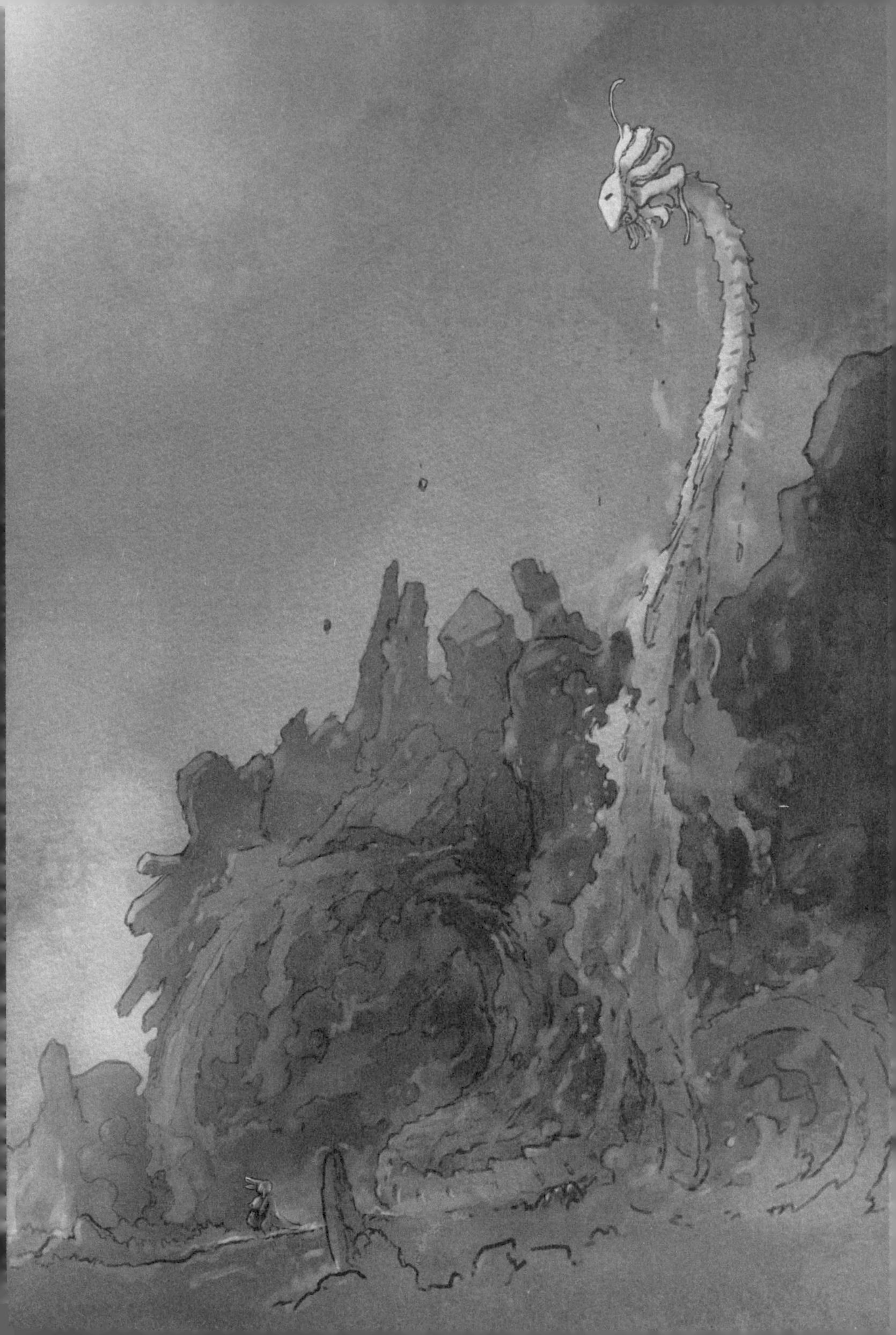

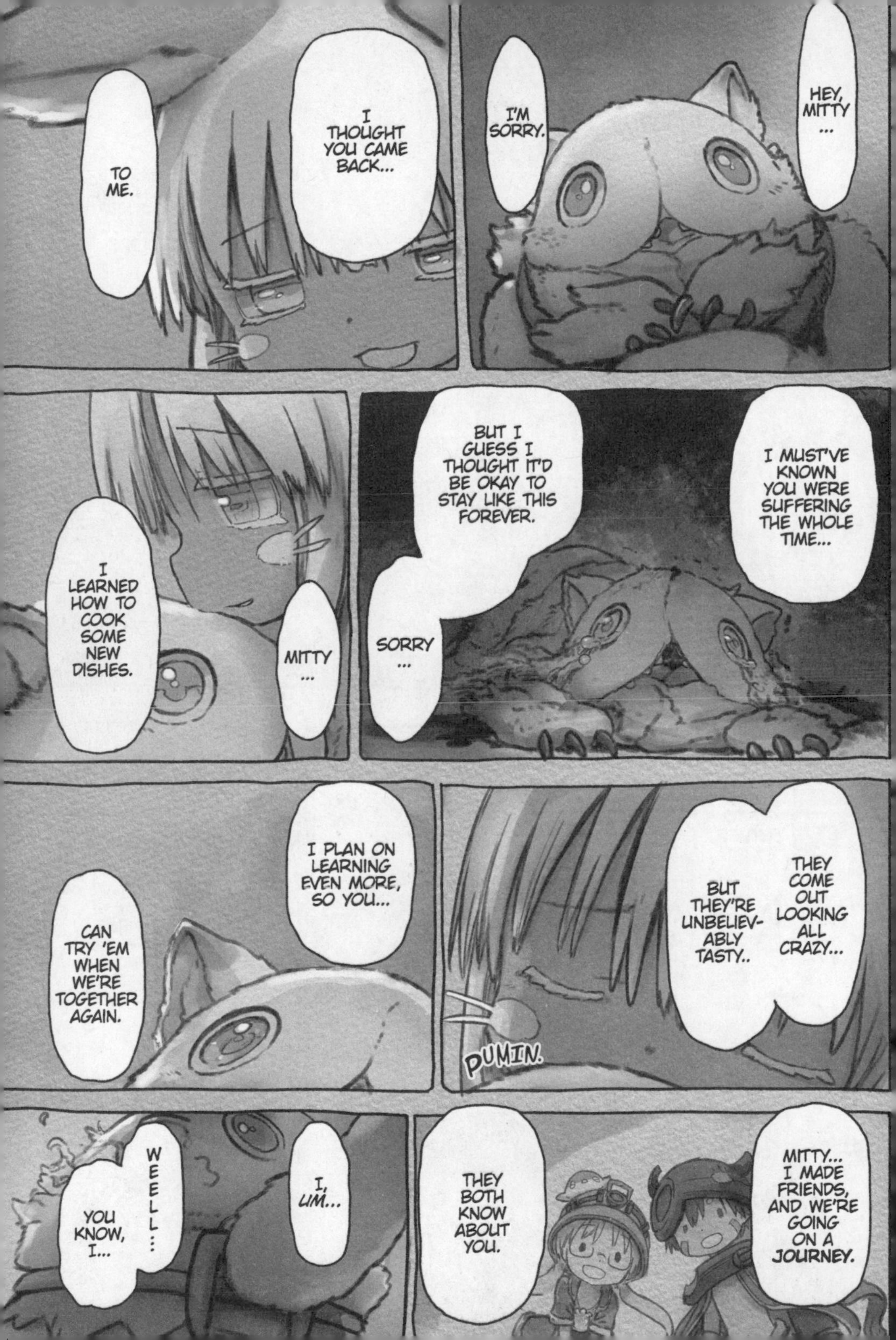

HEY, MITTY ...
I'M SORRY.
I THOUGHT YOU CAME BACK...
TO ME.
I MUST'VE KNOWN YOU WERE SUFFERING THE WHOLE TIME...
BUT I GUESS I THOUGHT IT'D BE OKAY TO STAY LIKE THIS FOREVER.
SORRY ...
MITTY ...
I LEARNED HOW TO COOK SOME NEW DISHES.
THEY COME OUT LOOKING ALL CRAZY...
BUT THEY'RE UNBELIEV-ABLY TASTY..
PUMIN.
I PLAN ON LEARNING EVEN MORE, SO YOU...
CAN TRY 'EM WHEN WE'RE TOGETHER AGAIN.
MITTY... I MADE FRIENDS, AND WE'RE GOING ON A JOURNEY.
THEY BOTH KNOW ABOUT YOU.
I, UM...
WEELL...
YOU KNOW, I...

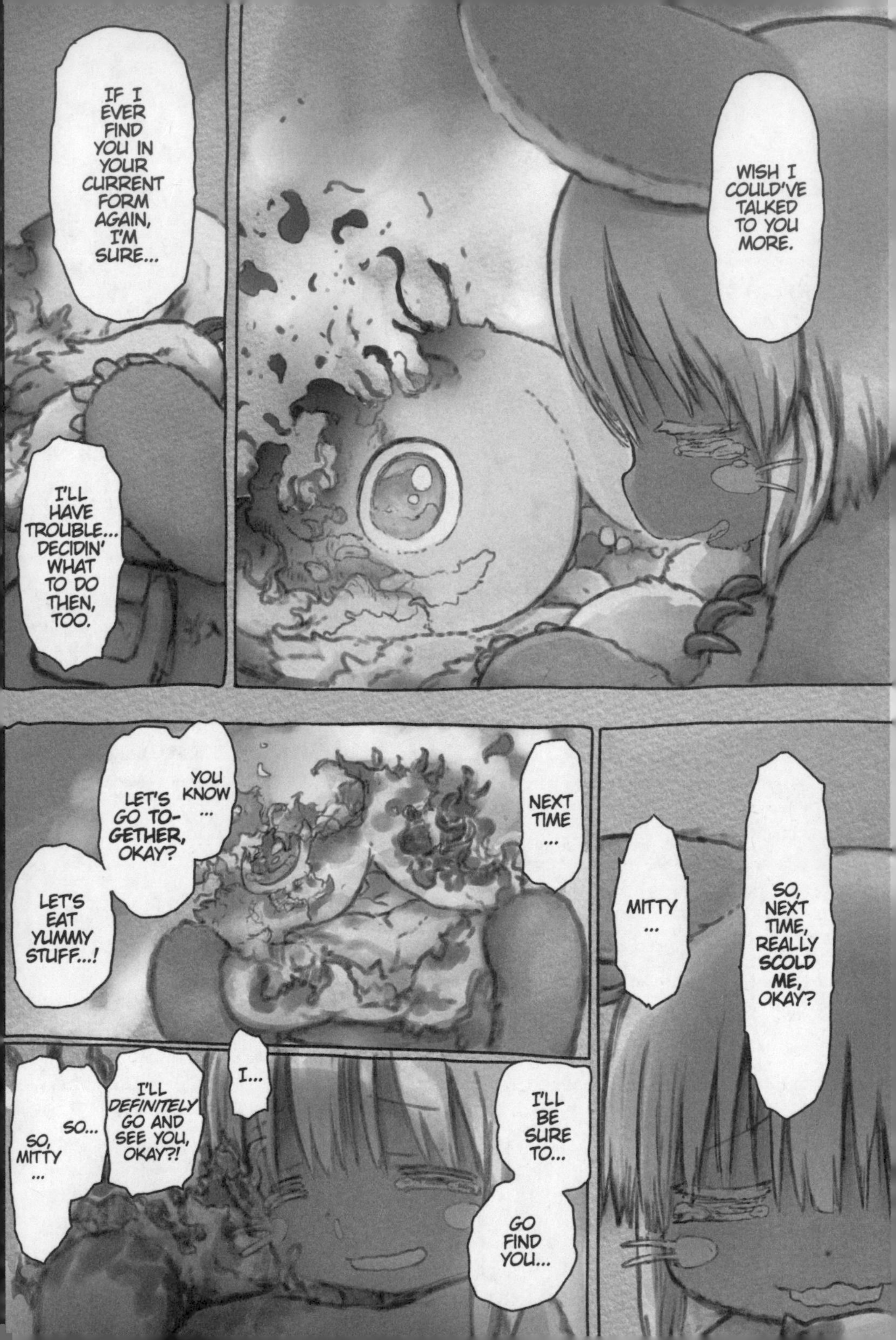
WISH I COULD'VE TALKED TO YOU MORE.
IF I EVER FIND YOU IN YOUR CURRENT FORM AGAIN, I'M SURE...
I'LL HAVE TROUBLE... DECIDIN' WHAT TO DO THEN, TOO.
SO, NEXT TIME, REALLY SCOLD ME, OKAY?
MITTY ...
NEXT TIME ...
YOU KNOW ...
LET'S GO TO-GETHER, OKAY?
LET'S EAT YUMMY STUFF...!
I'LL BE SURE TO...
GO FIND YOU...
I...
I'LL *DEFINITELY* GO AND SEE YOU, OKAY?!
SO...
SO, MITTY ...

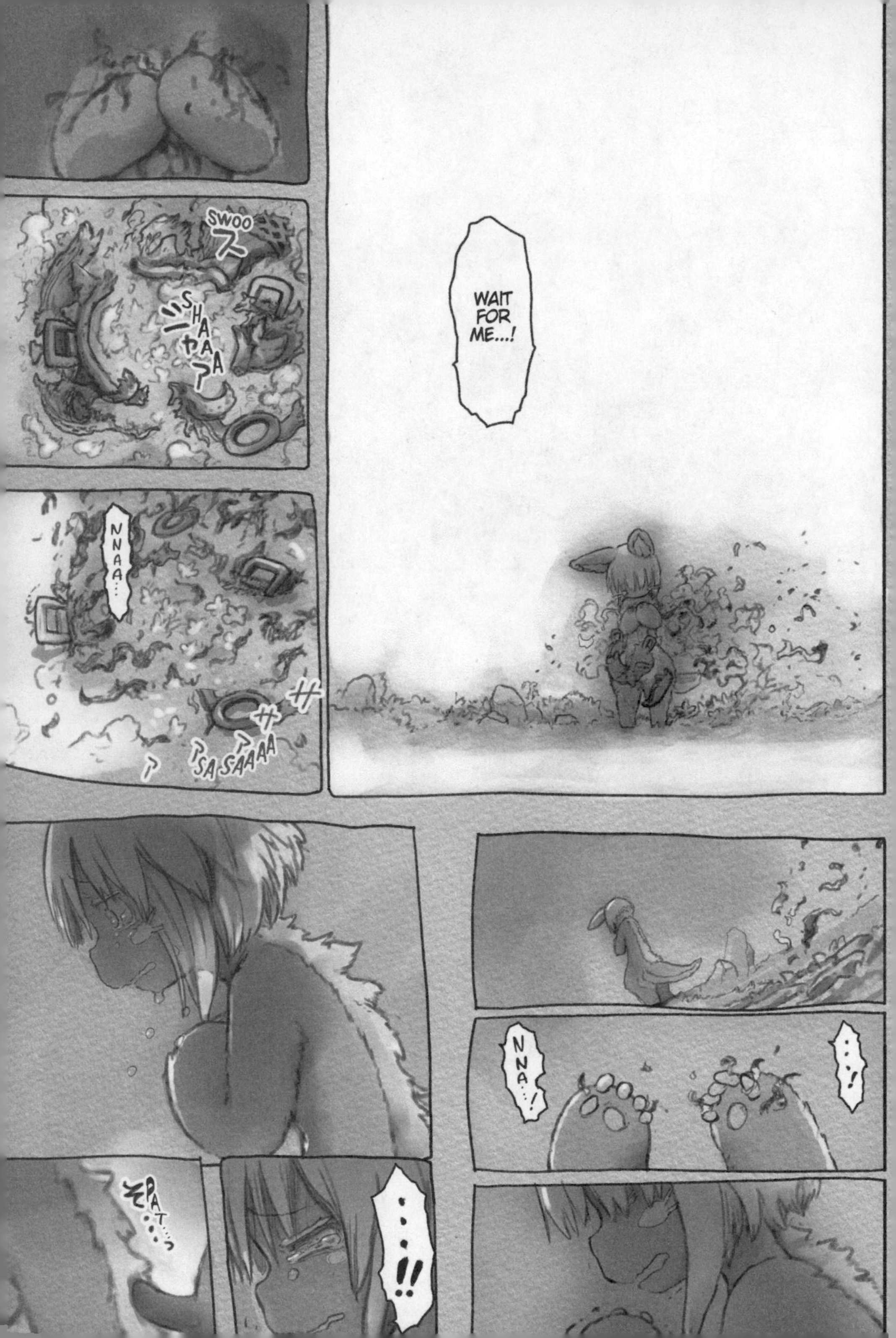
WAIT FOR ME...!
SWOO
SHAAAA
NNAA...
TSA SAAAA
...!
NNA...!
...!!
PAT...

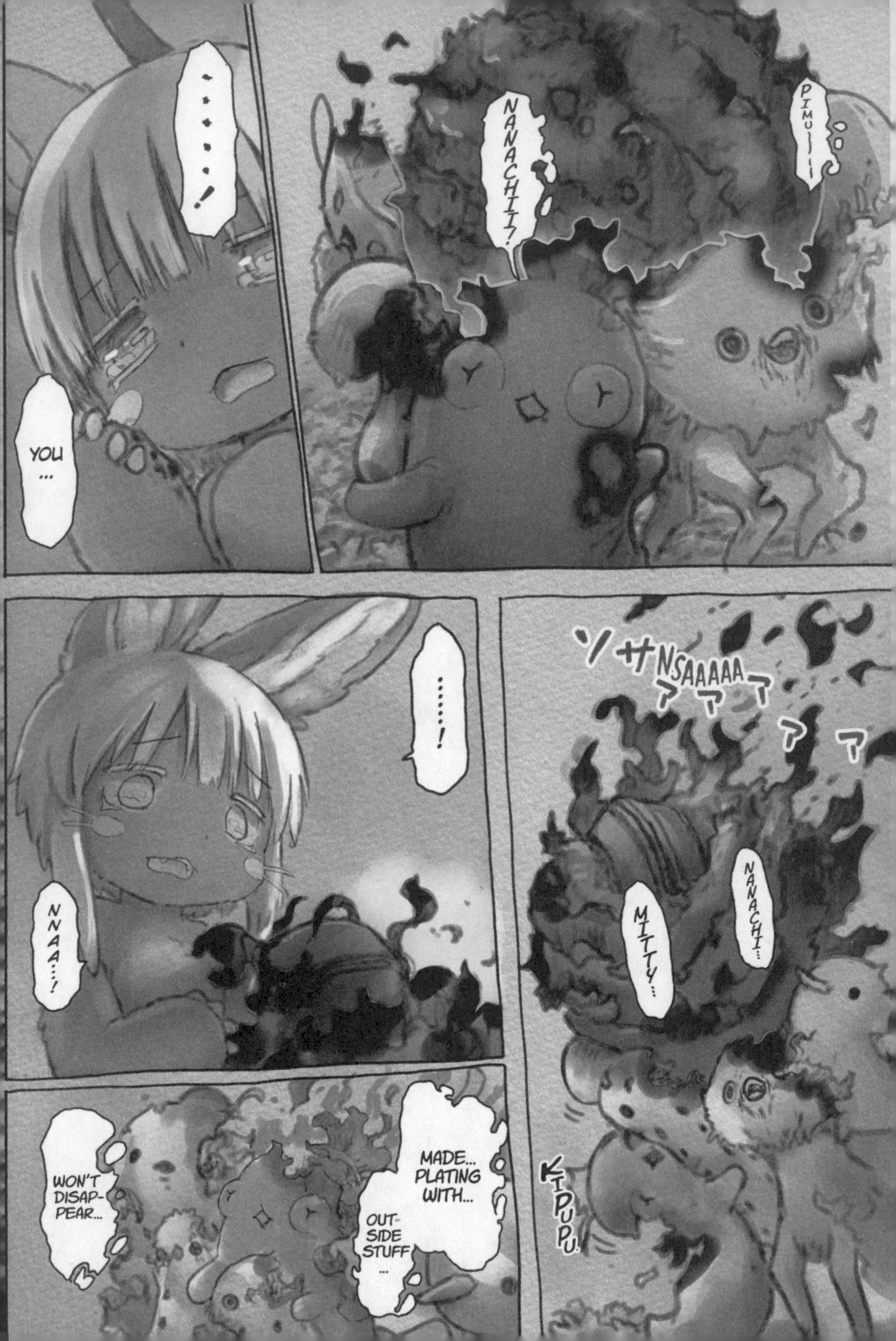
PIMU!!!
NANACHI!?
......!
YOU...
NSAAAAA
NANACHI...
MITTY...
KIPUPU.
......!
NNAA...!?
MADE... PLATING WITH... OUTSIDE STUFF...
WON'T DISAPPEAR...

TAKE WITH YOU...

IMPURITY
...

ゴ゛
RMB

ゴ゛
RMB

ゴ゛
RMB

LONG-ING...

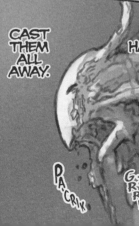

CAST THEM ALL AWAY.

I HAVE
...

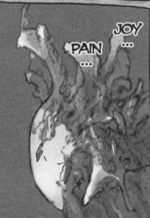

PAIN
...

JOY
...

パ-CRIK

G-R-R-ゴ゛ッ RRゴP゛...

ゴ゛
RMB

ゴ゛
RMB

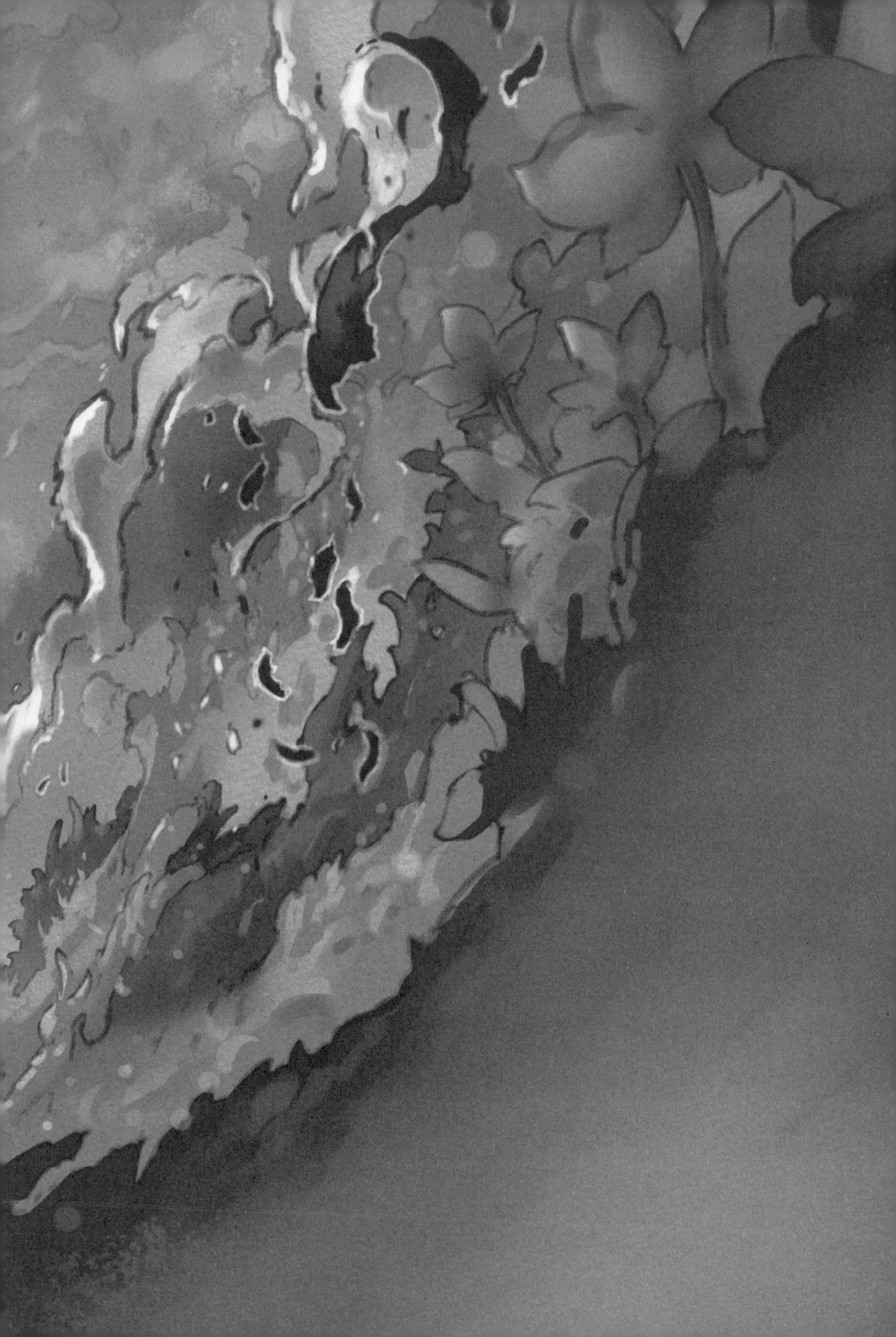

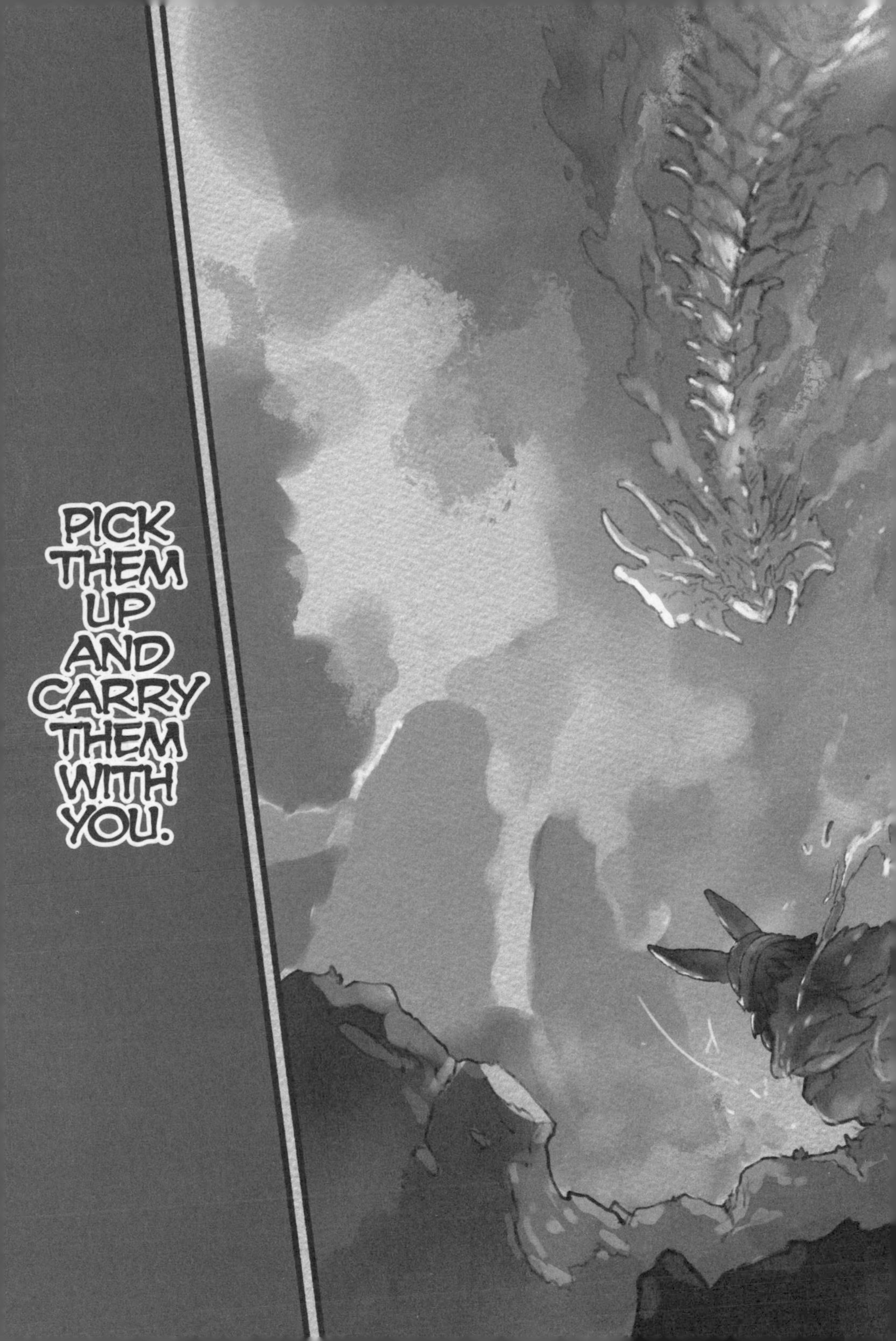
PICK THEM UP AND CARRY THEM WITH YOU.

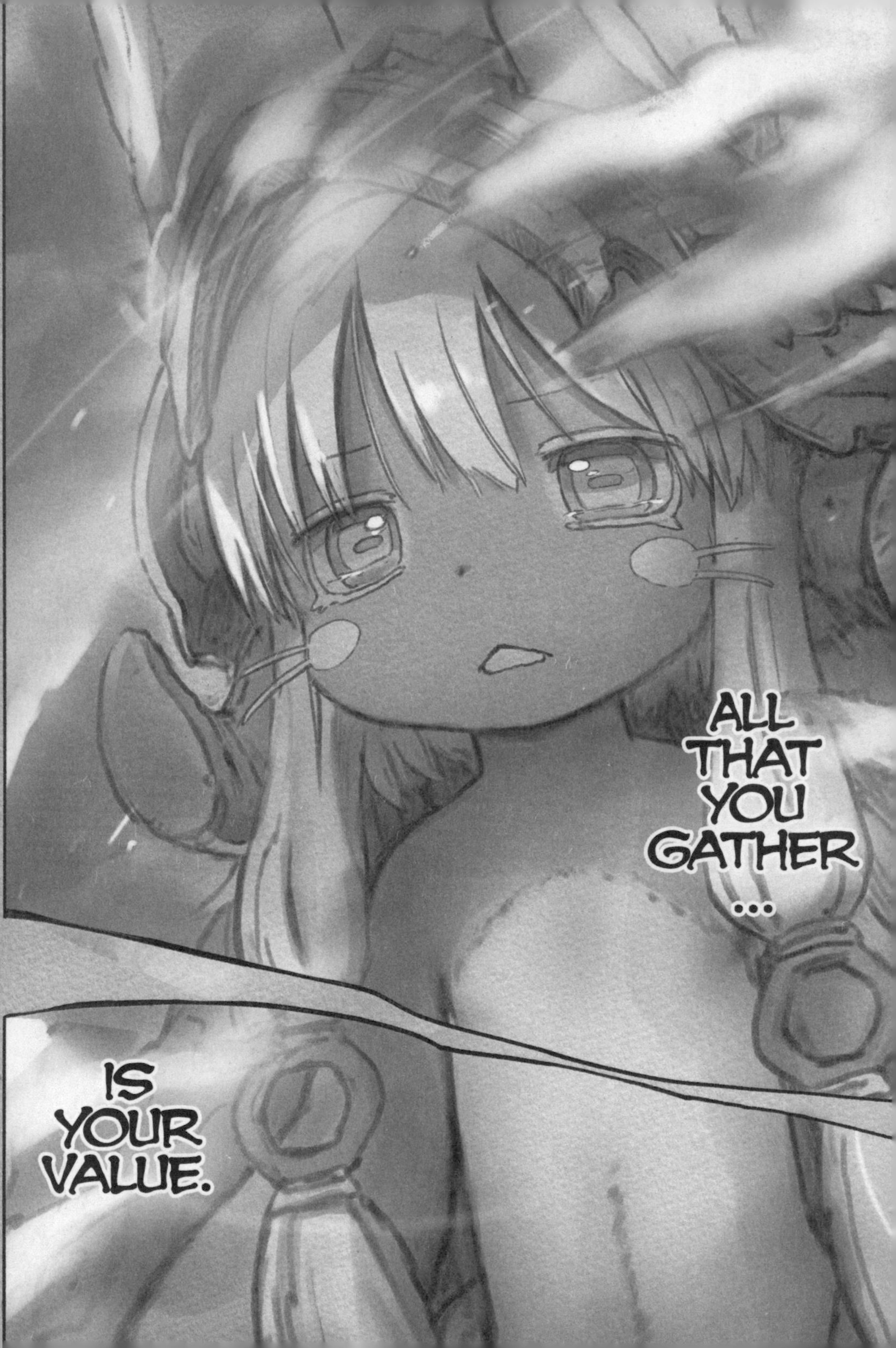
ALL THAT YOU GATHER ...
IS YOUR VALUE.

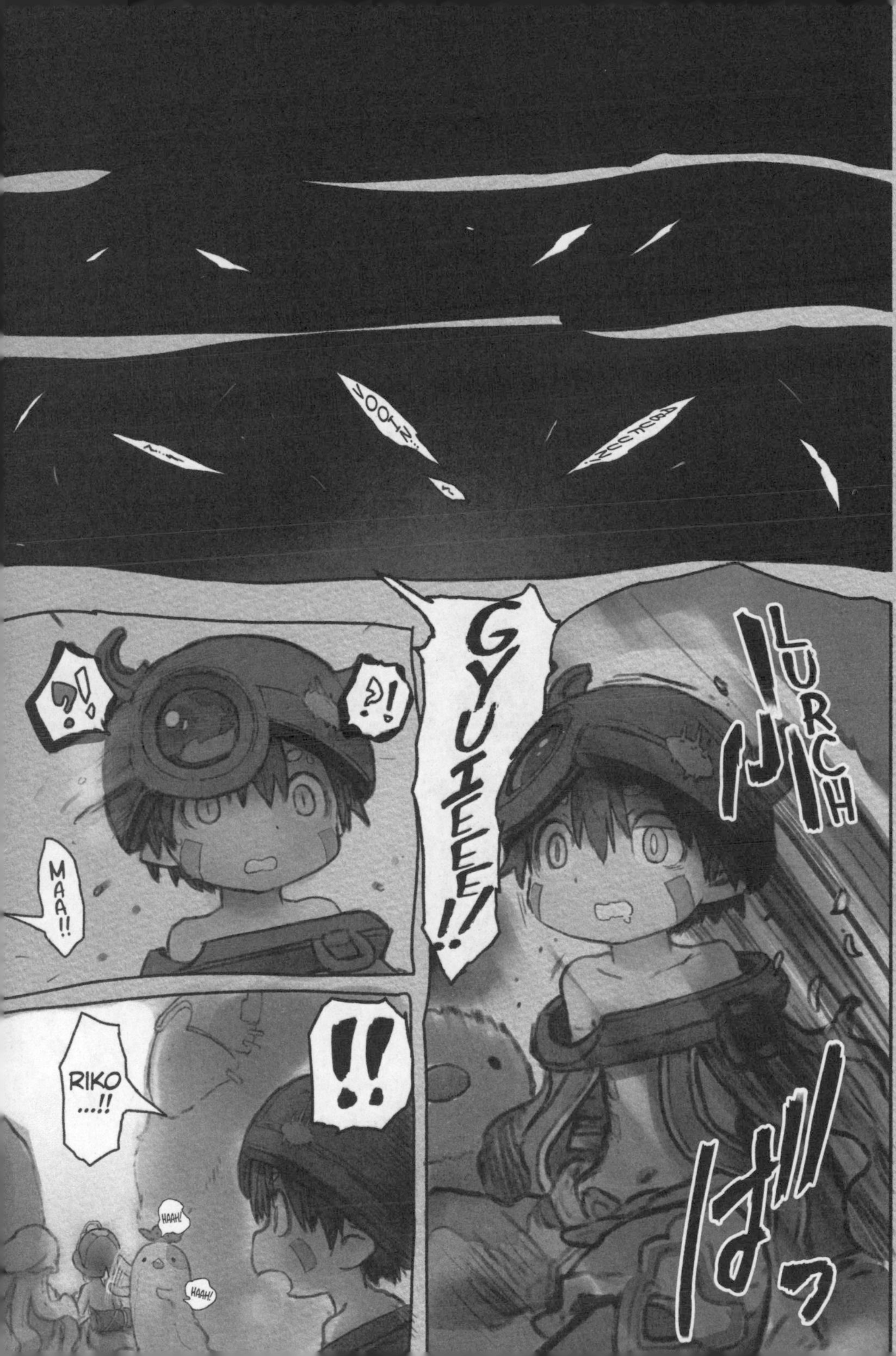

GYUIEEE!!
LURCH
?!
?!
MAA!!
はっ
!!
RIKO ...!!
HAAH!
HAAH!

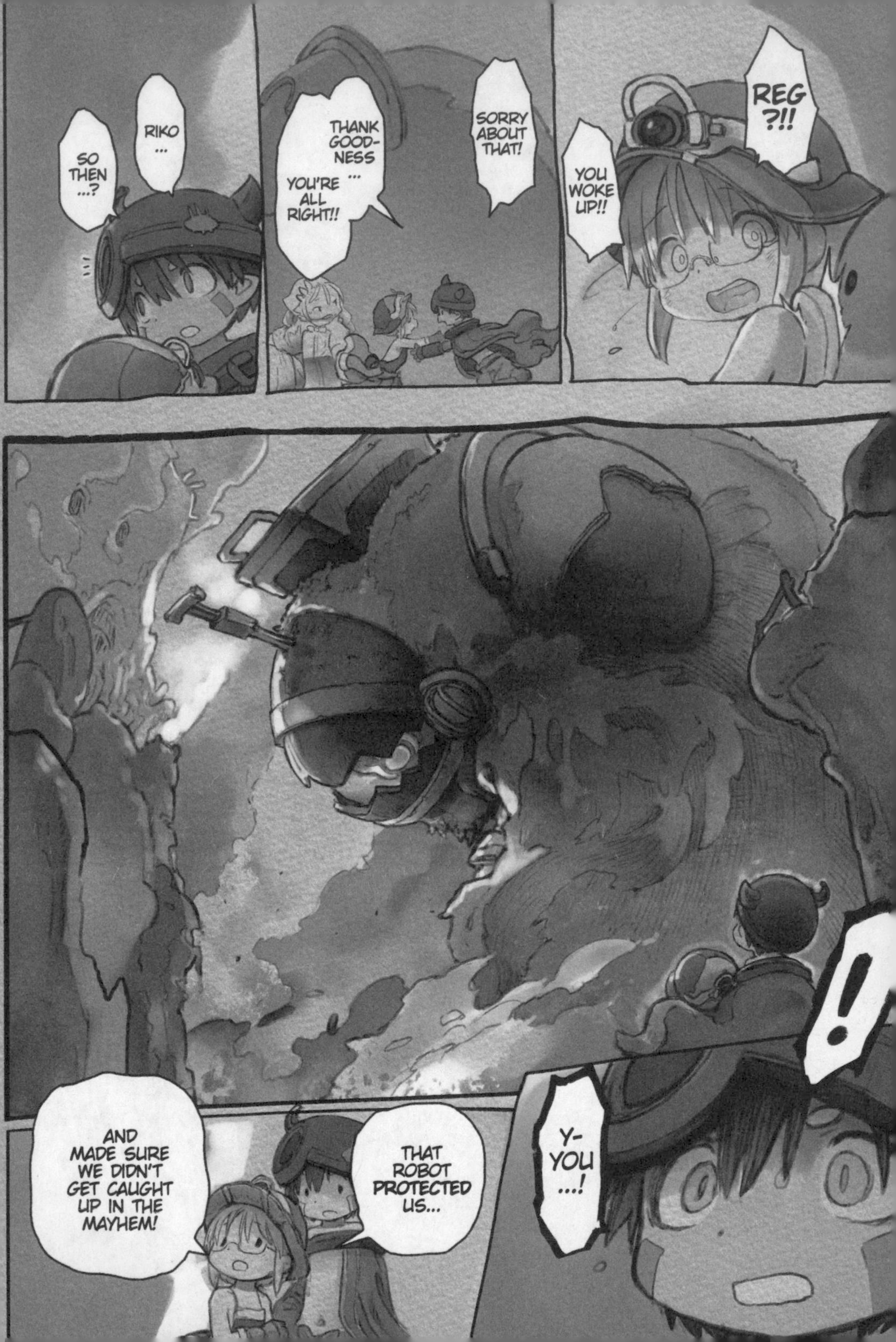
REG ?!!
YOU WOKE UP!!
SORRY ABOUT THAT!
THANK GOOD-NESS ...
YOU'RE ALL RIGHT!!
RIKO ...
SO THEN ...?
!
Y-YOU ...!
THAT ROBOT PROTECTED US...
AND MADE SURE WE DIDN'T GET CAUGHT UP IN THE MAYHEM!

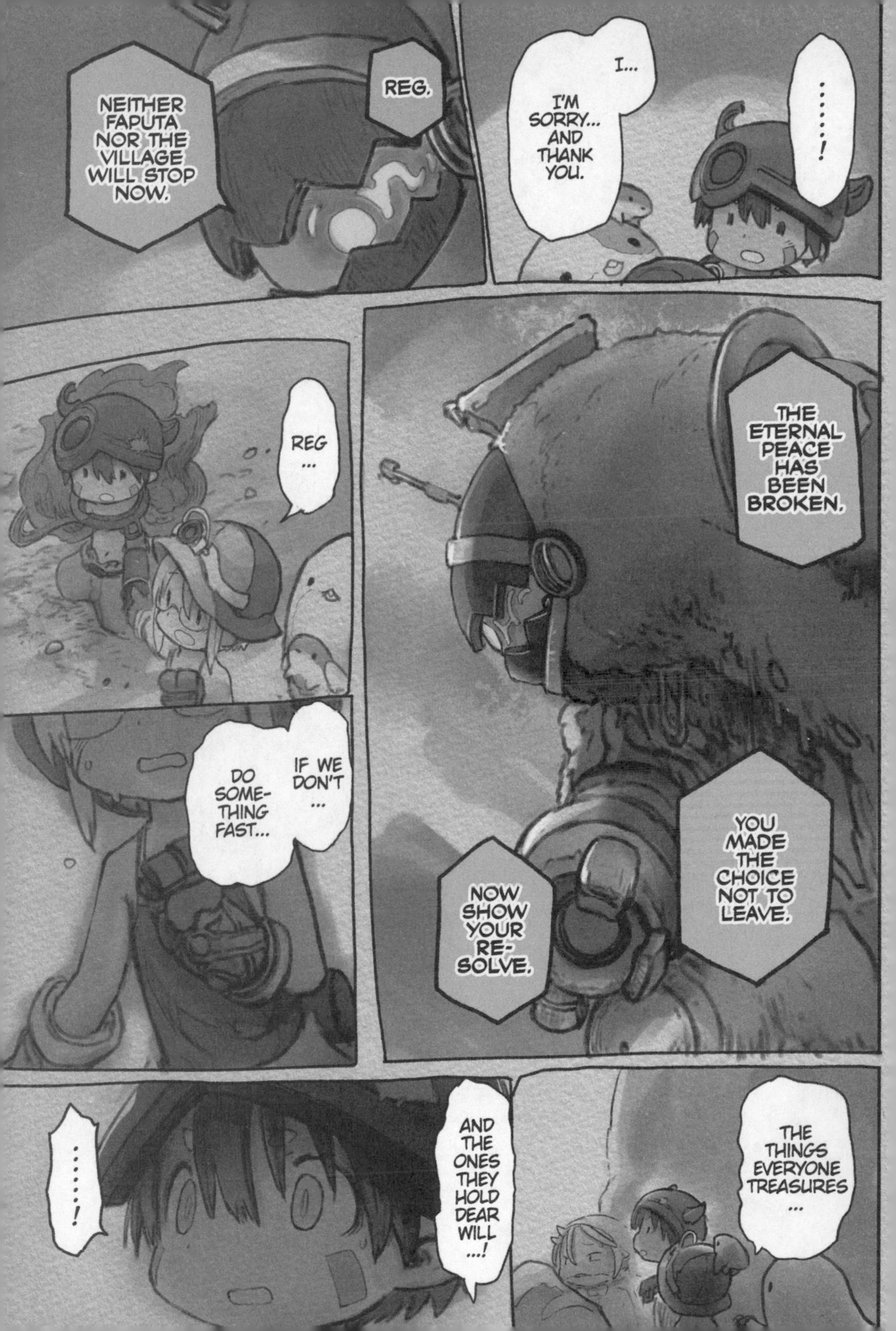
......!
I...
I'M SORRY... AND THANK YOU.
REG.
NEITHER FAPUTA NOR THE VILLAGE WILL STOP NOW.
THE ETERNAL PEACE HAS BEEN BROKEN.
YOU MADE THE CHOICE NOT TO LEAVE.
NOW SHOW YOUR RE-SOLVE.
REG...
IF WE DON'T... DO SOME-THING FAST...
THE THINGS EVERYONE TREASURES...
AND THE ONES THEY HOLD DEAR WILL...!
......!

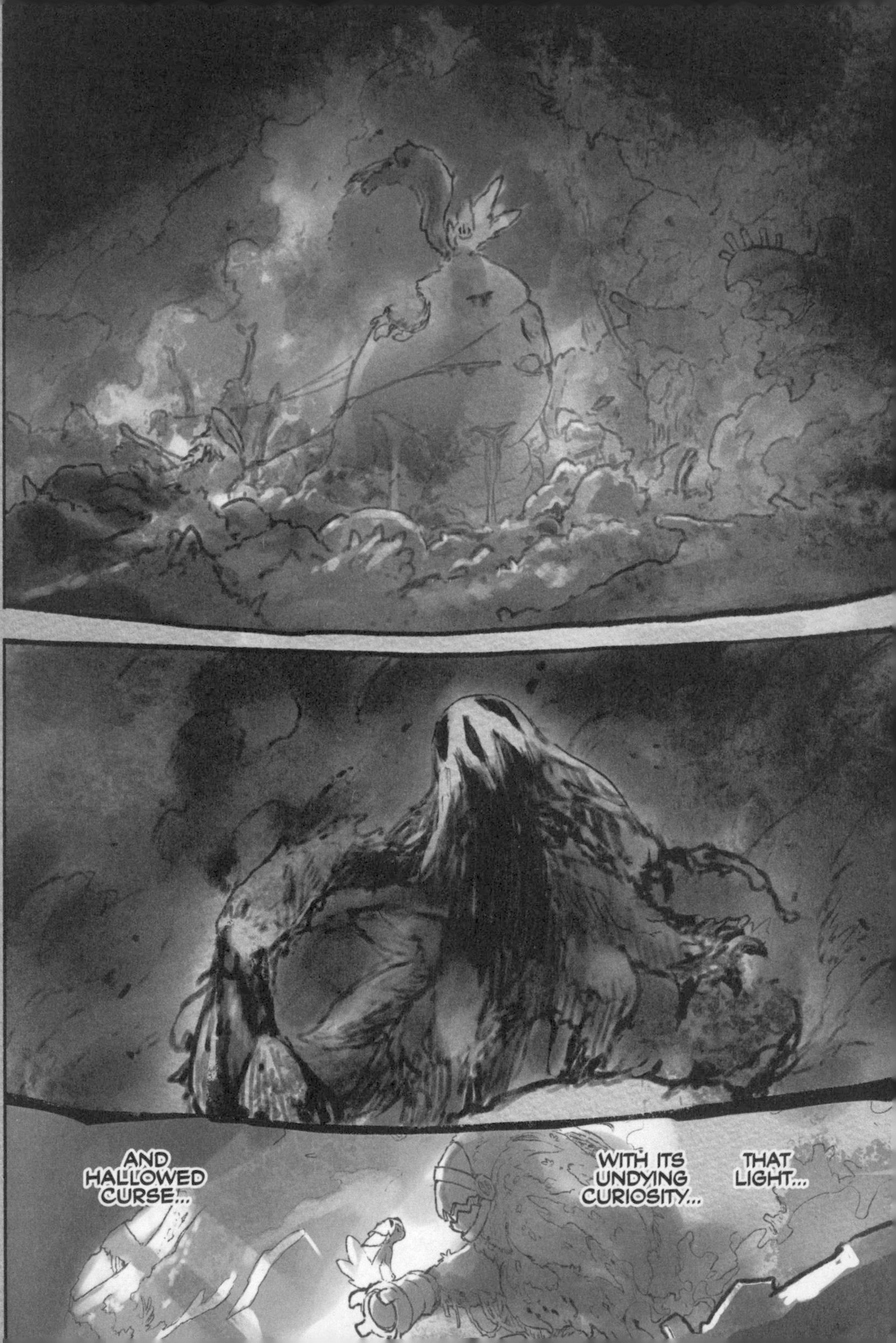
THAT LIGHT...
WITH ITS UNDYING CURIOSITY...
AND HALLOWED CURSE...

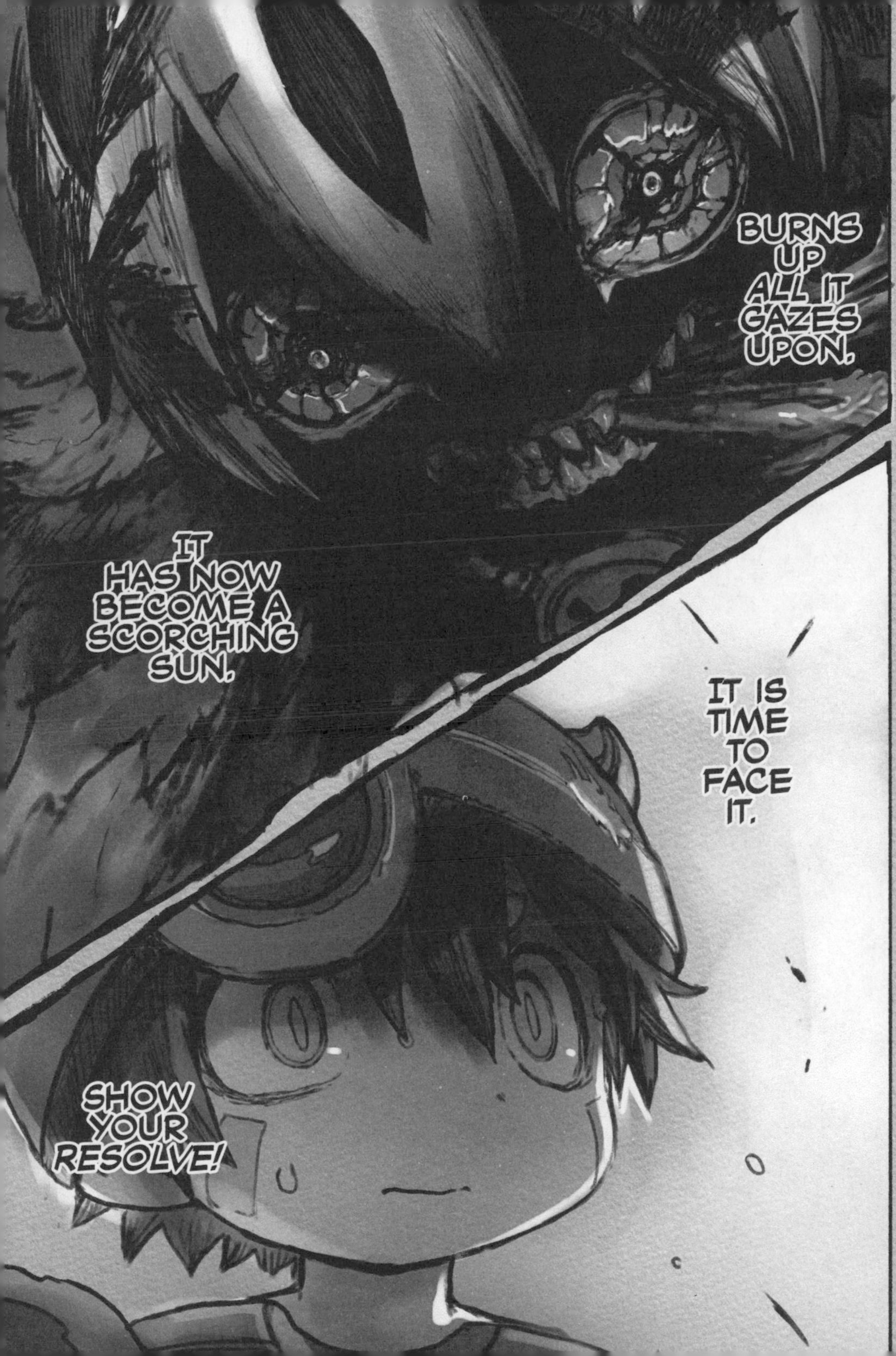
BURNS UP ALL IT GAZES UPON.
IT HAS NOW BECOME A SCORCHING SUN.
IT IS TIME TO FACE IT.
SHOW YOUR RESOLVE!

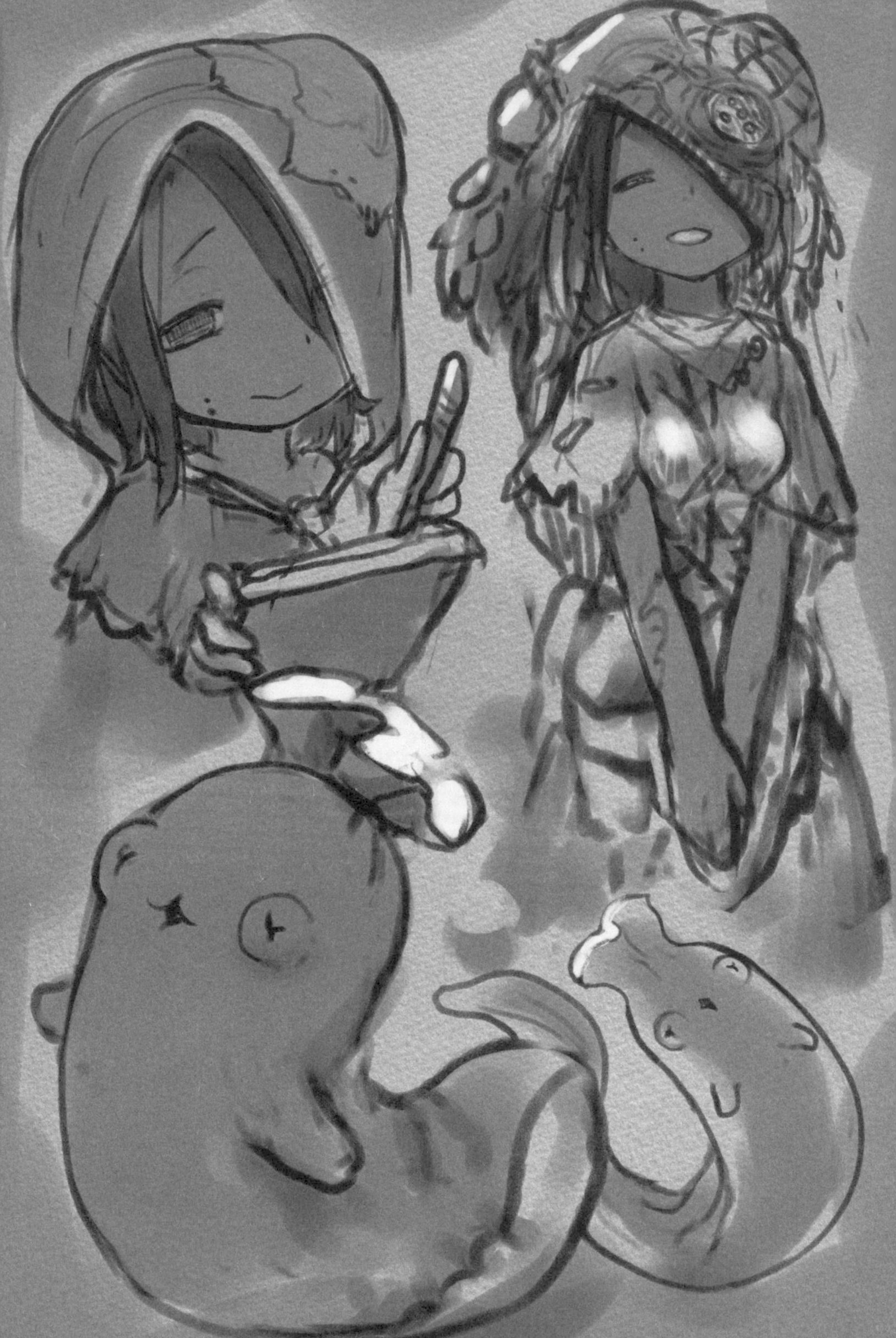

MADE IN ABYSS

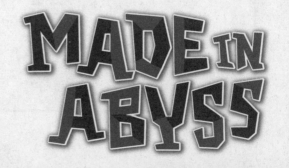

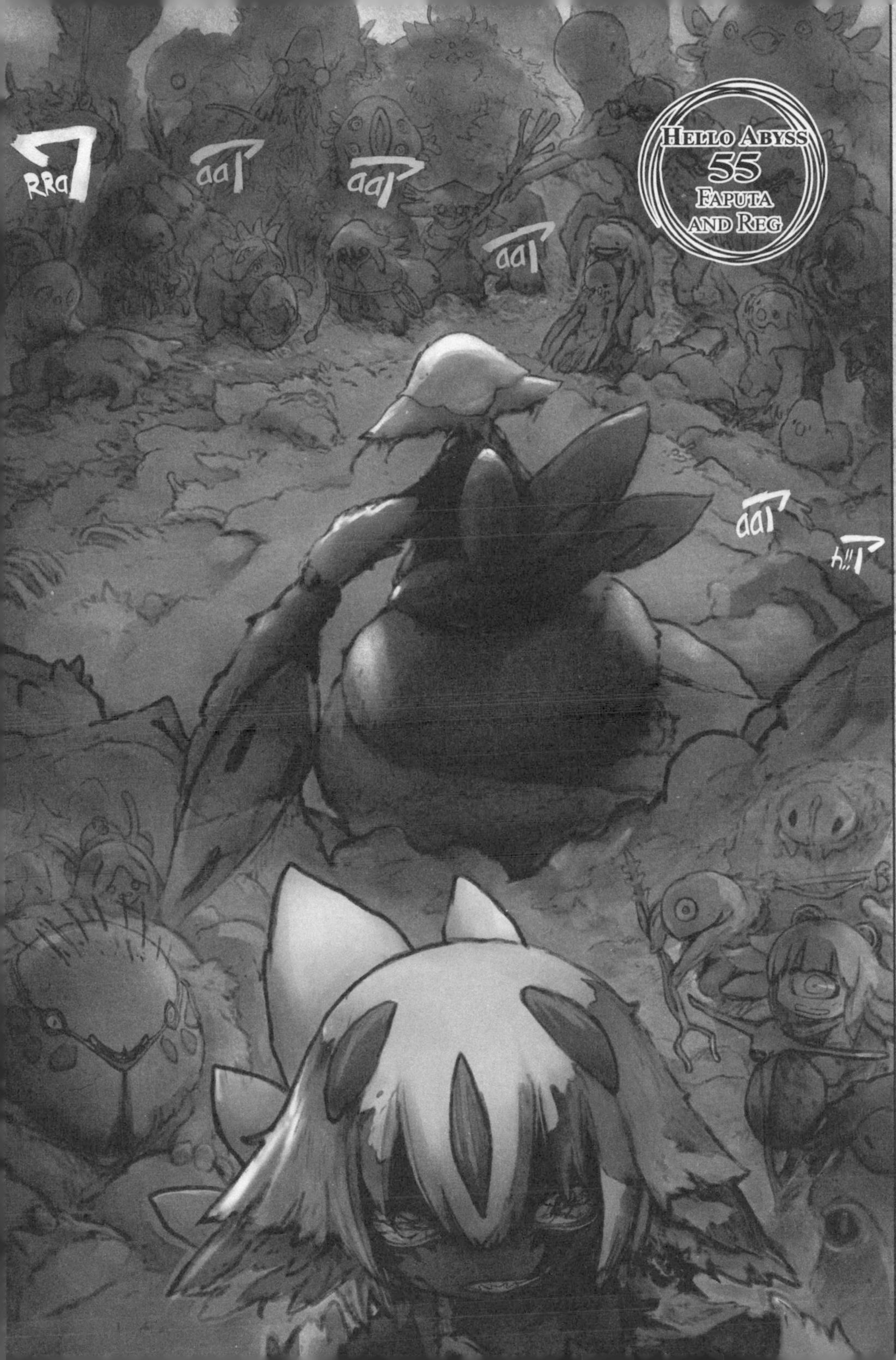
HELLO ABYSS
55
FAPUTA AND REG
aa
aa
aa
RRa
aa
h!!

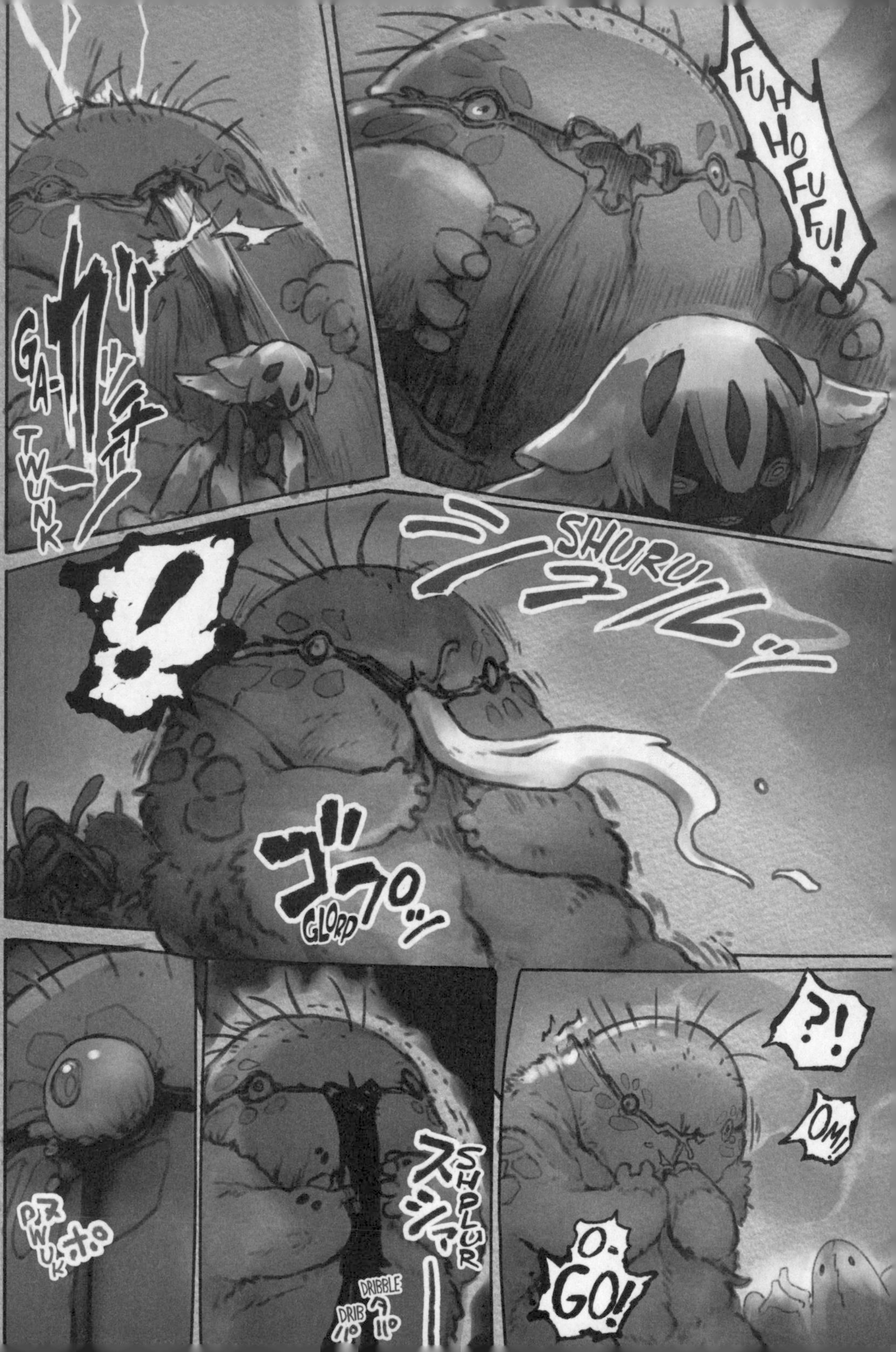

FUHHOFUFU!
GA-TWUNK
!
SHURU
GLORP
?!
OM!
O-GO!
SHPLUR
DRIBBLE
DRIB
PWUK

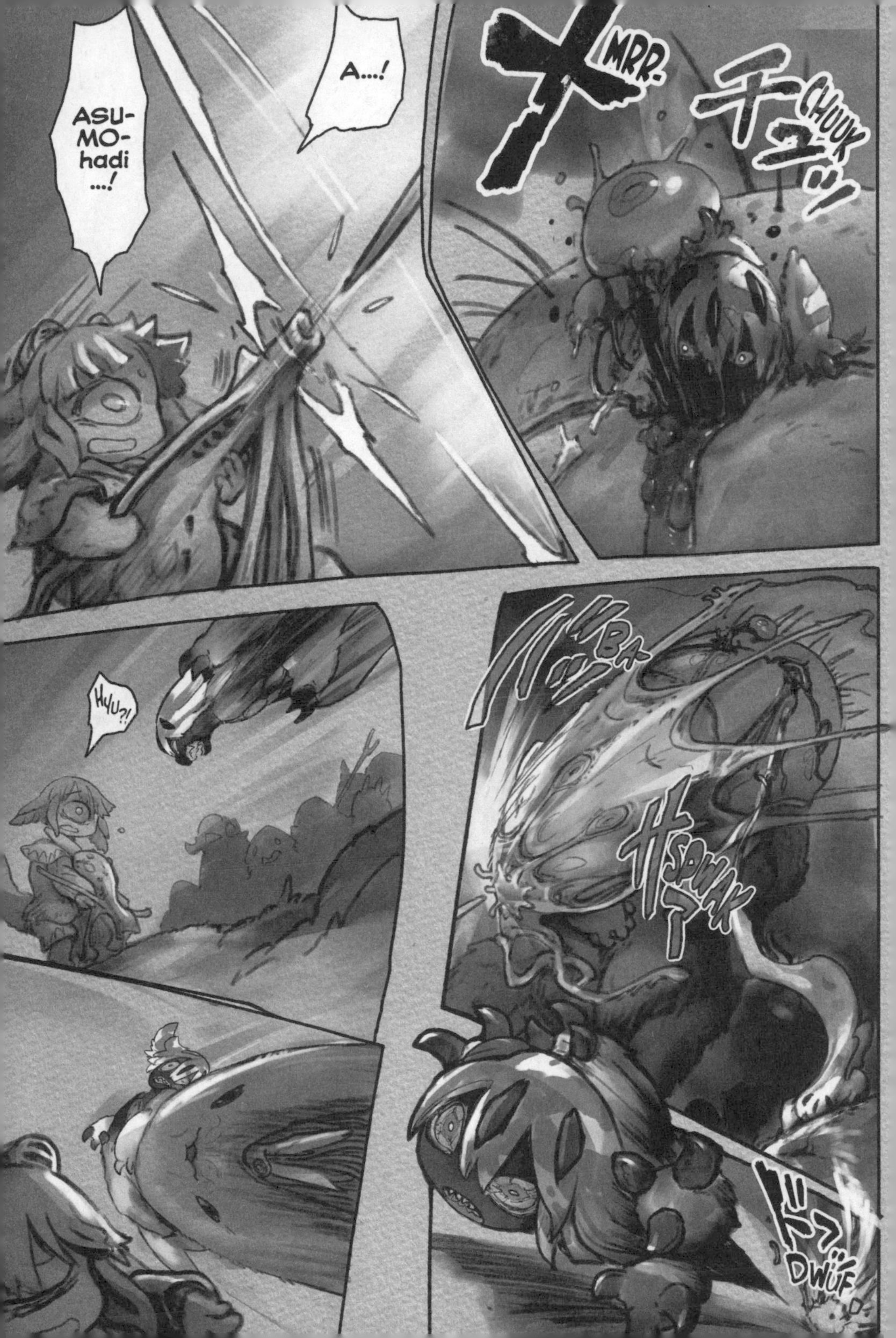
MRR.
CHUUK
A...!
ASU-MO-hadi ...!
MBA
SPWAK
DWÜF
HYU?!

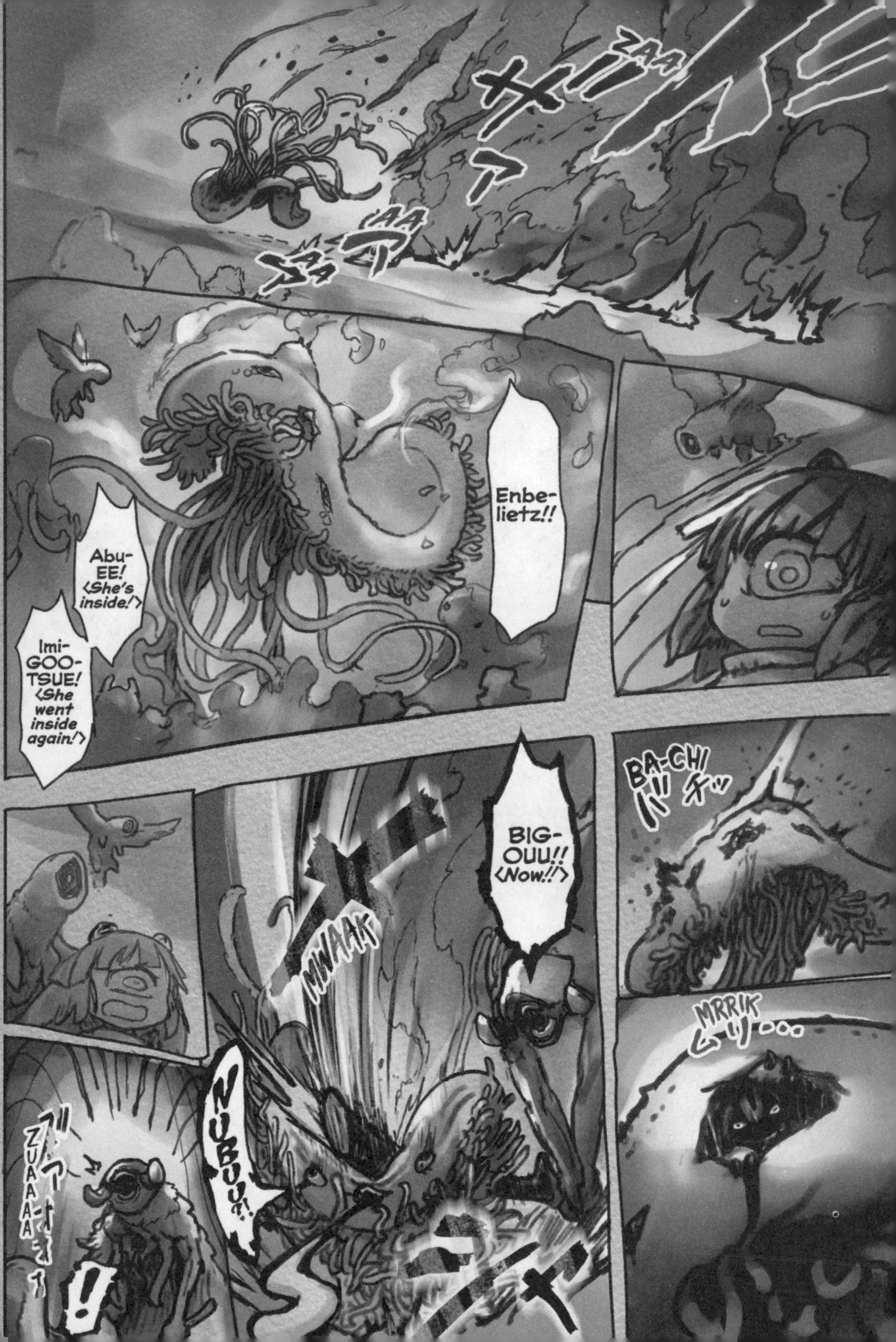
ZAA
ZAA
ZAA
Enbe-
lietz!!
Abu-
EE!
<She's
inside!>
Imi-
GOO-
TSUE!
<She
went
inside
again!>
BA-CHI
MRRIK
BIG-
OUU!!
<Now!!>
MWAAK
NUBUU?!
ZUAAAA
!

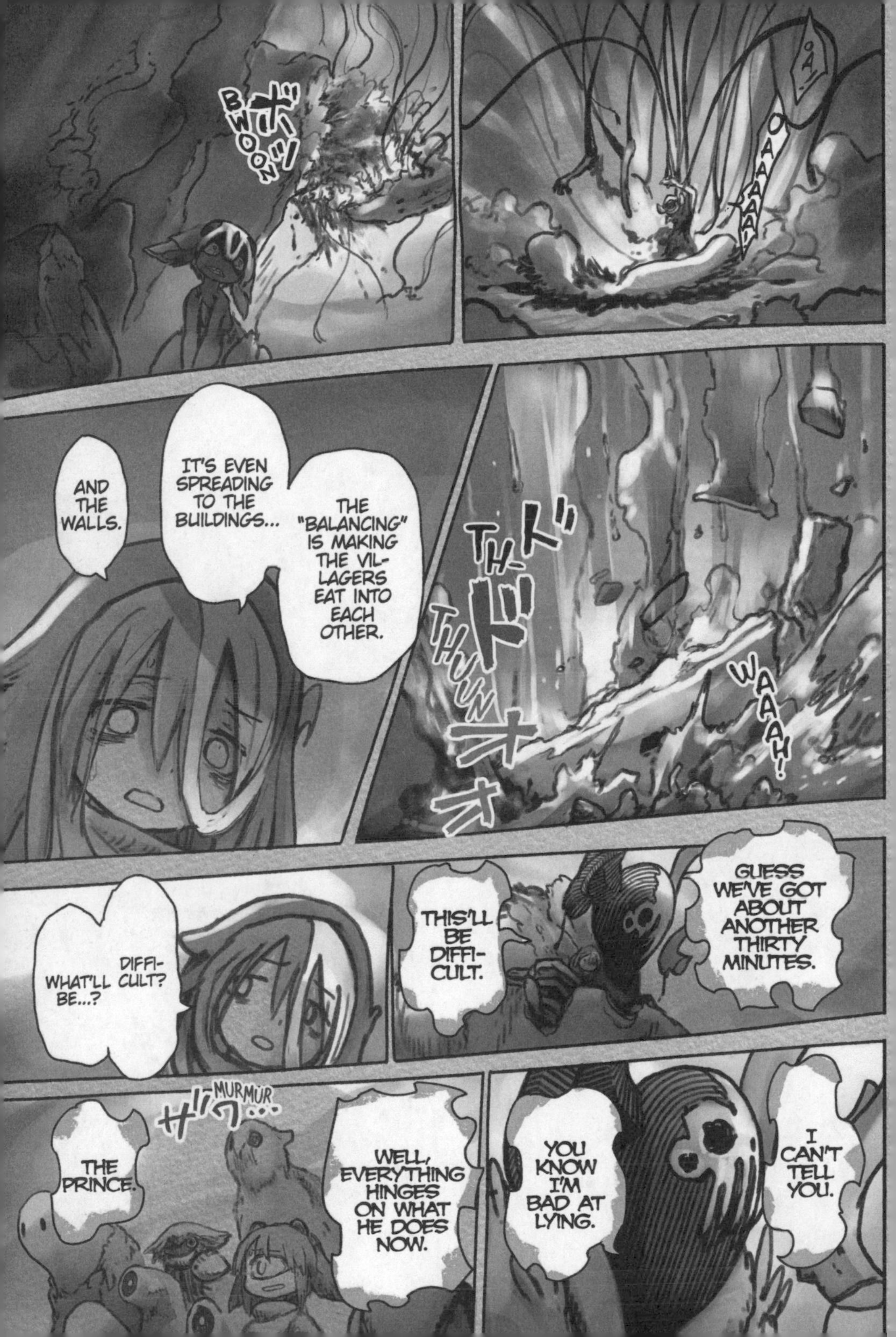
OA...!
OAAAAA!
BWOOON
THUN
WAAAH!
TH-
THE "BALANCING" IS MAKING THE VILLAGERS EAT INTO EACH OTHER.
IT'S EVEN SPREADING TO THE BUILDINGS...
AND THE WALLS.
GUESS WE'VE GOT ABOUT ANOTHER THIRTY MINUTES.
THIS'LL BE DIFFICULT.
DIFFICULT? WHAT'LL BE...?
I CAN'T TELL YOU.
YOU KNOW I'M BAD AT LYING.
WELL, EVERYTHING HINGES ON WHAT HE DOES NOW.
MURMUR
THE PRINCE.

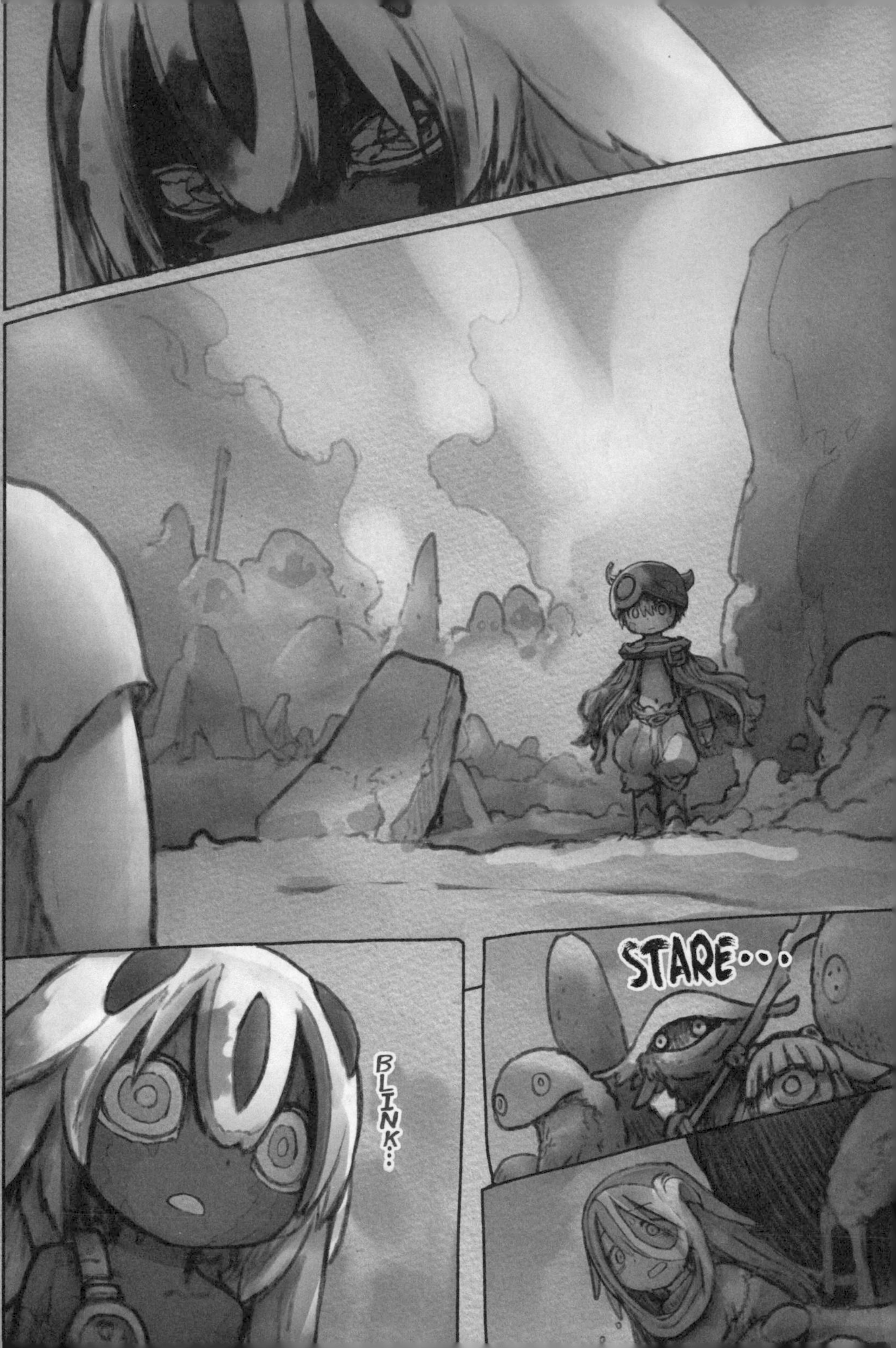
STARE...
BLINK...

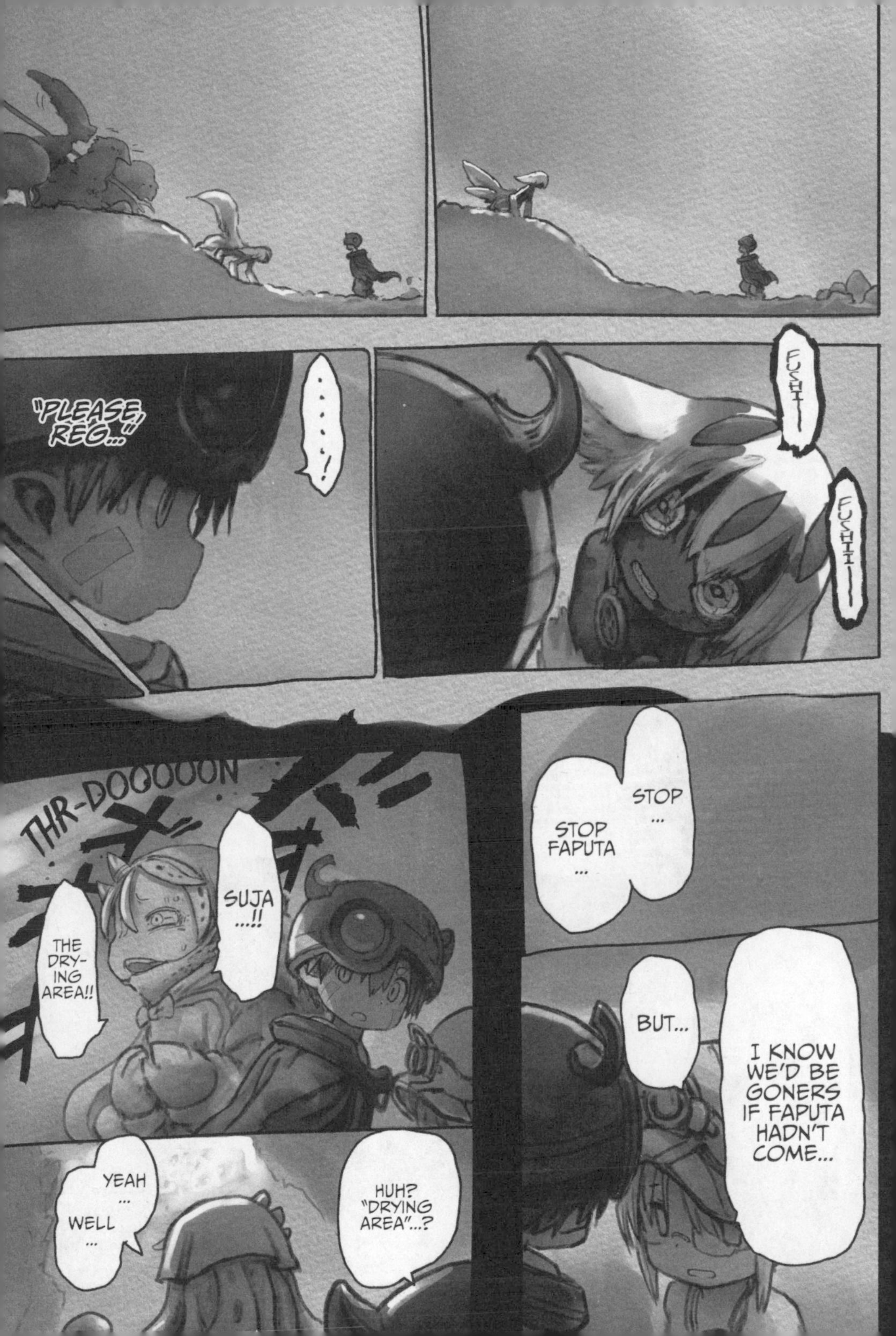
FUSHI—
FUSHI——
......?!
"PLEASE, REG..."
STOP... STOP FAPUTA...
BUT...
I KNOW WE'D BE GONERS IF FAPUTA HADN'T COME...
THR-DOOOOON
SUJA...!!
THE DRYING AREA!!
HUH? "DRYING AREA"...?
YEAH... WELL...

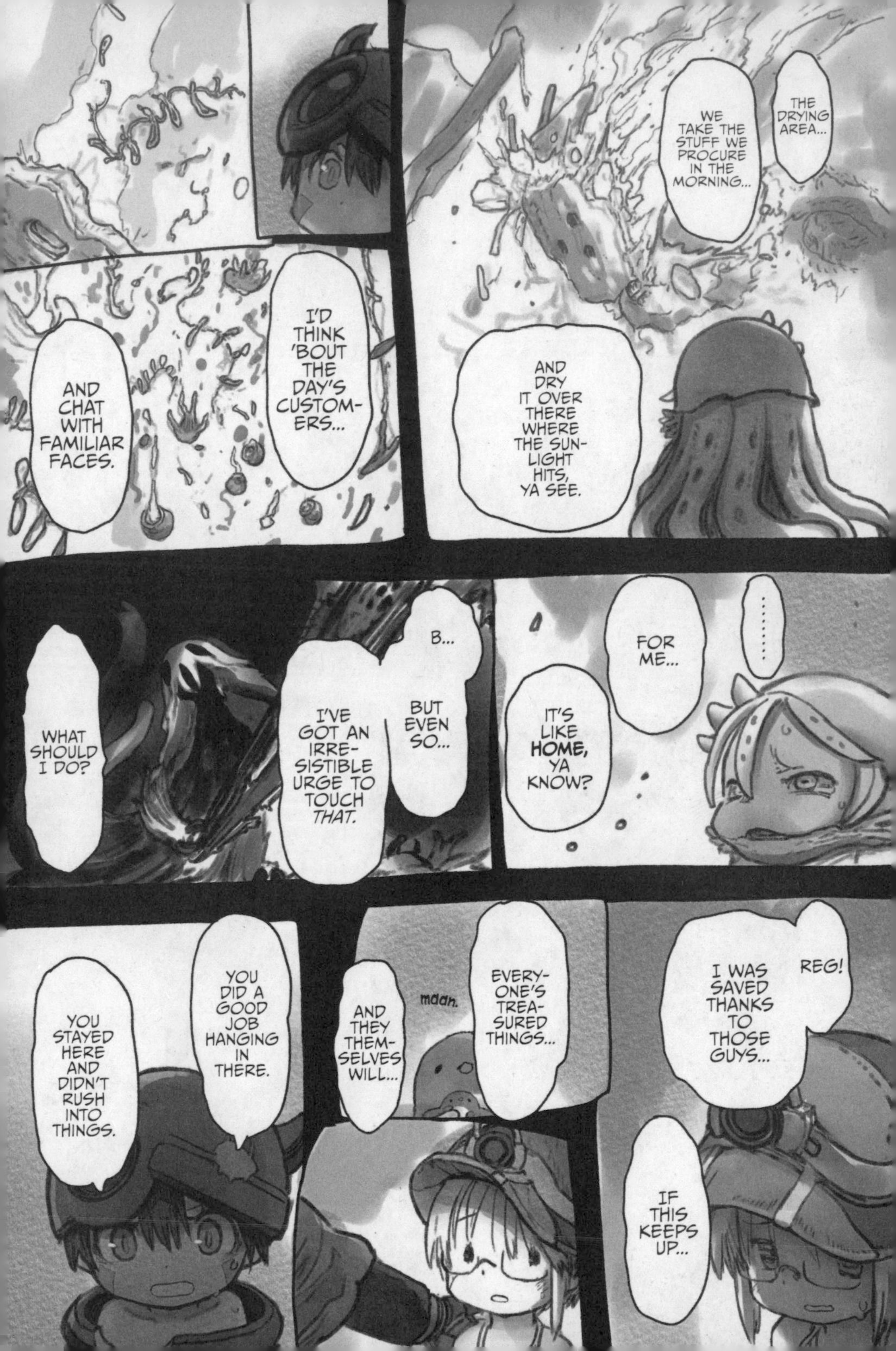
THE DRYING AREA...
WE TAKE THE STUFF WE PROCURE IN THE MORNING...
AND DRY IT OVER THERE WHERE THE SUNLIGHT HITS, YA SEE.
I'D THINK 'BOUT THE DAY'S CUSTOMERS...
AND CHAT WITH FAMILIAR FACES.
......
FOR ME...
IT'S LIKE **HOME,** YA KNOW?
B...
BUT EVEN SO...
I'VE GOT AN IRRESISTIBLE URGE TO TOUCH *THAT.*
WHAT SHOULD I DO?
REG!
I WAS SAVED THANKS TO THOSE GUYS...
IF THIS KEEPS UP...
EVERYONE'S TREASURED THINGS...
maan.
AND THEY THEMSELVES WILL...
YOU DID A GOOD JOB HANGING IN THERE.
YOU STAYED HERE AND DIDN'T RUSH INTO THINGS.

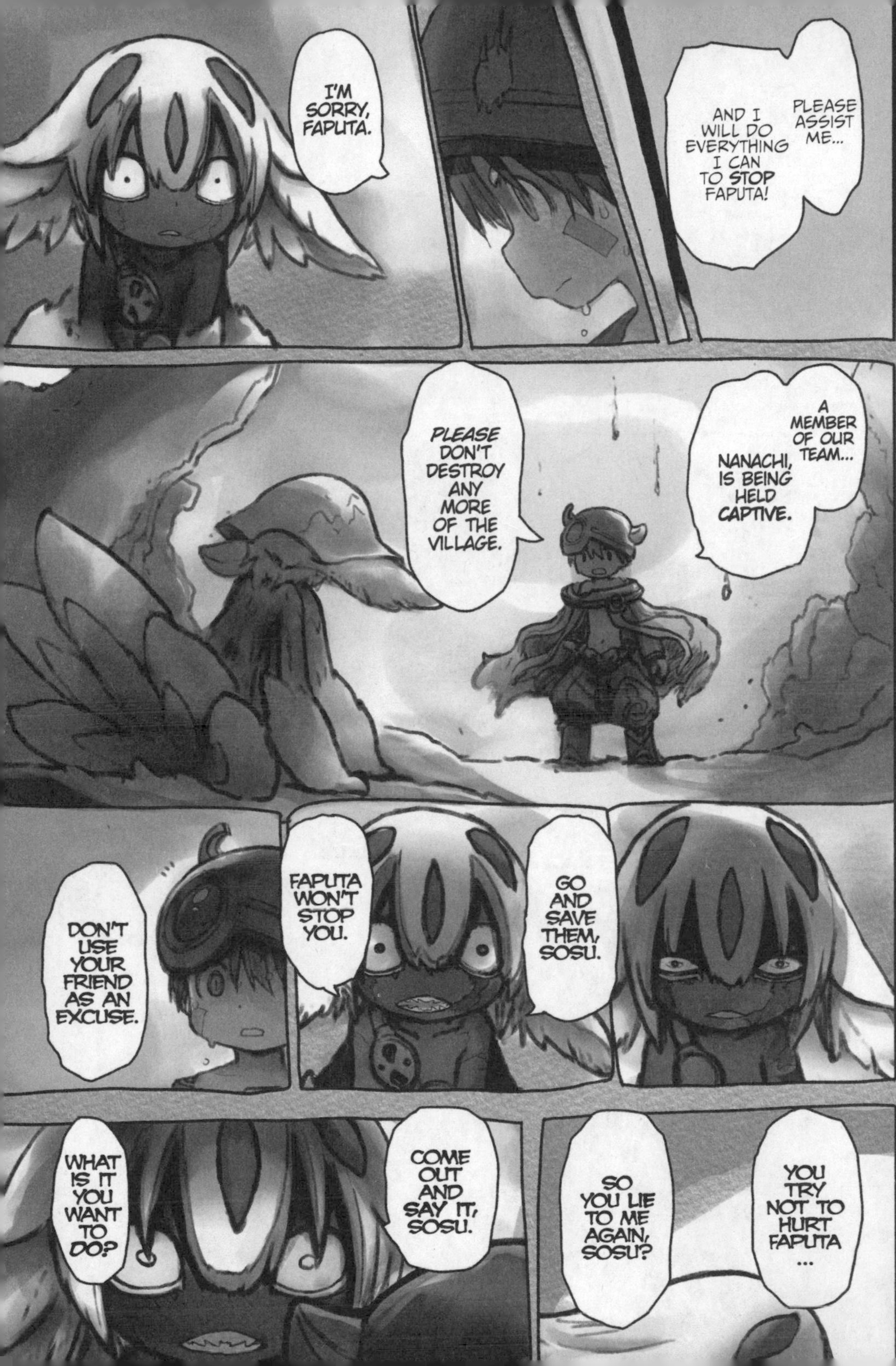
PLEASE ASSIST ME...
AND I WILL DO EVERYTHING I CAN TO STOP FAPUTA!
I'M SORRY, FAPUTA.
A MEMBER OF OUR TEAM... NANACHI, IS BEING HELD CAPTIVE.
PLEASE DON'T DESTROY ANY MORE OF THE VILLAGE.
GO AND SAVE THEM, SOSU.
FAPUTA WON'T STOP YOU.
DON'T USE YOUR FRIEND AS AN EXCUSE.
YOU TRY NOT TO HURT FAPUTA ...
SO YOU LIE TO ME AGAIN, SOSU?
COME OUT AND SAY IT, SOSU.
WHAT IS IT YOU WANT TO DO?

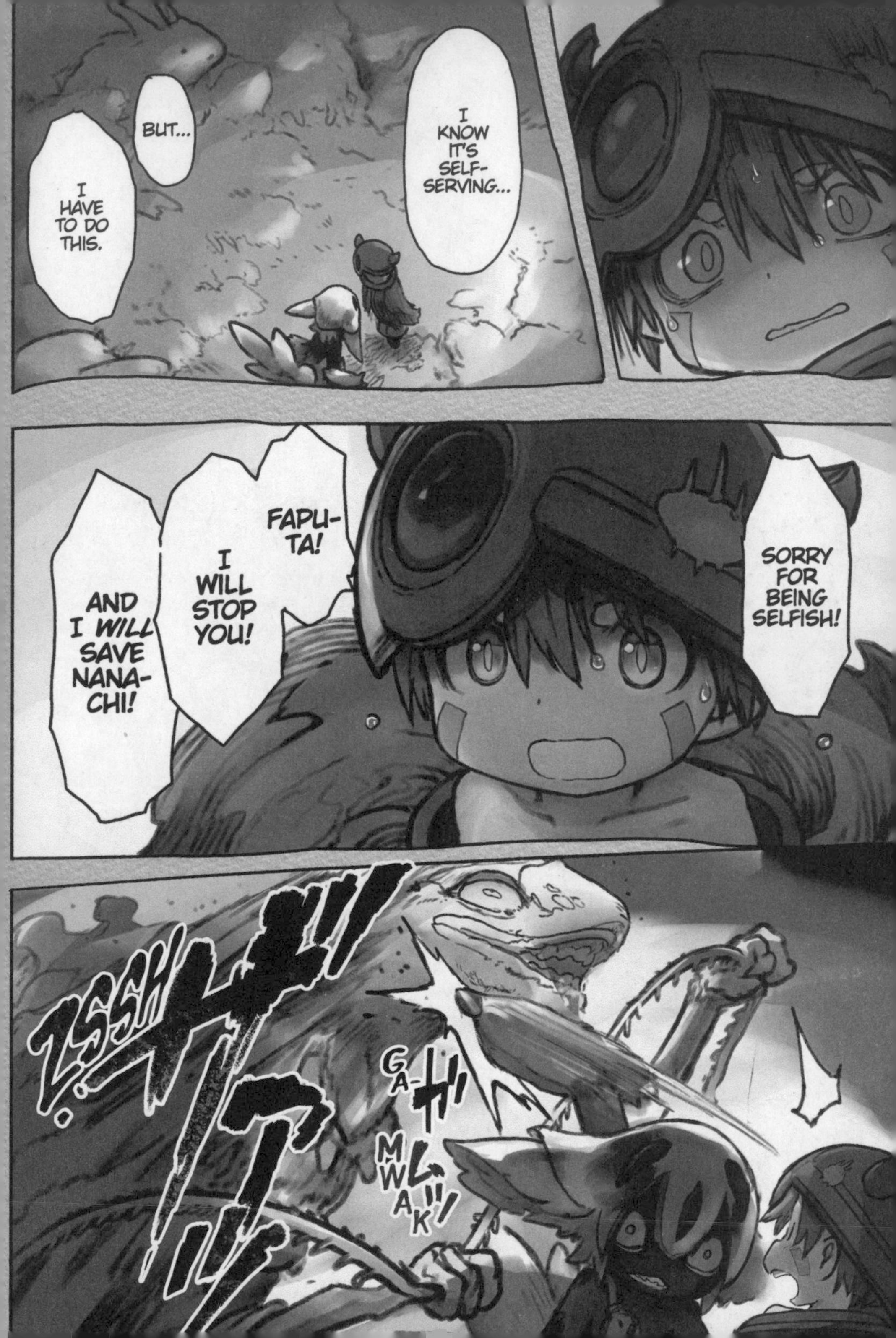
I KNOW IT'S SELF-SERVING...
BUT...
I HAVE TO DO THIS.
SORRY FOR BEING SELFISH!
FAPU-TA!
I WILL STOP YOU!
AND I *WILL* SAVE NANA-CHI!
GA-
MWAK
ZSSH

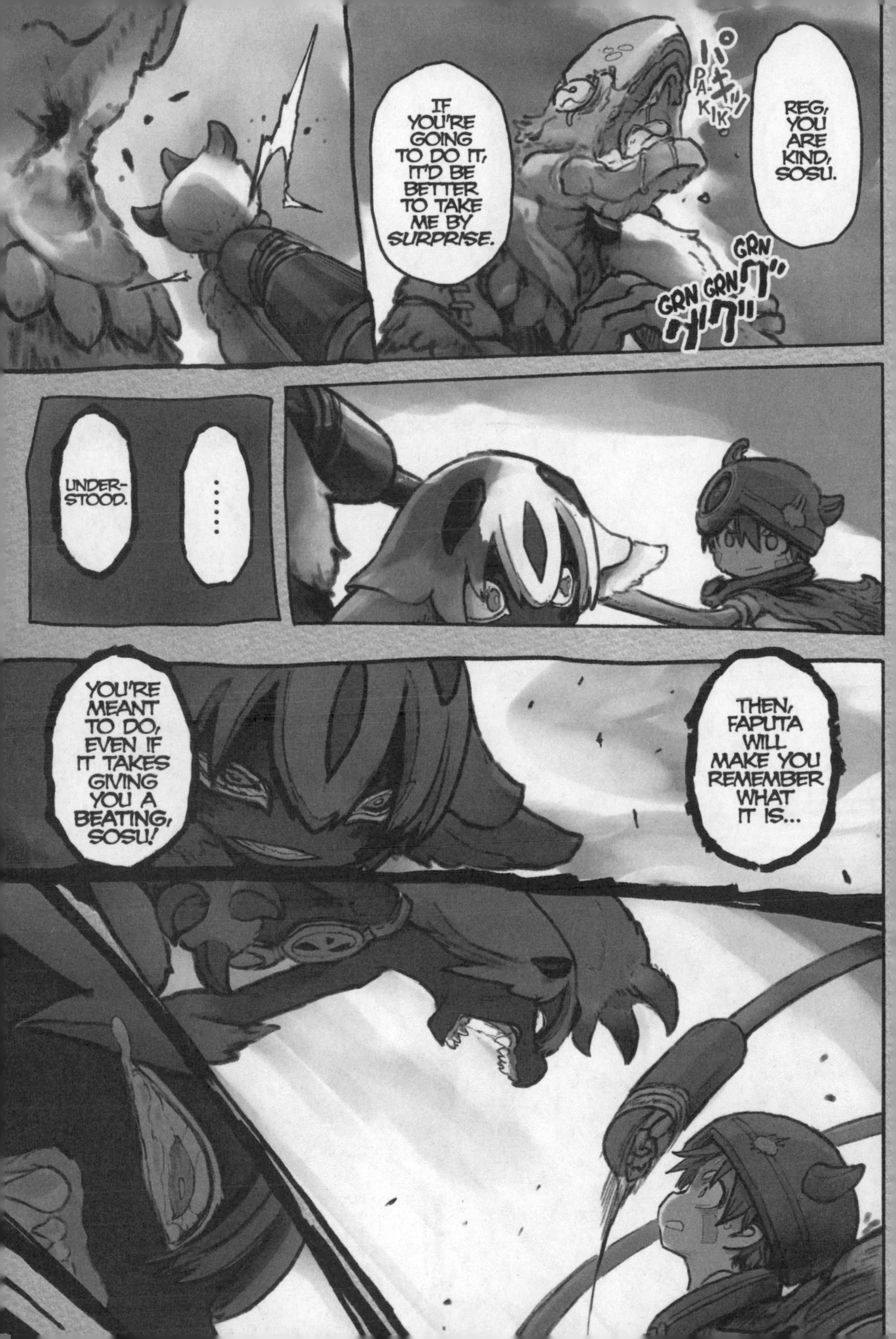
REG, YOU ARE KIND, SOSU.
パキッ
PA-KIK
IF YOU'RE GOING TO DO IT, IT'D BE BETTER TO TAKE ME BY SURPRISE.
GRN GRN GRN
......
UNDER-STOOD.
THEN, FAPUTA WILL MAKE YOU REMEMBER WHAT IT IS...
YOU'RE MEANT TO DO, EVEN IF IT TAKES GIVING YOU A BEATING, SOSU!

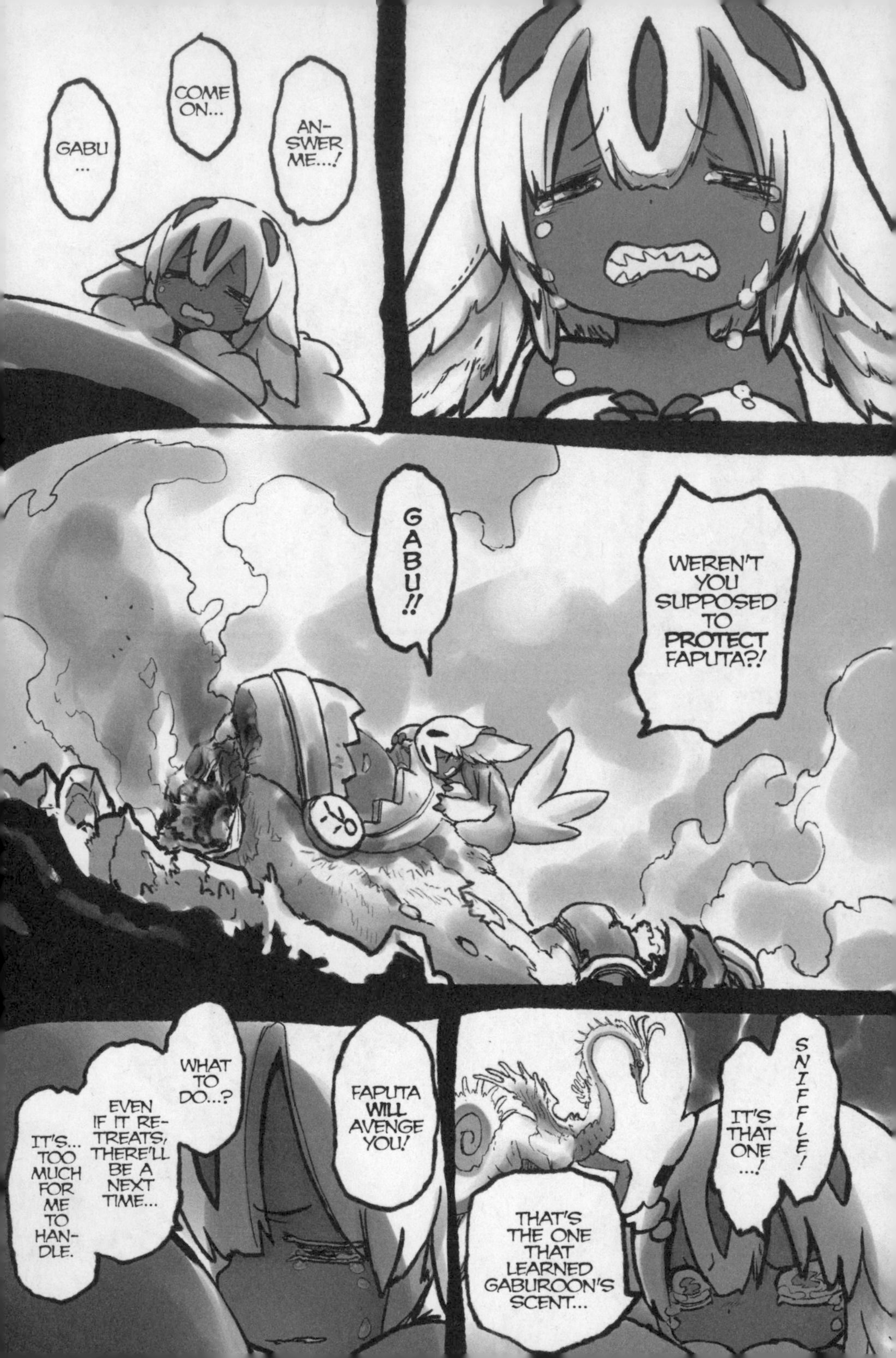
ANSWER ME...!
COME ON...
GABU ...
WEREN'T YOU SUPPOSED TO PROTECT FAPUTA?!
GABU!!
SNIFFLE!
IT'S THAT ONE ...!
THAT'S THE ONE THAT LEARNED GABUROON'S SCENT...
FAPUTA WILL AVENGE YOU!
WHAT TO DO...?
EVEN IF IT RETREATS, THERE'LL BE A NEXT TIME...
IT'S... TOO MUCH FOR ME TO HANDLE.

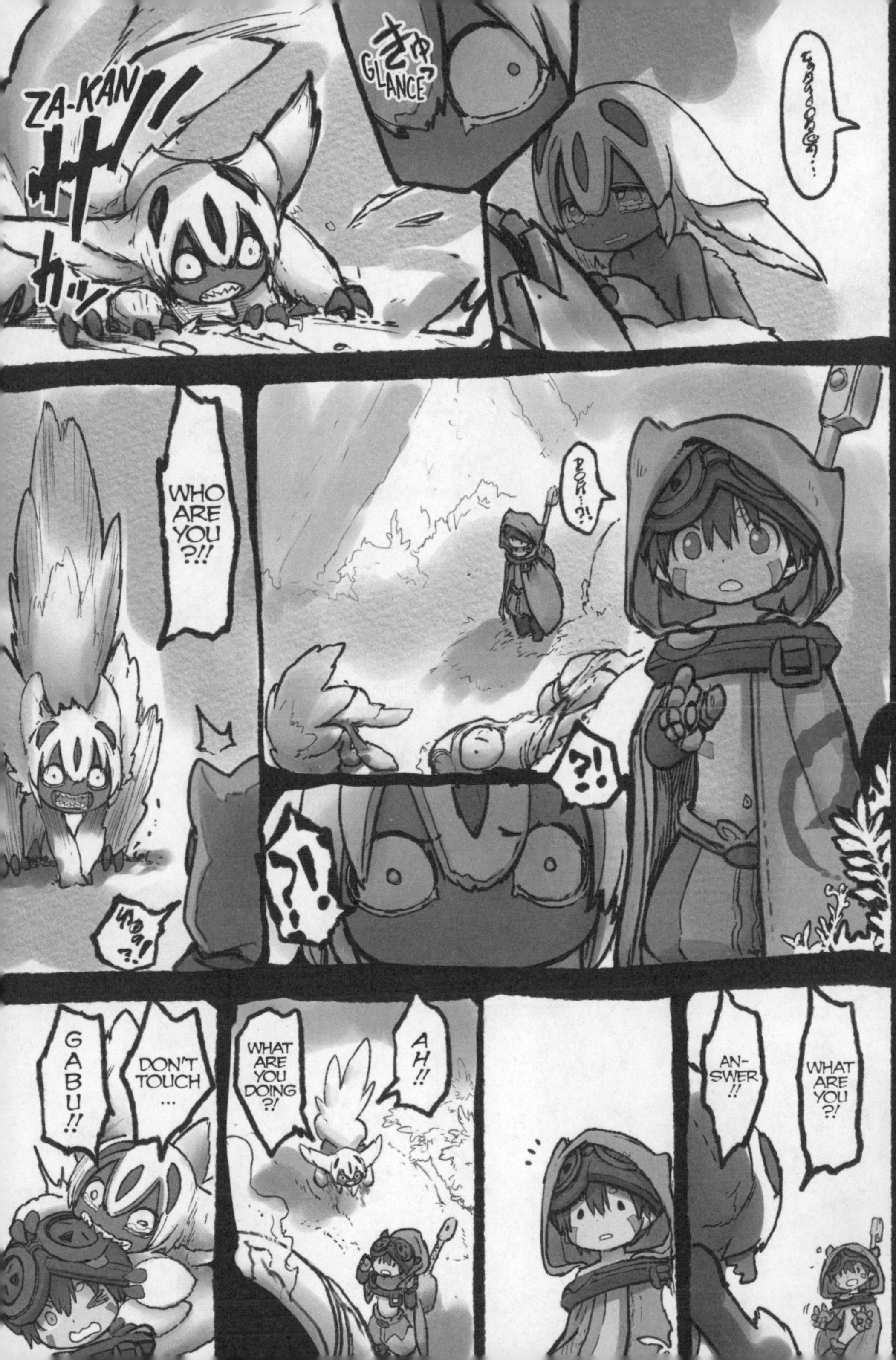
きゅっ
GLANCE
ZA-KAN
カッ
DOH...?!
?!
?!
WHO ARE YOU?!!
WHAT ARE YOU?!
AN-SWER!!
AH!!
WHAT ARE YOU DOING?!
DON'T TOUCH ...
GABU!!

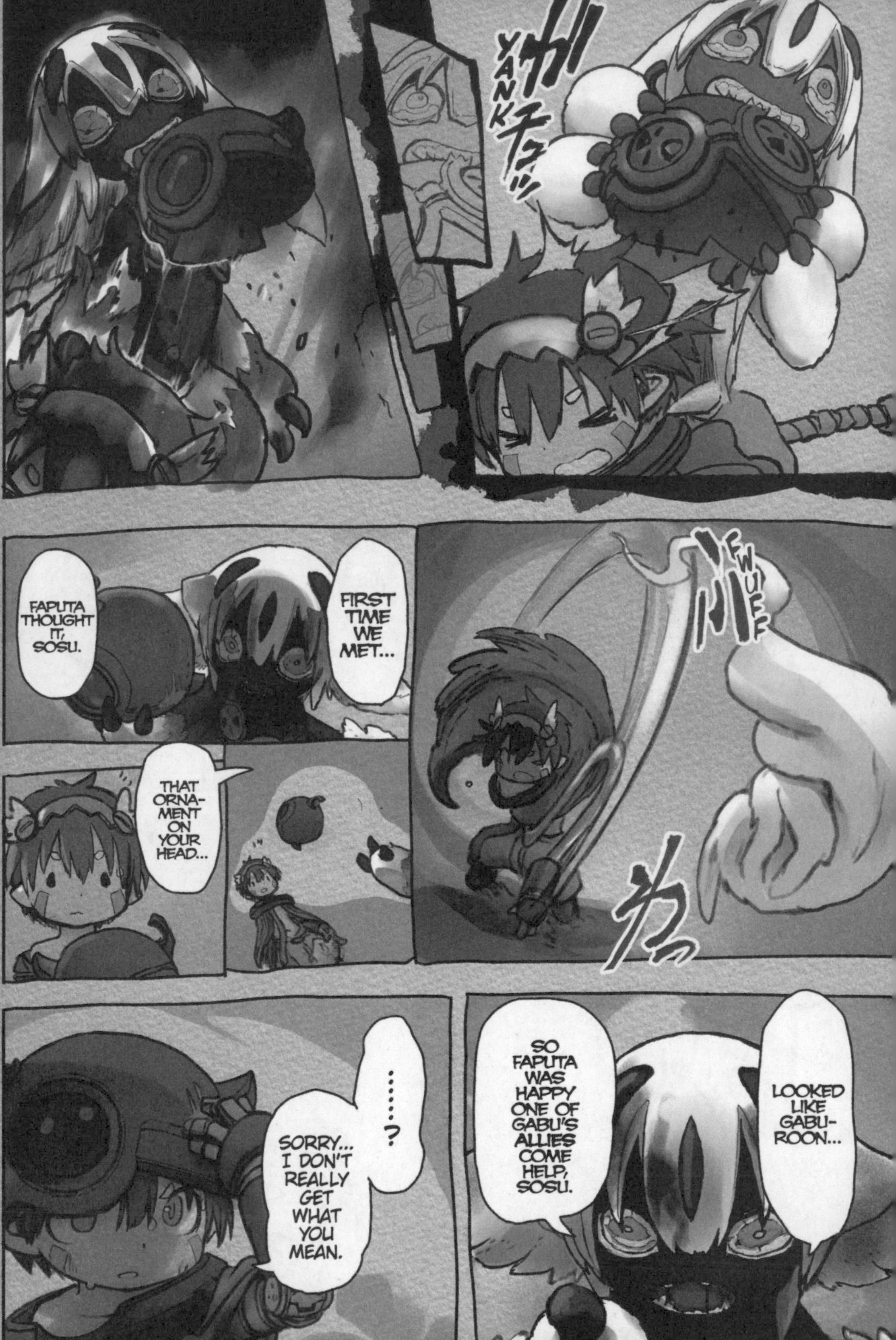
YANK
FWUFF
FIRST TIME WE MET...
FAPUTA THOUGHT IT, SOSU.
THAT ORNAMENT ON YOUR HEAD...
LOOKED LIKE GABUROON...
SO FAPUTA WAS HAPPY ONE OF GABU'S ALLIES COME HELP, SOSU.
......?
SORRY... I DON'T REALLY GET WHAT YOU MEAN.

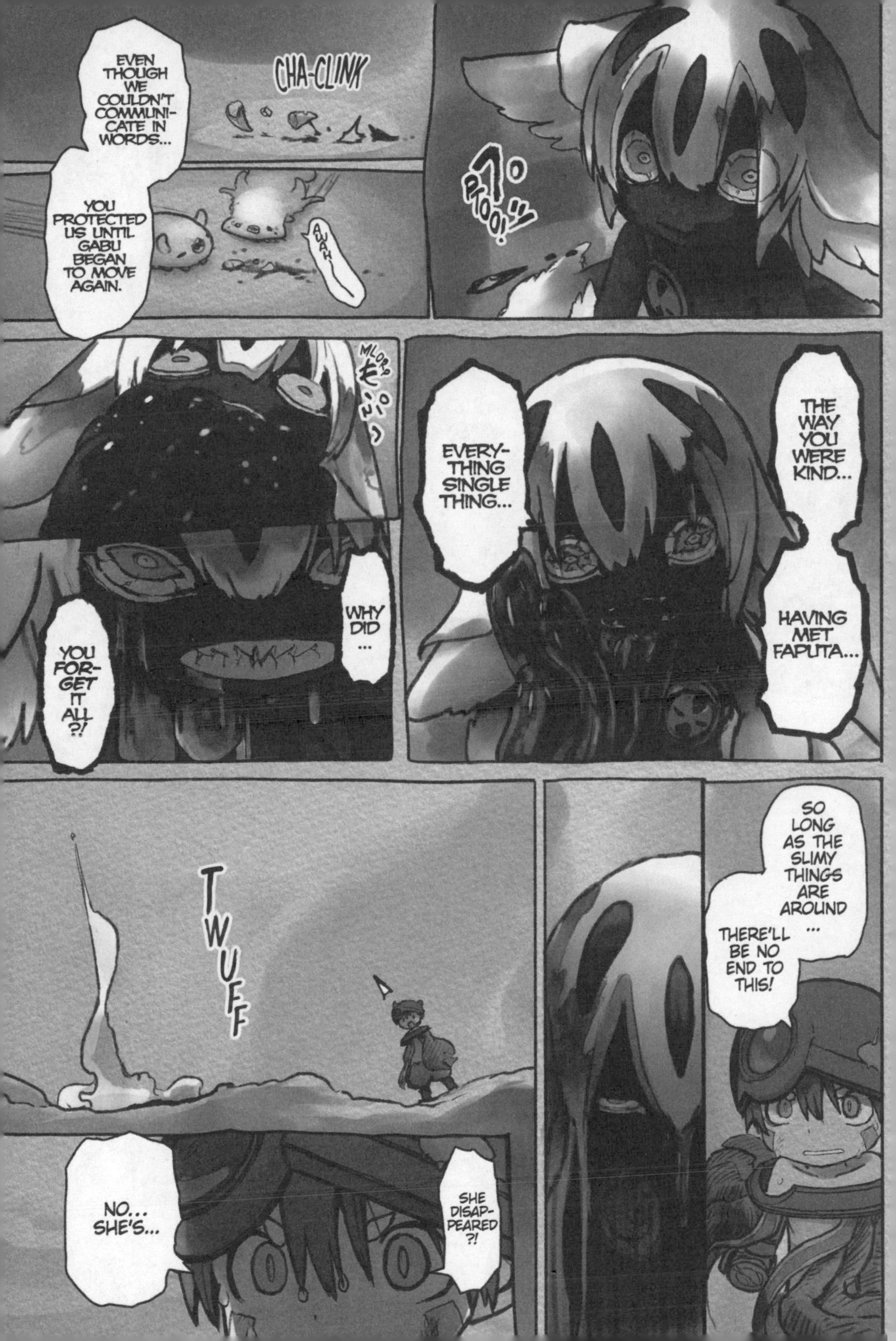
PTOO!!
CHA-CLINK
EVEN THOUGH WE COULDN'T COMMUNI-CATE IN WORDS...
YOU PROTECTED US UNTIL GABU BEGAN TO MOVE AGAIN.
AUAH...
THE WAY YOU WERE KIND...
EVERY-THING SINGLE THING...
HAVING MET FAPUTA...
MLORP
WHY DID ...
YOU FOR-GET IT ALL?!
SO LONG AS THE SLIMY THINGS ARE AROUND...
THERE'LL BE NO END TO THIS!
TWUFF
SHE DISAP-PEARED?!
NO... SHE'S...

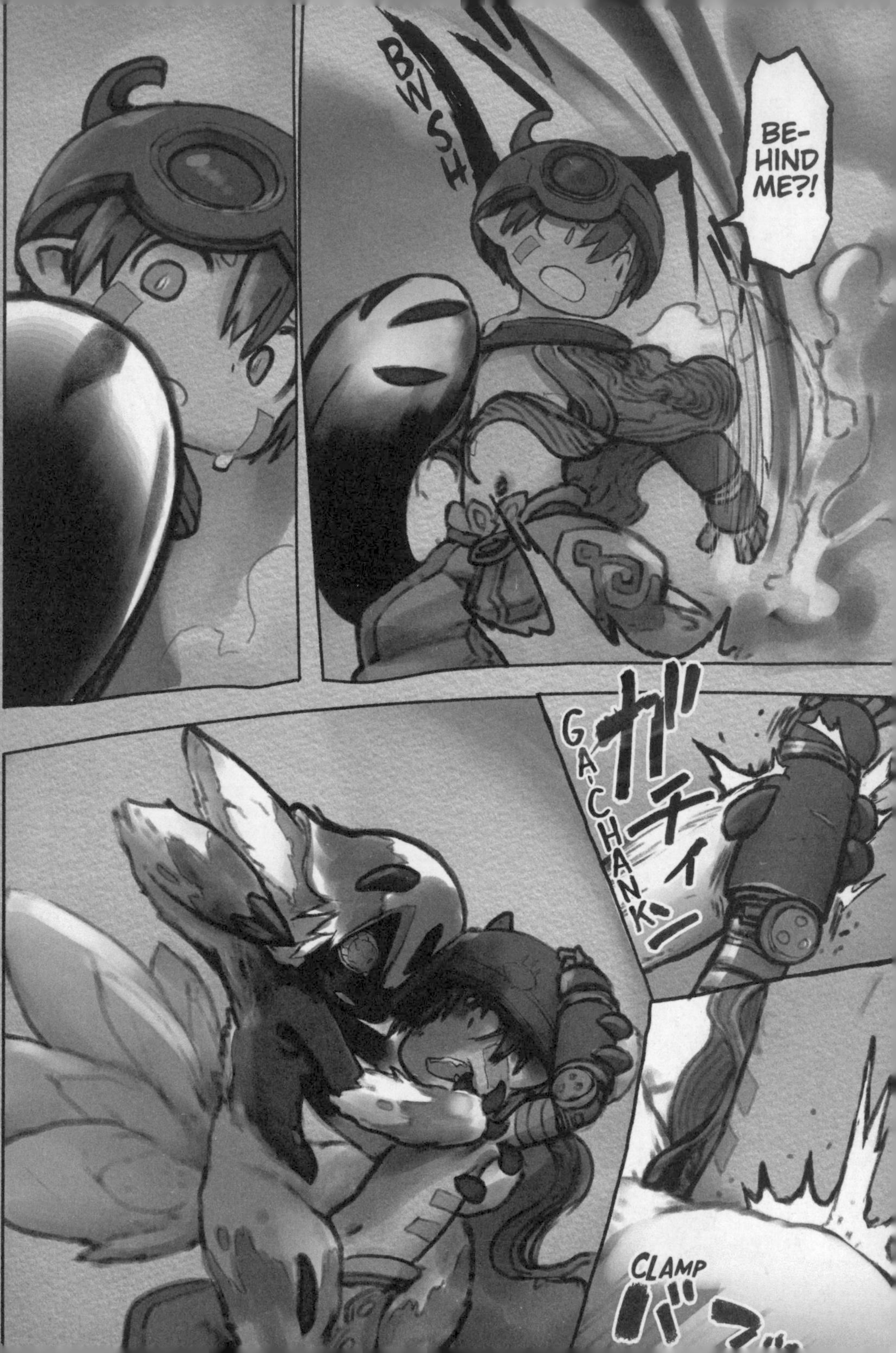
BWSH
BE-HIND ME?!
GACHANK
CLAMP

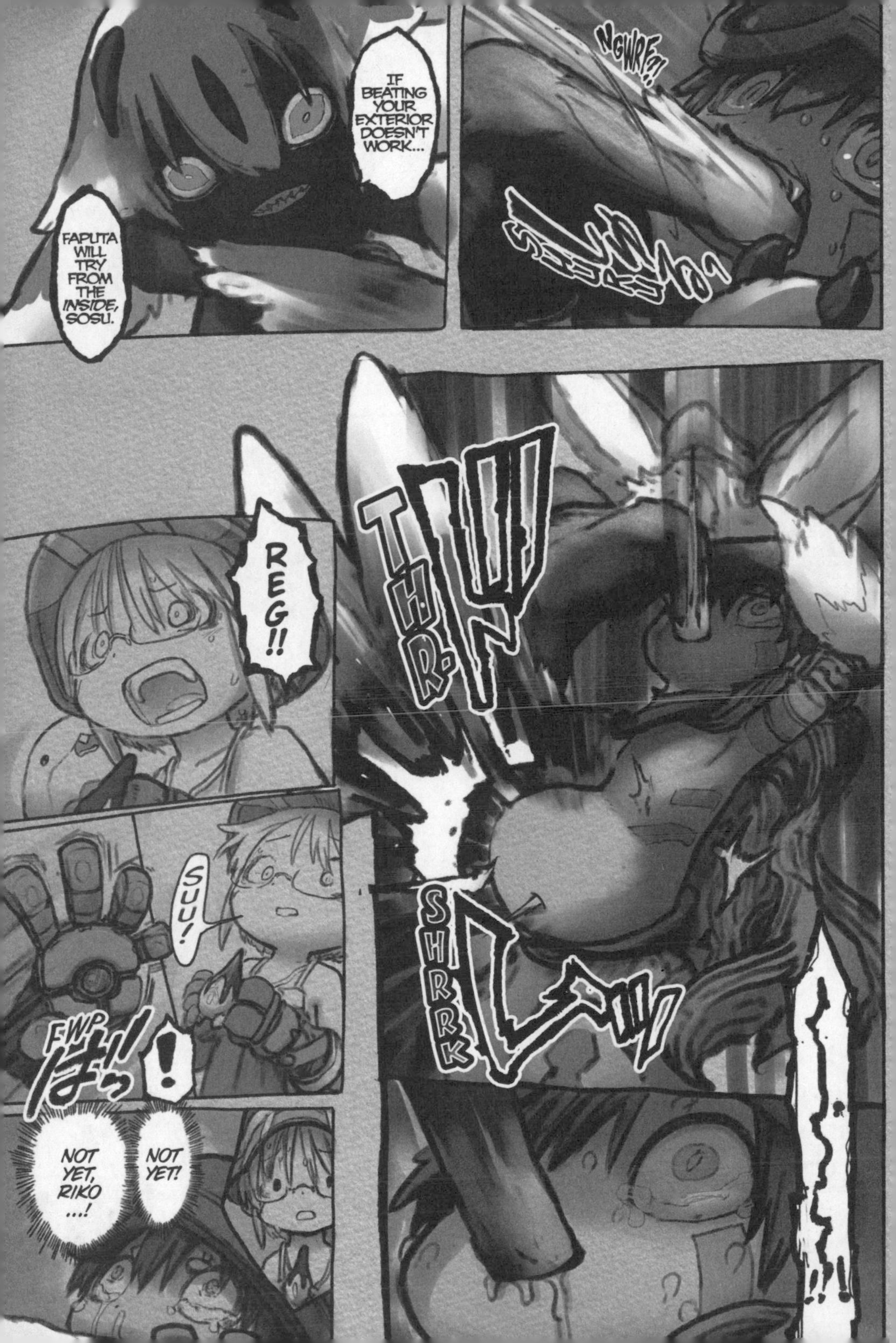
NGWRE?!
IF BEATING YOUR EXTERIOR DOESN'T WORK...
FAPUTA WILL TRY FROM THE INSIDE, SOSU.
THRR
SHRRK
REG!!
SUU!
!
FWP
!!?!!
NOT YET!
NOT YET, RIKO ...!

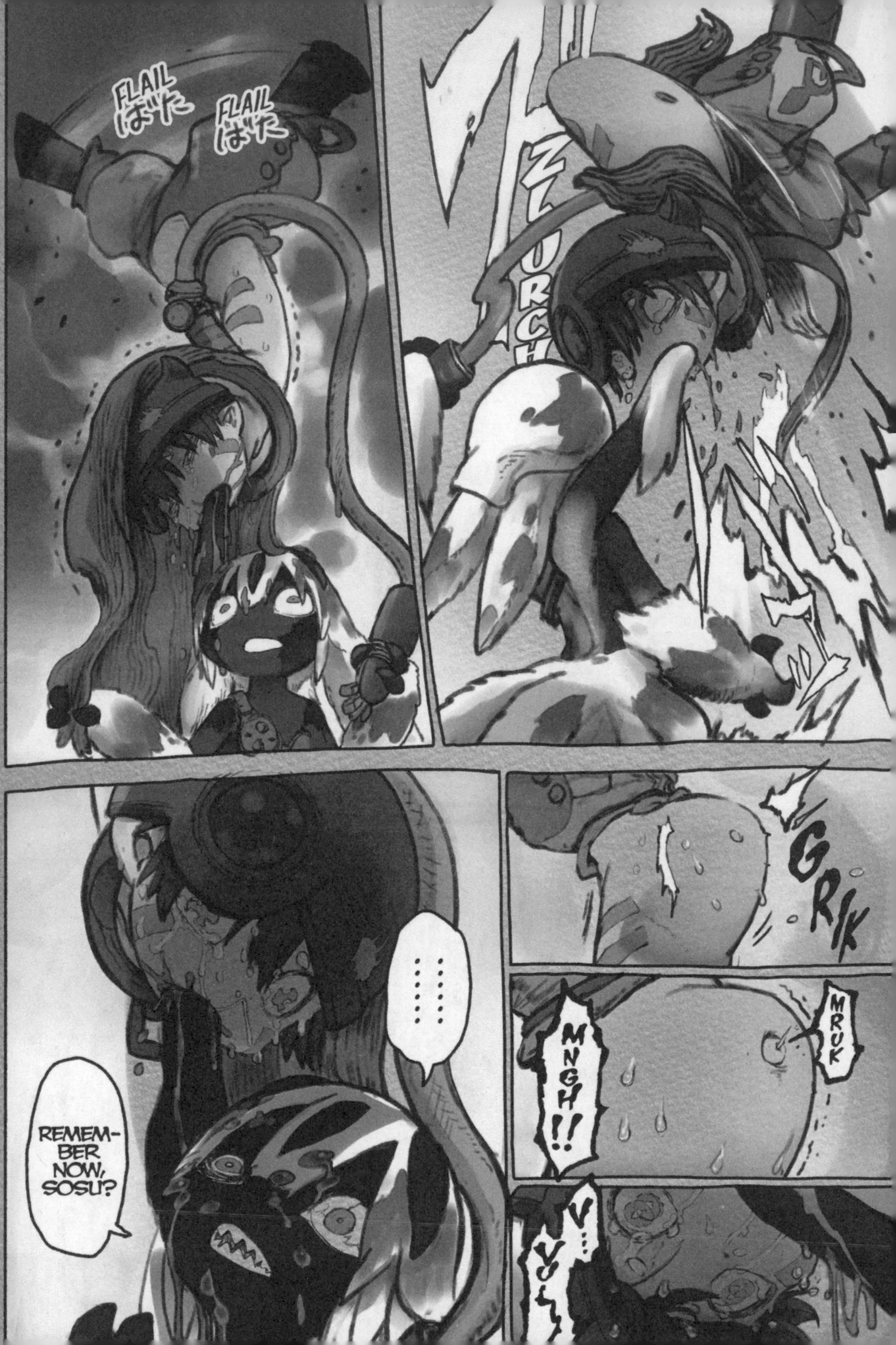
ZLURCH
FLAIL ばた
FLAIL ばた
GRIK
MRUK
MNGH!!
V...
VU...
......
REMEMBER NOW, SOSU?

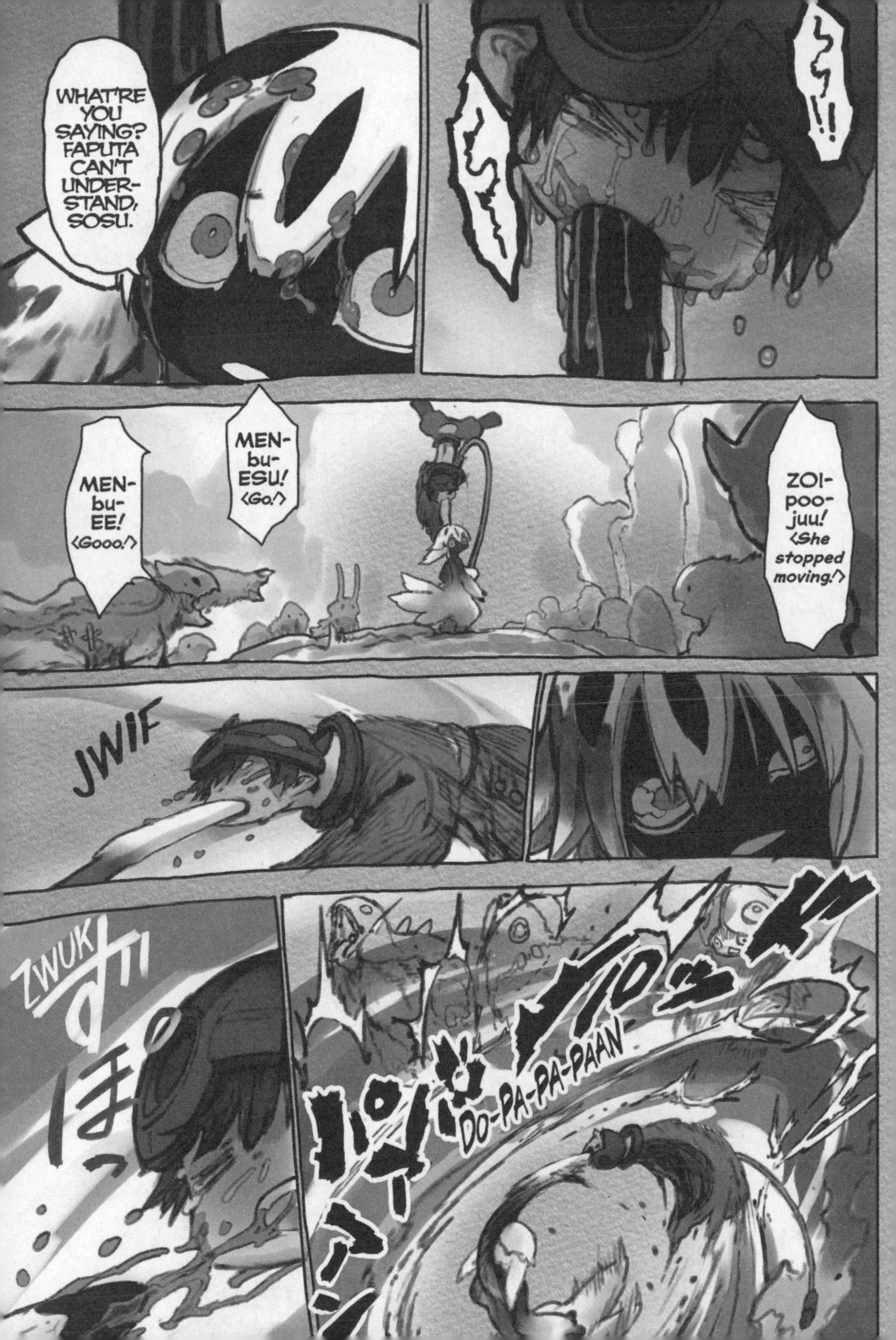
WHAT'RE YOU SAYING? FAPUTA CAN'T UNDER-STAND, SOSU.
ZOI-poo-juu! <She stopped moving!>
MEN-bu-ESU! <Go!>
MEN-bu-EE! <Gooo!>
JWIF
DO-PA-PA-PAAN
ZWUK

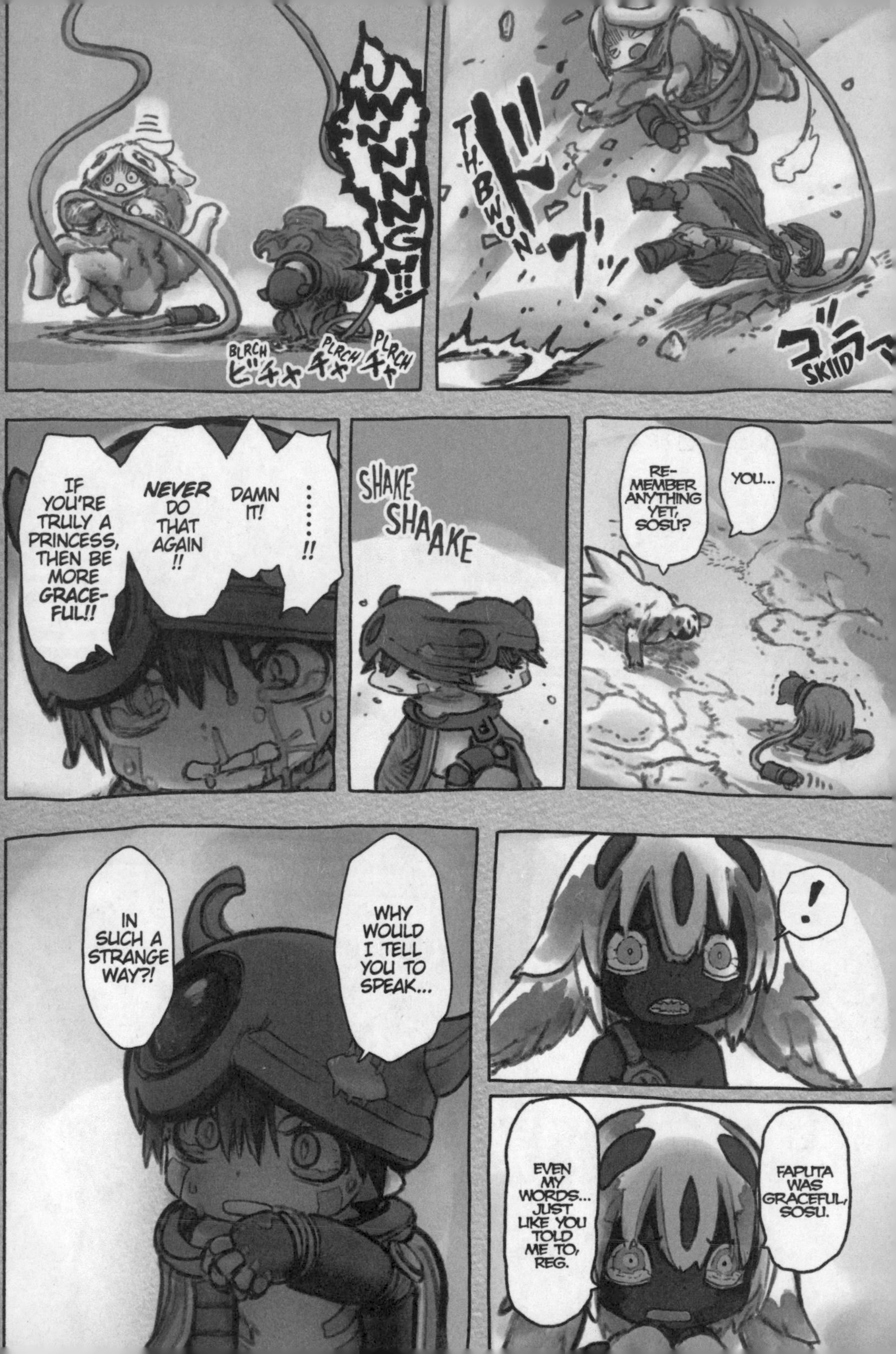
TH-BWUN
SKIID
UWNNNNGH!!
BLRCH
PLRCH
PLRCH
YOU...
RE-MEMBER ANYTHING YET, SOSU?
SHAKE SHAAKE
......!!
DAMN IT!
NEVER DO THAT AGAIN!!
IF YOU'RE TRULY A PRINCESS, THEN BE MORE GRACE-FUL!!
!
FAPUTA WAS GRACEFUL, SOSU.
EVEN MY WORDS... JUST LIKE YOU TOLD ME TO, REG.
WHY WOULD I TELL YOU TO SPEAK...
IN SUCH A STRANGE WAY?!

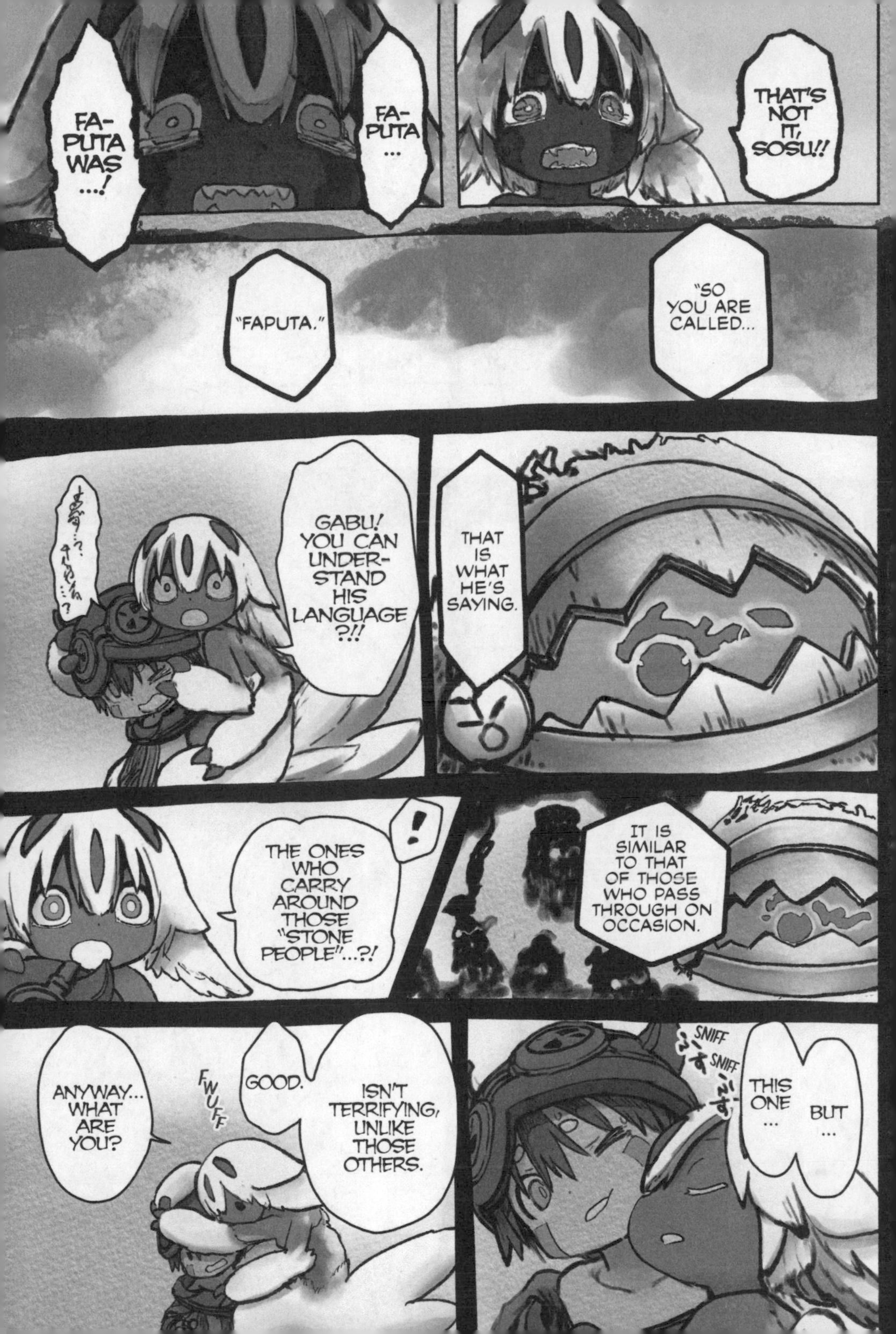
THAT'S NOT IT, SOSU!!
FA-PUTA ...
FA-PUTA WAS ...!
"SO YOU ARE CALLED...
"FAPUTA."
THAT IS WHAT HE'S SAYING.
GABU! YOU CAN UNDER-STAND HIS LANGUAGE ?!!
IT IS SIMILAR TO THAT OF THOSE WHO PASS THROUGH ON OCCASION.
!
THE ONES WHO CARRY AROUND THOSE "STONE PEOPLE"...?!
SNIFF ふす
SNIFF ふす
BUT ...
THIS ONE ...
ISN'T TERRIFYING, UNLIKE THOSE OTHERS.
GOOD.
FWUFF
ANYWAY... WHAT ARE YOU?

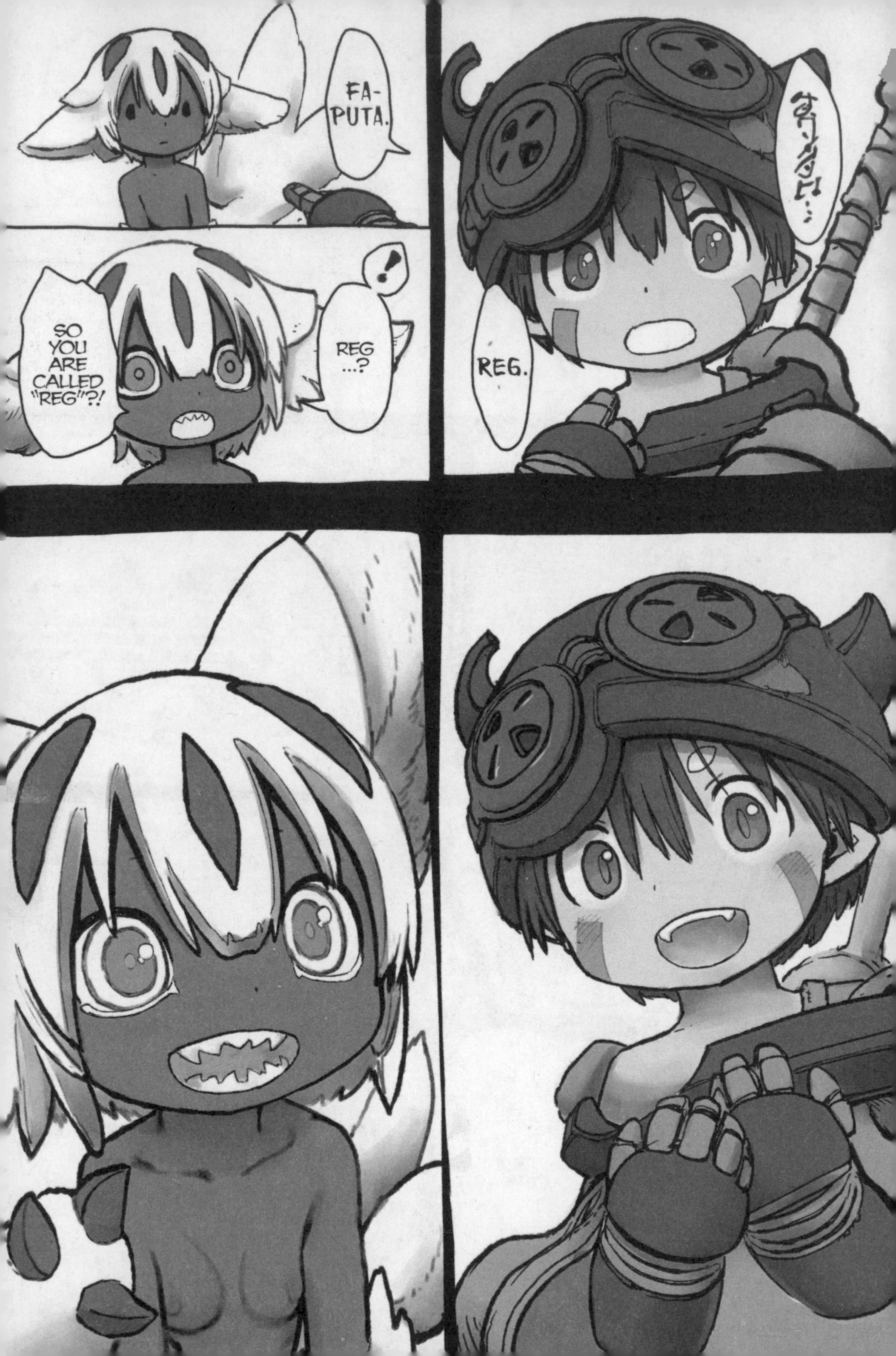
REG.
FA-PUTA.
!
REG ...?
SO YOU ARE CALLED "REG"?!

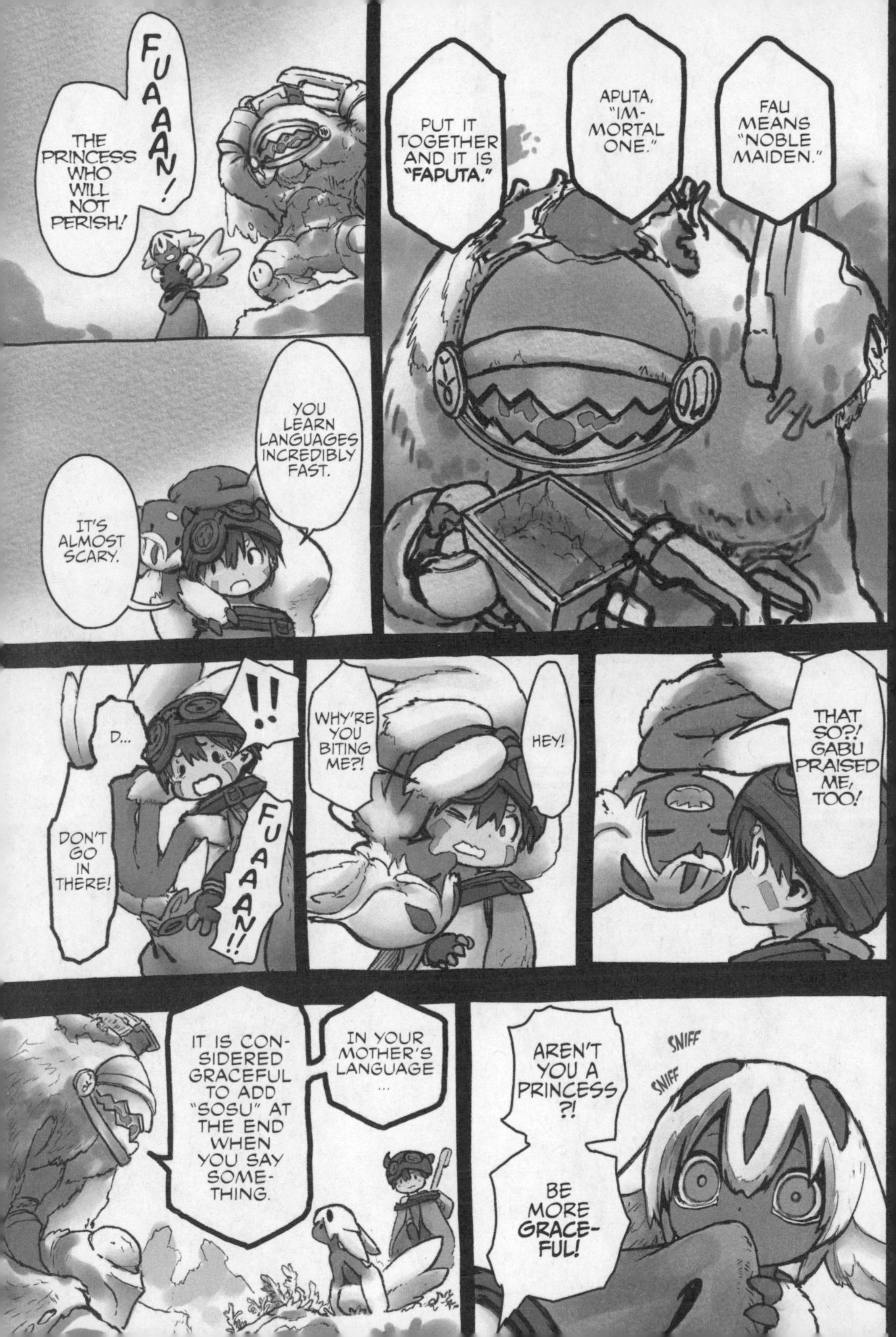
FAU MEANS "NOBLE MAIDEN."
APUTA, "IM-MORTAL ONE."
PUT IT TOGETHER AND IT IS **"FAPUTA."**
FUAAAAN!
THE PRINCESS WHO WILL NOT PERISH!
YOU LEARN LANGUAGES INCREDIBLY FAST.
IT'S ALMOST SCARY.
THAT SO?! GABU PRAISED ME, TOO!
HEY!
WHY'RE YOU BITING ME?!
!!
FUAAAAN!!
D...
DON'T GO IN THERE!
SNIFF
SNIFF
AREN'T YOU A PRINCESS?!
BE MORE **GRACE-FUL!**
IN YOUR MOTHER'S LANGUAGE ...
IT IS CON-SIDERED GRACEFUL TO ADD "SOSU" AT THE END WHEN YOU SAY SOME-THING.

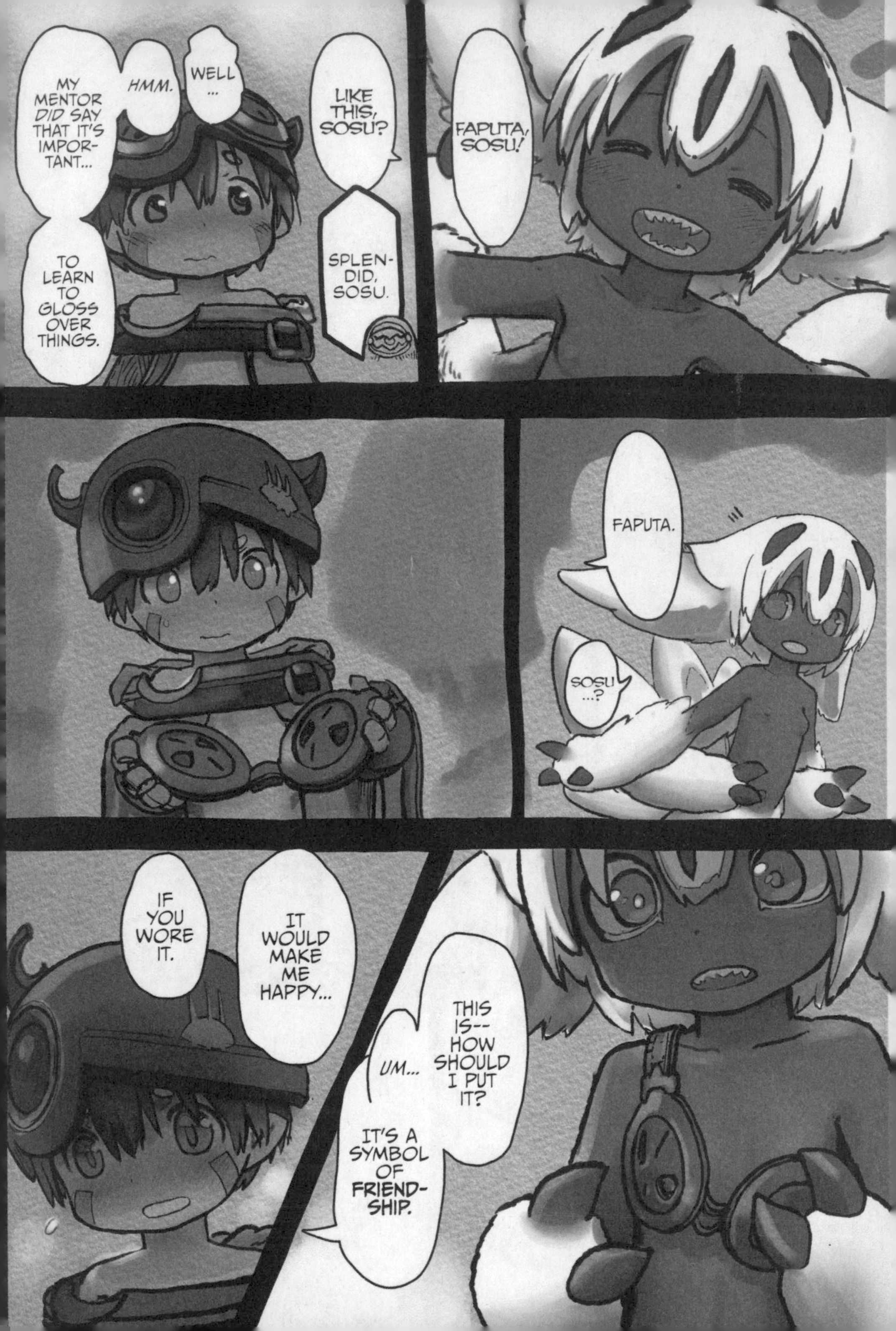
FAPUTA, SOSU!
LIKE THIS, SOSU?
SPLENDID, SOSU.
WELL ...
HMM.
MY MENTOR *DID* SAY THAT IT'S IMPORTANT...
TO LEARN TO GLOSS OVER THINGS.
FAPUTA.
SOSU ...?
THIS IS-- HOW SHOULD I PUT IT?
UM...
IT'S A SYMBOL OF FRIENDSHIP.
IT WOULD MAKE ME HAPPY...
IF YOU WORE IT.

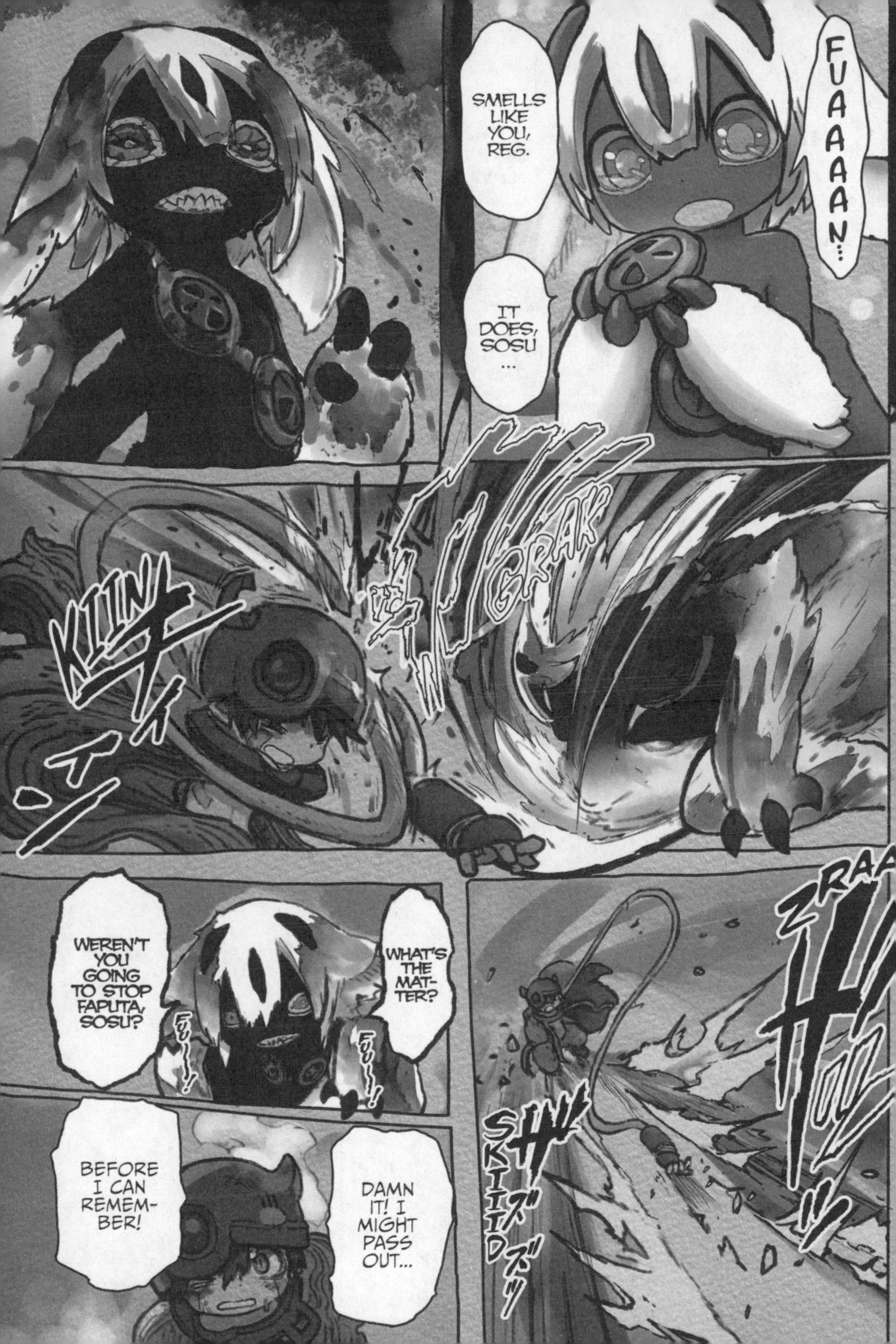
FUAAAAAN...
SMELLS LIKE YOU, REG.
IT DOES, SOSU ...
GRAK
KIIIN
ZRAA
SH
SKIIID
WHAT'S THE MATTER?
WEREN'T YOU GOING TO STOP FAPUTA, SOSU?
DAMN IT! I MIGHT PASS OUT...
BEFORE I CAN REMEMBER!

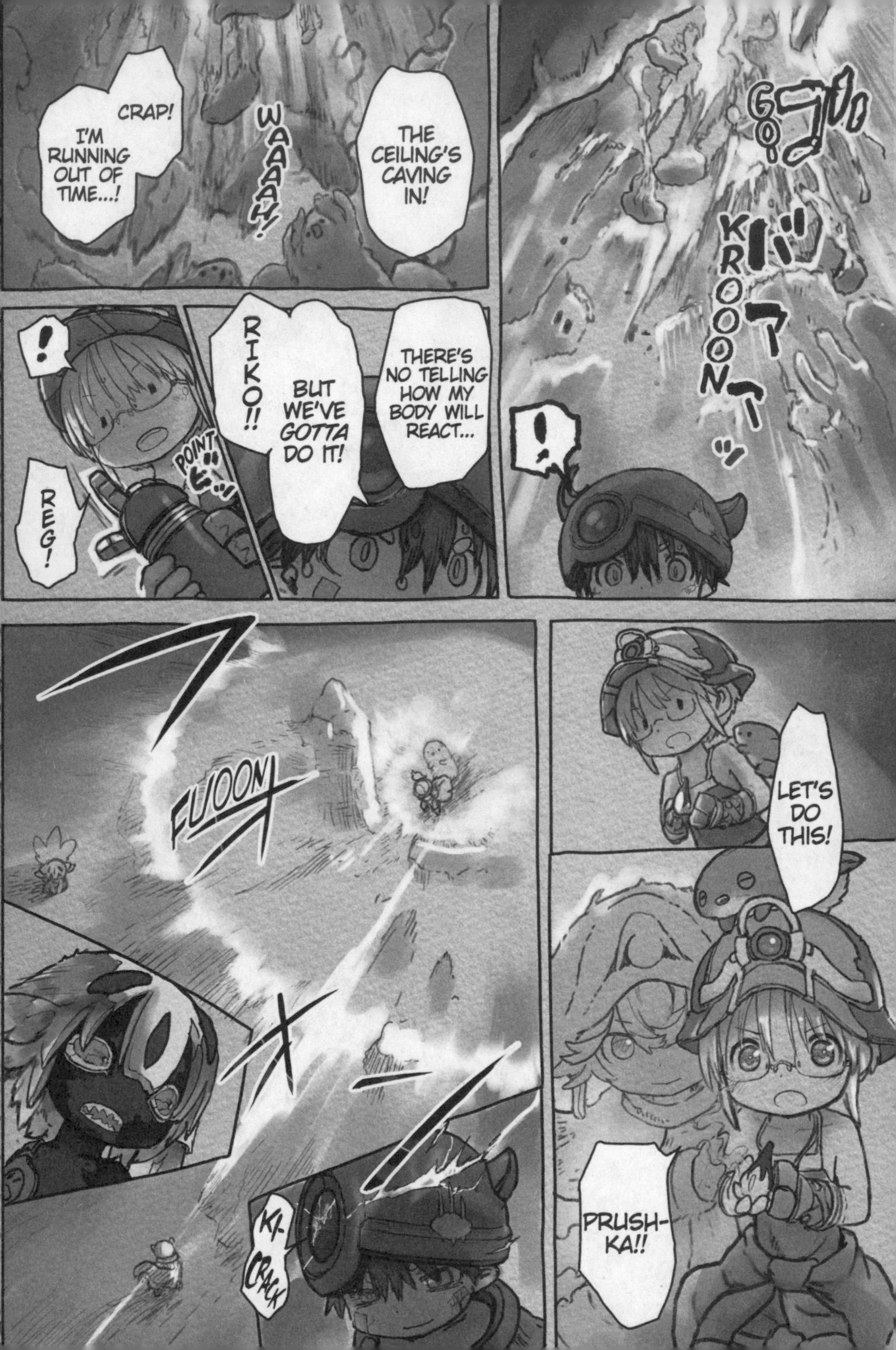
GO
KROOOON
!
THE CEILING'S CAVING IN!
WAAAAH!
CRAP!
I'M RUNNING OUT OF TIME...!
THERE'S NO TELLING HOW MY BODY WILL REACT...
BUT WE'VE GOTTA DO IT!
RIKO!!
!
POINT
REG!
LET'S DO THIS!
PRUSHKA!!
FUOON
KI-CRACK

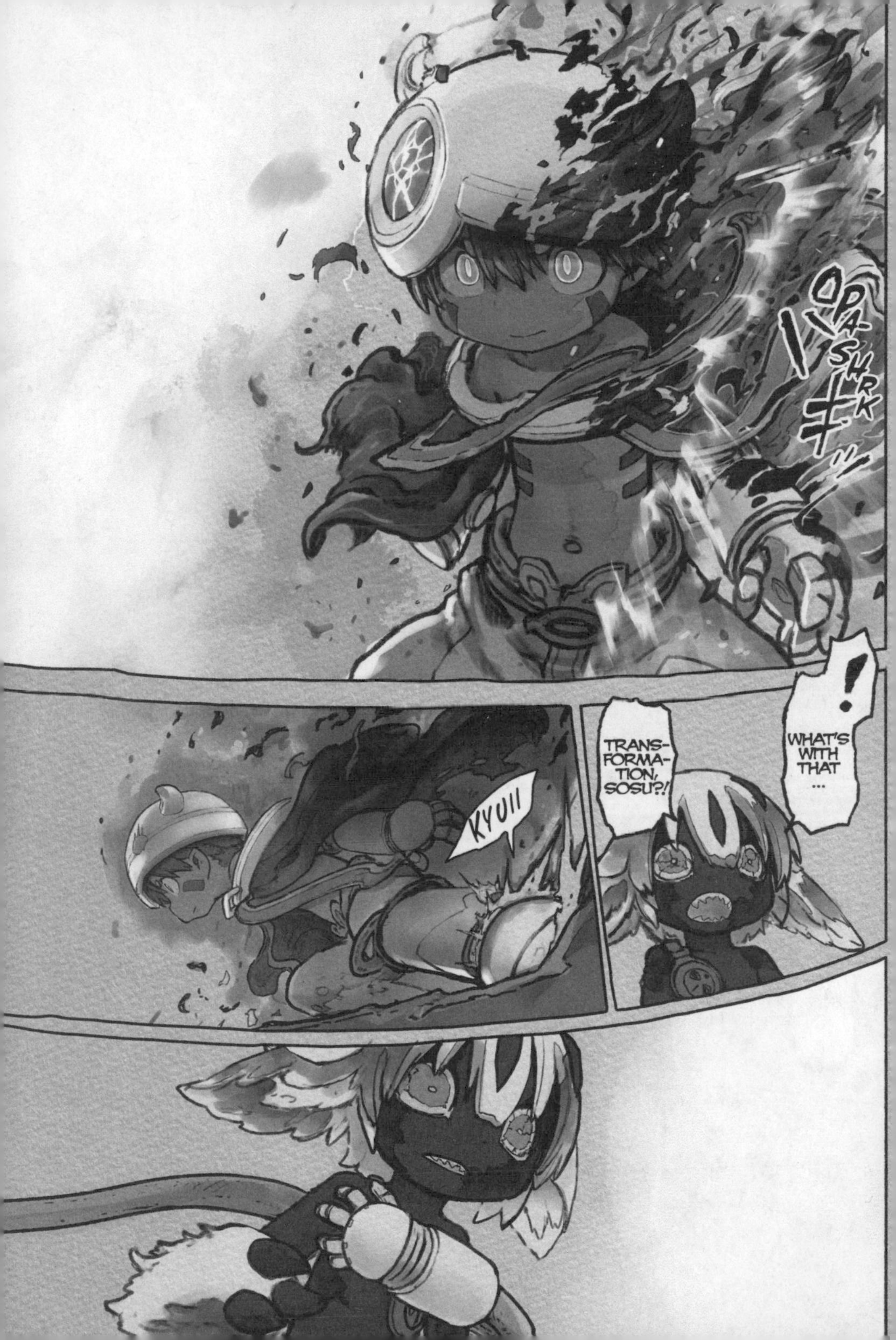
DPASHRK
!
WHAT'S WITH THAT ...
TRANS-FORMA-TION, SOSU?!
KYUII

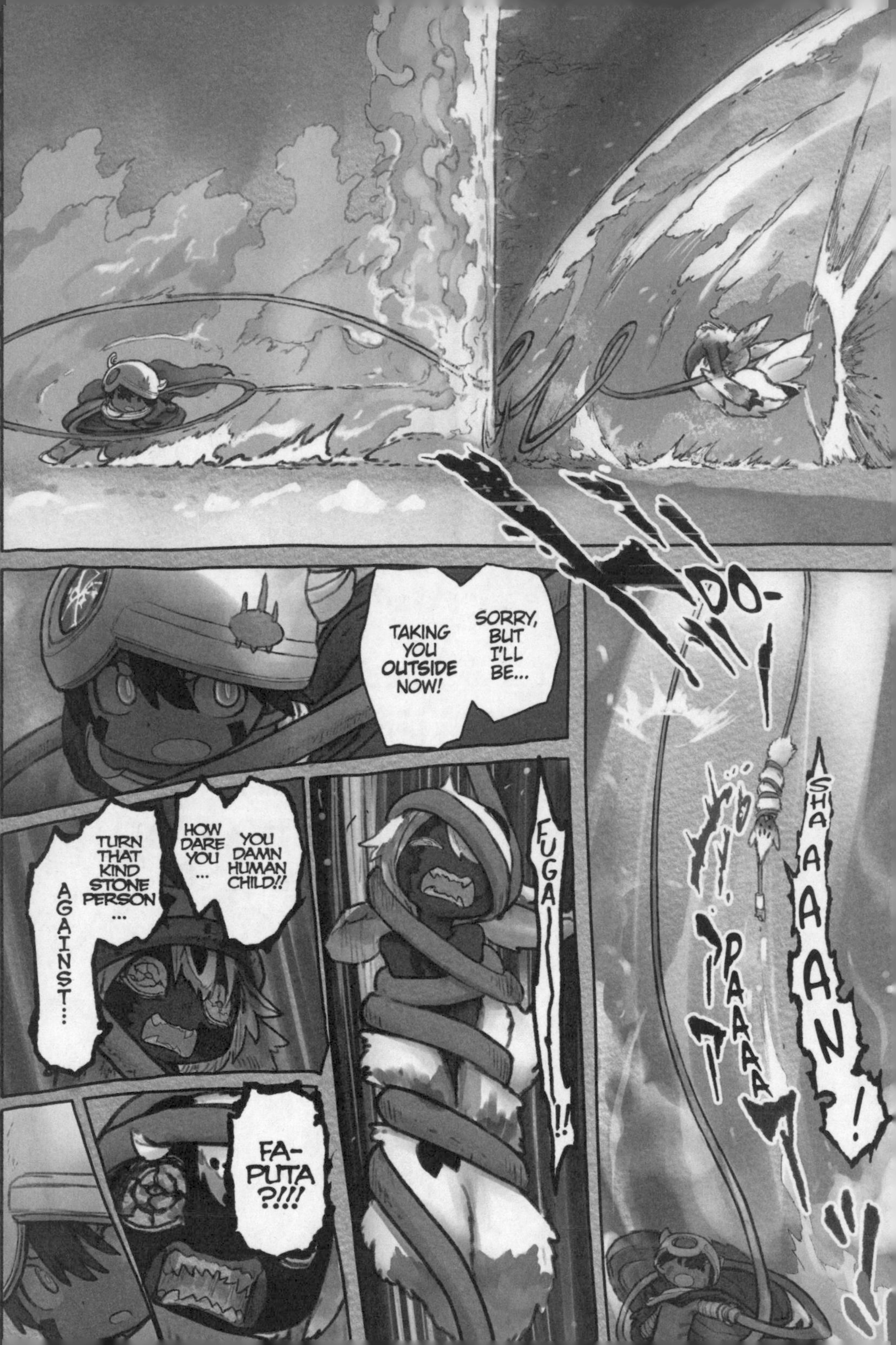
DO-
SHAAAAN!
PAAAA
SORRY, BUT I'LL BE...
TAKING YOU OUTSIDE NOW!
FUGA!!
YOU DAMN HUMAN CHILD!!
HOW DARE YOU...
TURN THAT KIND STONE PERSON...
AGAINST...
FA-PUTA?!!!

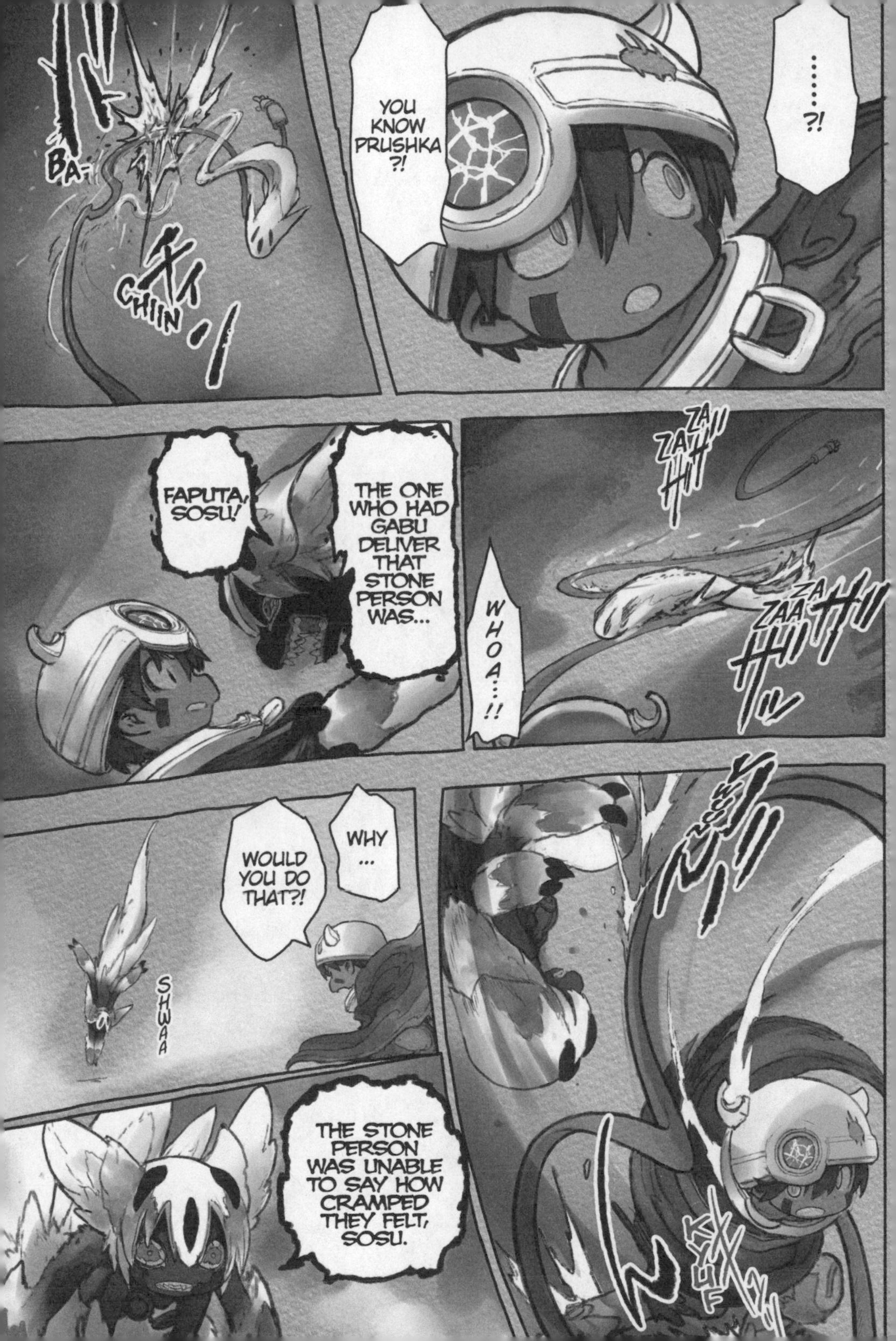
......?!
YOU KNOW PRUSHKA ?!
BA-
KI
CHIIN
ZA ZAHH
WHOA...!!
ZA ZAAHHH
THE ONE WHO HAD GABU DELIVER THAT STONE PERSON WAS...
FAPUTA, SOSU!
KYUF
WHY ...
WOULD YOU DO THAT?!
SHWAA
THE STONE PERSON WAS UNABLE TO SAY HOW CRAMPED THEY FELT, SOSU.

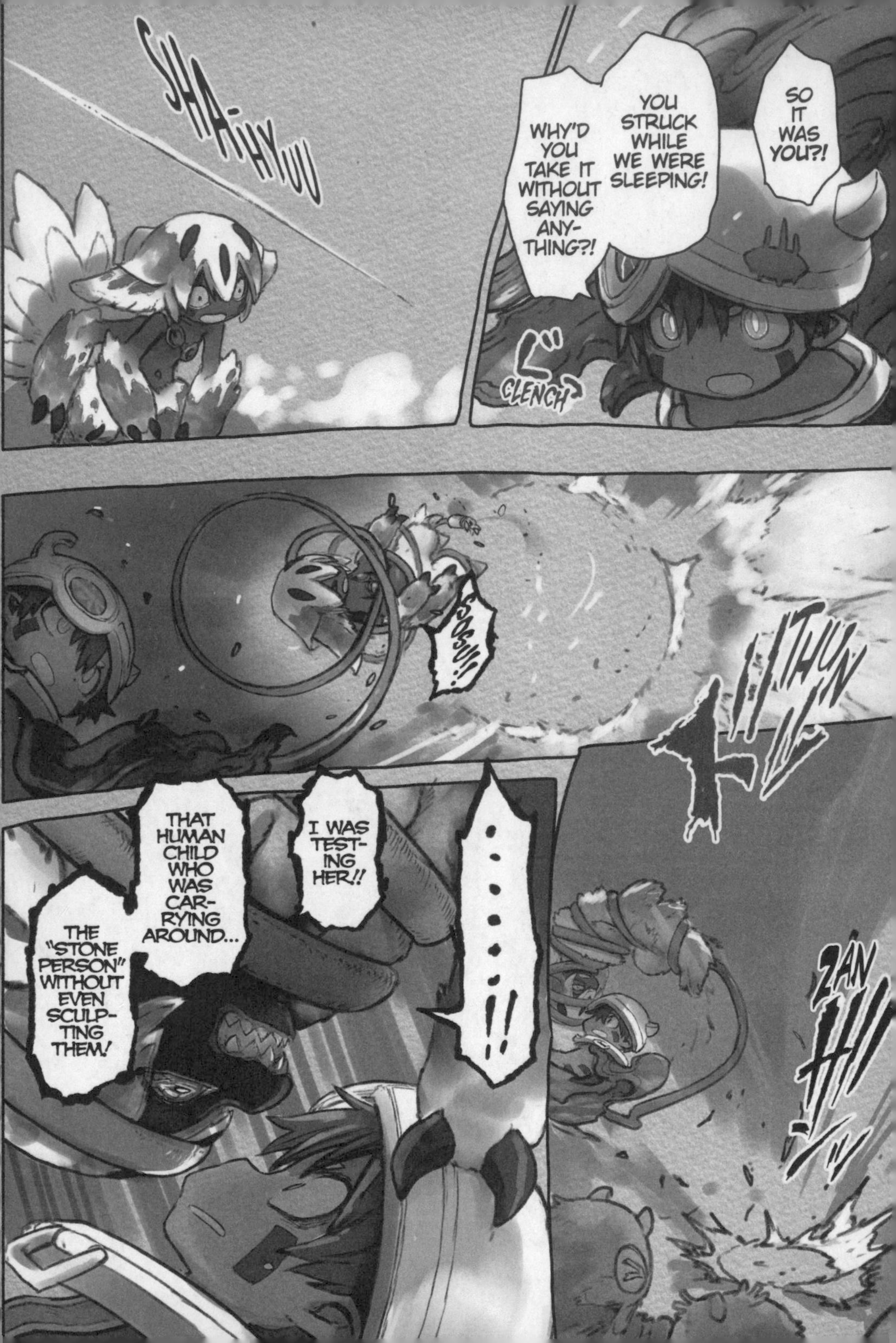
SO IT WAS YOU?!
YOU STRUCK WHILE WE WERE SLEEPING!
WHY'D YOU TAKE IT WITHOUT SAYING ANY-THING?!
CLENCH
SHA-HYUU
SOSU!!
THUN
ZAN
...!!
I WAS TEST-ING HER!!
THAT HUMAN CHILD WHO WAS CAR-RYING AROUND...
THE "STONE PERSON" WITHOUT EVEN SCULP-TING THEM!

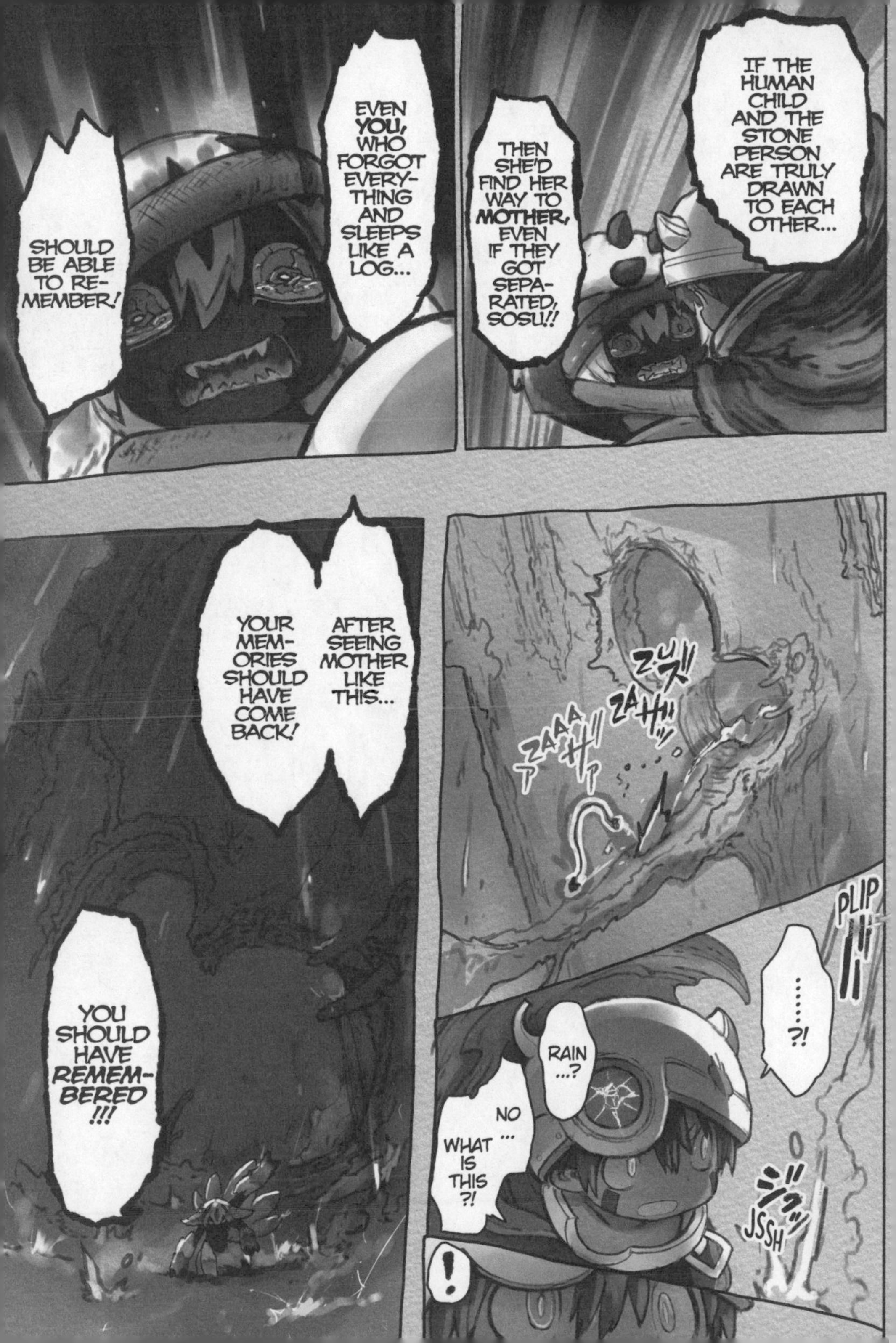
IF THE HUMAN CHILD AND THE STONE PERSON ARE TRULY DRAWN TO EACH OTHER...
THEN SHE'D FIND HER WAY TO MOTHER, EVEN IF THEY GOT SEPARATED, SOSU!!
EVEN YOU, WHO FORGOT EVERYTHING AND SLEEPS LIKE A LOG...
SHOULD BE ABLE TO REMEMBER!
ZU
ZA
ZAAA
PLIP
......?!
RAIN...?
NO... WHAT IS THIS?!
JSSH
!
AFTER SEEING MOTHER LIKE THIS...
YOUR MEMORIES SHOULD HAVE COME BACK!
YOU SHOULD HAVE REMEMBERED!!!

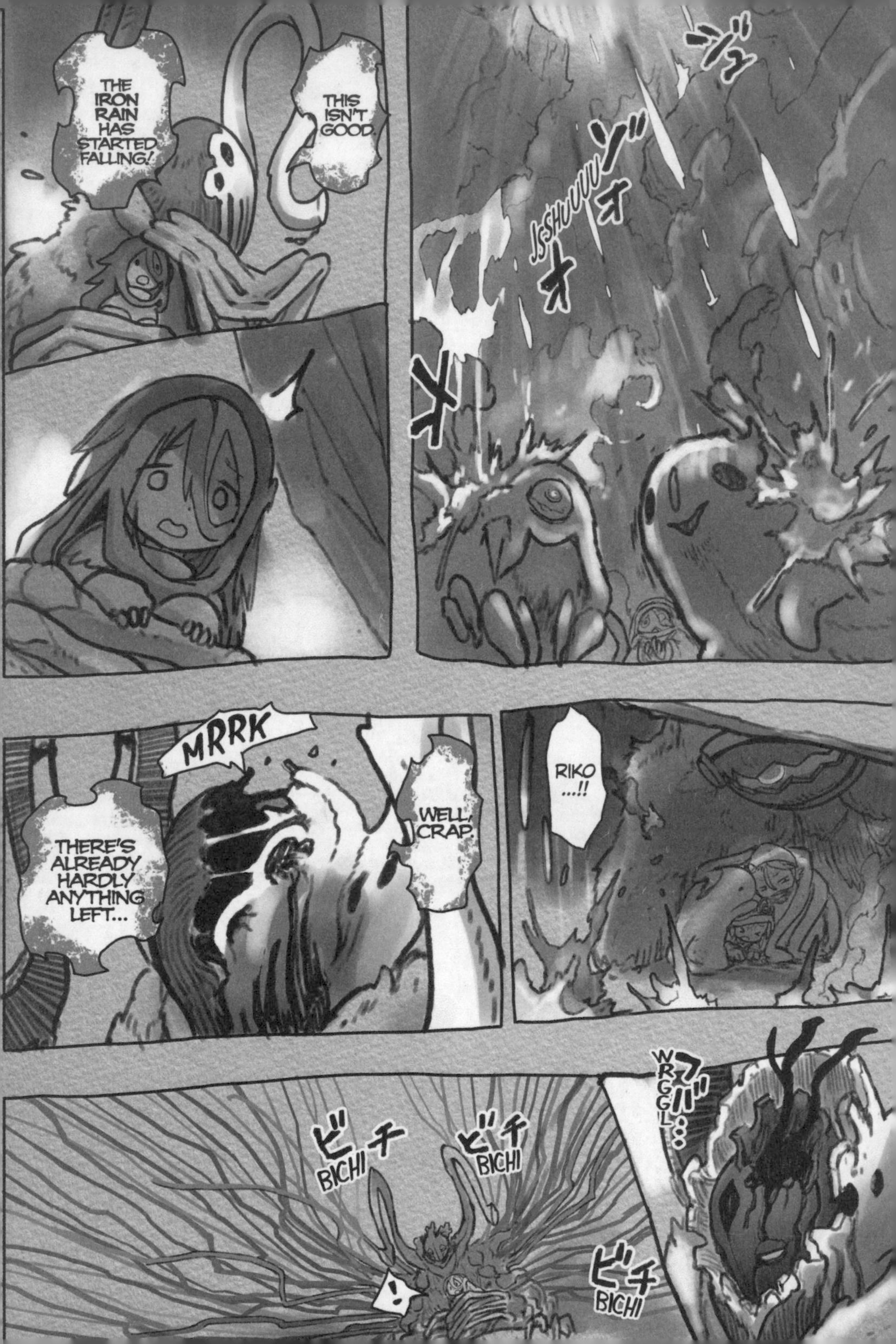
JSSHUUUU
THIS ISN'T GOOD.
THE IRON RAIN HAS STARTED FALLING!
RIKO ...!!
WELL, CRAP.
MRRK
THERE'S ALREADY HARDLY ANYTHING LEFT...
WRGGL...
BICHI
BICHI
BICHI
!

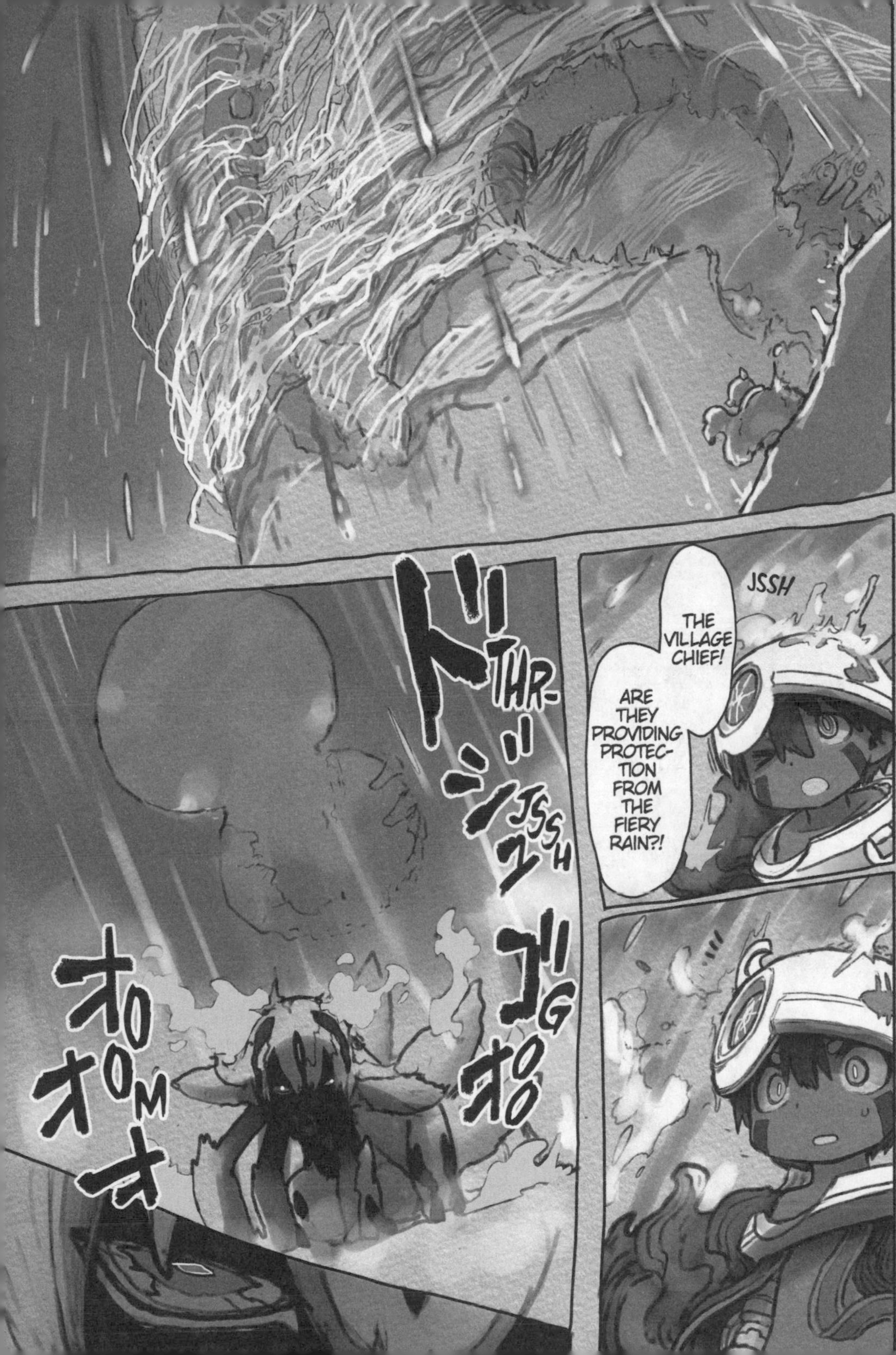
JSSH
THE VILLAGE CHIEF!
ARE THEY PROVIDING PROTECTION FROM THE FIERY RAIN?!
THR-
JSSH
G
O
OOM

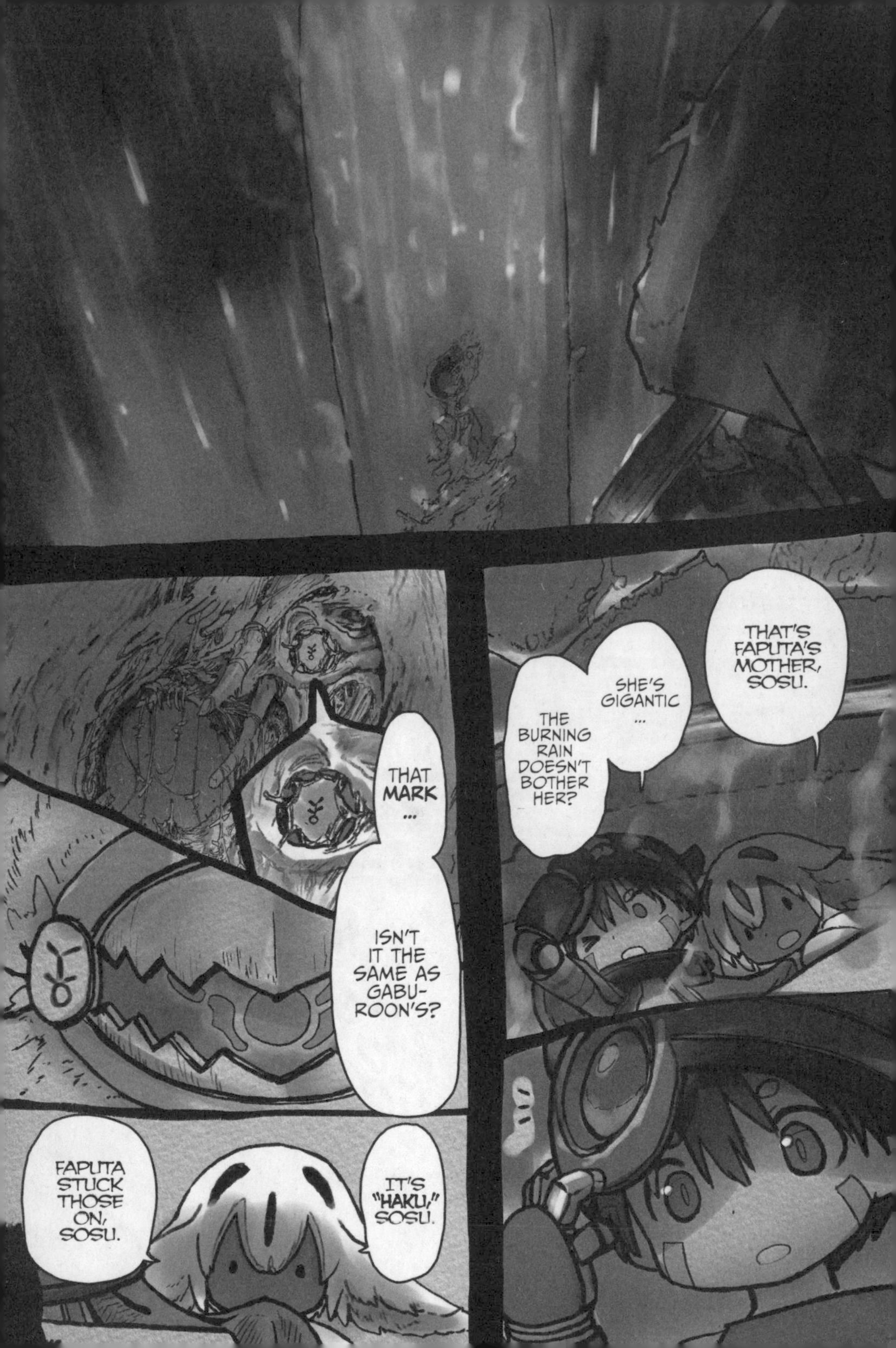
THAT'S FAPUTA'S MOTHER, SOSU.
SHE'S GIGANTIC ...
THE BURNING RAIN DOESN'T BOTHER HER?
THAT MARK ...
ISN'T IT THE SAME AS GABU-ROON'S?
IT'S "HAKU," SOSU.
FAPUTA STUCK THOSE ON, SOSU.

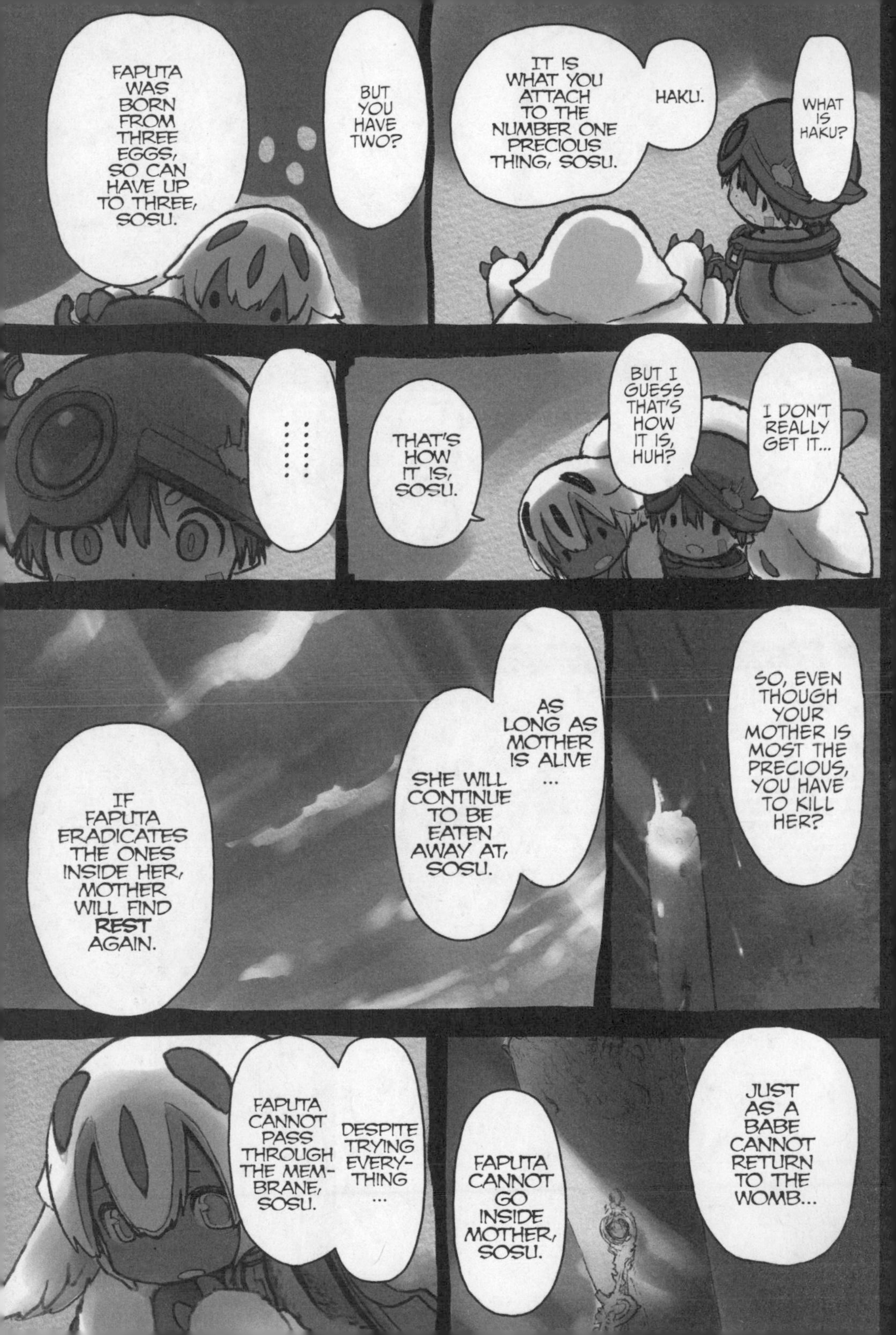
WHAT IS HAKU?
HAKU.
IT IS WHAT YOU ATTACH TO THE NUMBER ONE PRECIOUS THING, SOSU.
BUT YOU HAVE TWO?
FAPUTA WAS BORN FROM THREE EGGS, SO CAN HAVE UP TO THREE, SOSU.
I DON'T REALLY GET IT...
BUT I GUESS THAT'S HOW IT IS, HUH?
THAT'S HOW IT IS, SOSU.
......
SO, EVEN THOUGH YOUR MOTHER IS MOST THE PRECIOUS, YOU HAVE TO KILL HER?
AS LONG AS MOTHER IS ALIVE ...
SHE WILL CONTINUE TO BE EATEN AWAY AT, SOSU.
IF FAPUTA ERADICATES THE ONES INSIDE HER, MOTHER WILL FIND **REST** AGAIN.
JUST AS A BABE CANNOT RETURN TO THE WOMB...
FAPUTA CANNOT GO INSIDE MOTHER, SOSU.
DESPITE TRYING EVERY-THING ...
FAPUTA CANNOT PASS THROUGH THE MEM-BRANE, SOSU.

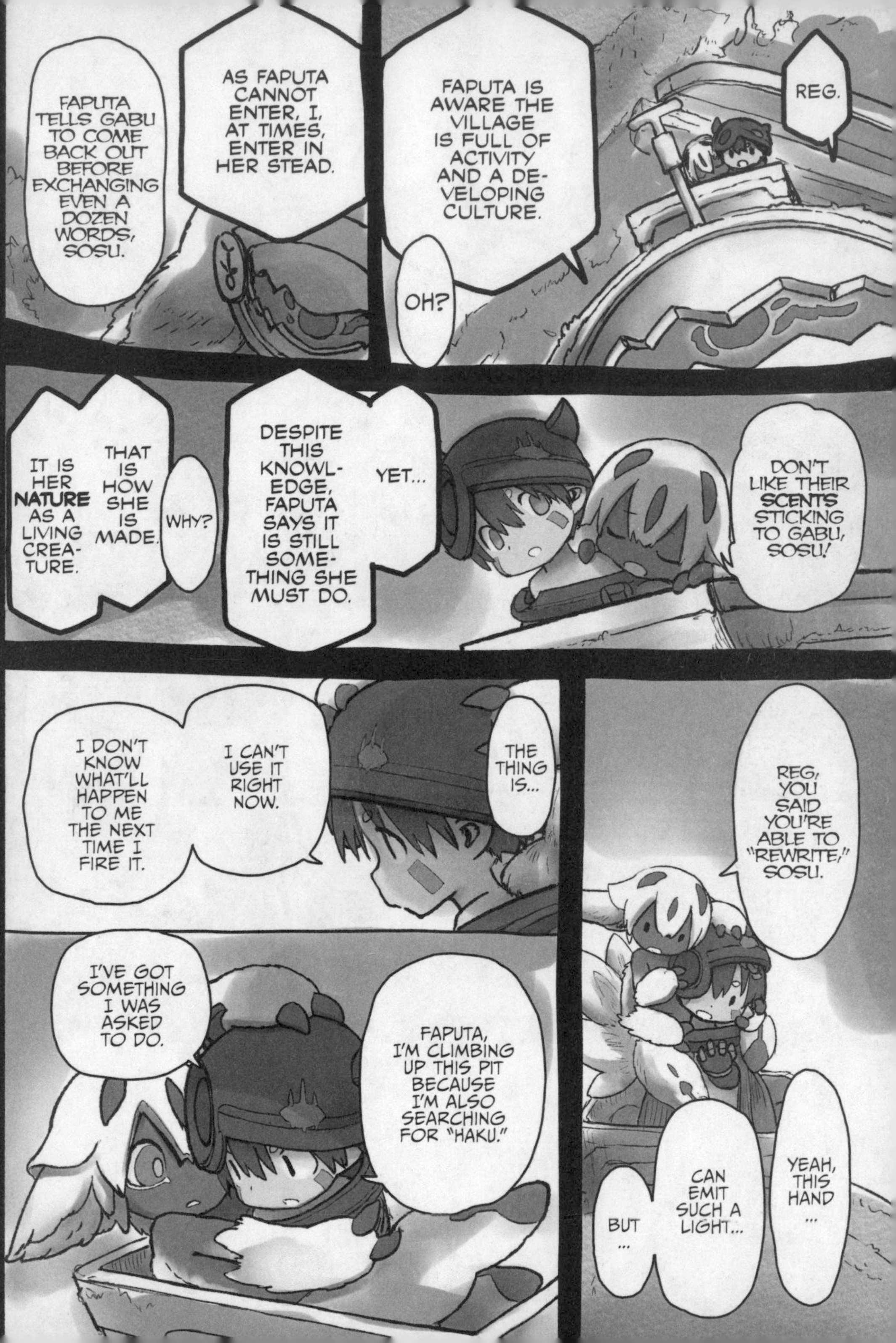
REG.
FAPUTA IS AWARE THE VILLAGE IS FULL OF ACTIVITY AND A DE-VELOPING CULTURE.
OH?
AS FAPUTA CANNOT ENTER, I, AT TIMES, ENTER IN HER STEAD.
FAPUTA TELLS GABU TO COME BACK OUT BEFORE EXCHANGING EVEN A DOZEN WORDS, SOSU.
DON'T LIKE THEIR **SCENTS** STICKING TO GABU, SOSU!
YET...
DESPITE THIS KNOWL-EDGE, FAPUTA SAYS IT IS STILL SOME-THING SHE MUST DO.
WHY?
THAT IS HOW SHE IS MADE.
IT IS HER **NATURE** AS A LIVING CREA-TURE.
REG, YOU SAID YOU'RE ABLE TO "REWRITE," SOSU.
YEAH, THIS HAND...
CAN EMIT SUCH A LIGHT...
BUT...
THE THING IS...
I CAN'T USE IT RIGHT NOW.
I DON'T KNOW WHAT'LL HAPPEN TO ME THE NEXT TIME I FIRE IT.
FAPUTA, I'M CLIMBING UP THIS PIT BECAUSE I'M ALSO SEARCHING FOR "HAKU."
I'VE GOT SOMETHING I WAS ASKED TO DO.

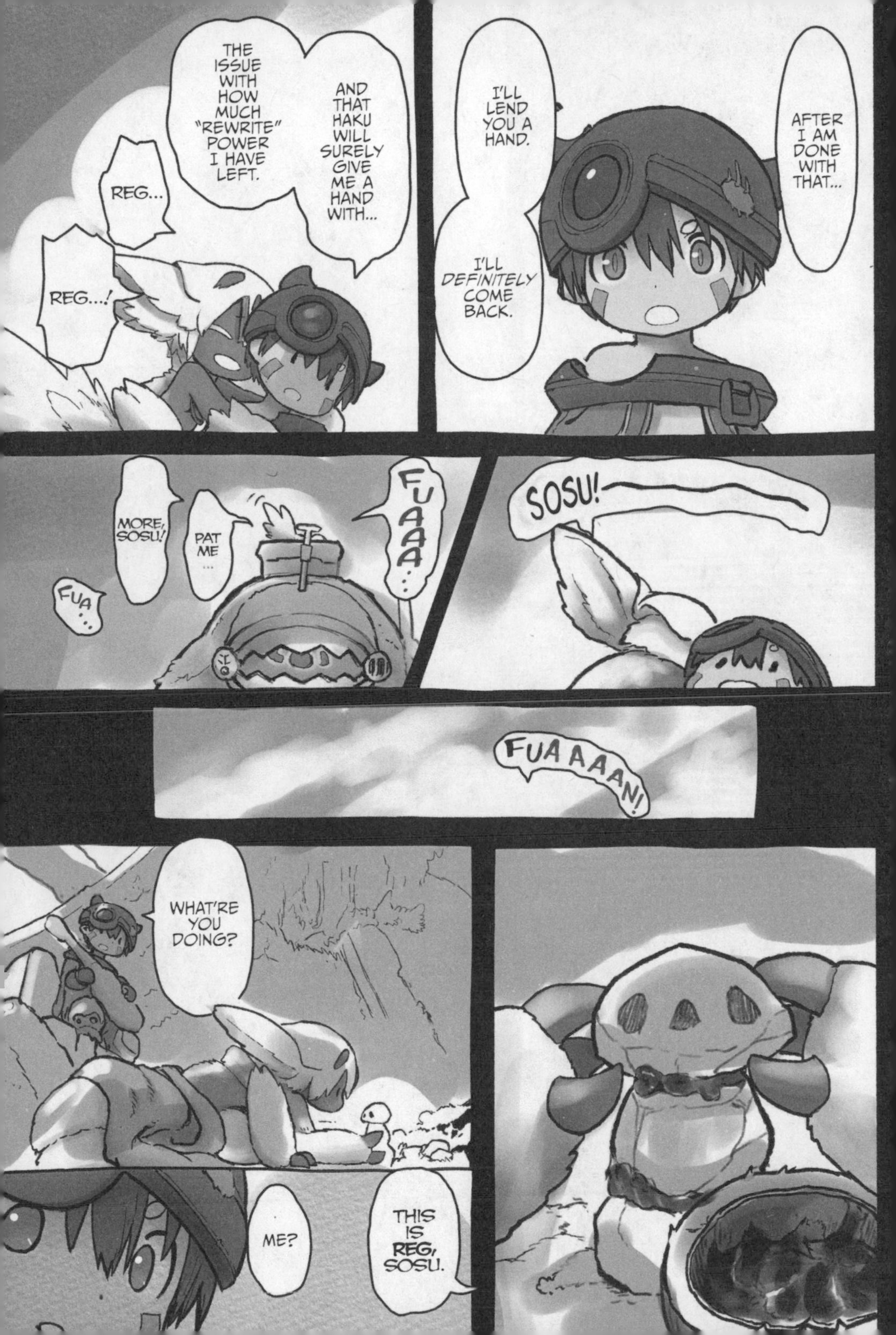
AFTER I AM DONE WITH THAT...
I'LL LEND YOU A HAND.
I'LL DEFINITELY COME BACK.
AND THAT HAKU WILL SURELY GIVE ME A HAND WITH...
THE ISSUE WITH HOW MUCH "REWRITE" POWER I HAVE LEFT.
REG...
REG...!
SOSU!
FUAAAA...
PAT ME...
MORE, SOSU!
FUA...
FUA AAAAN!
WHAT'RE YOU DOING?
THIS IS REG, SOSU.
ME?

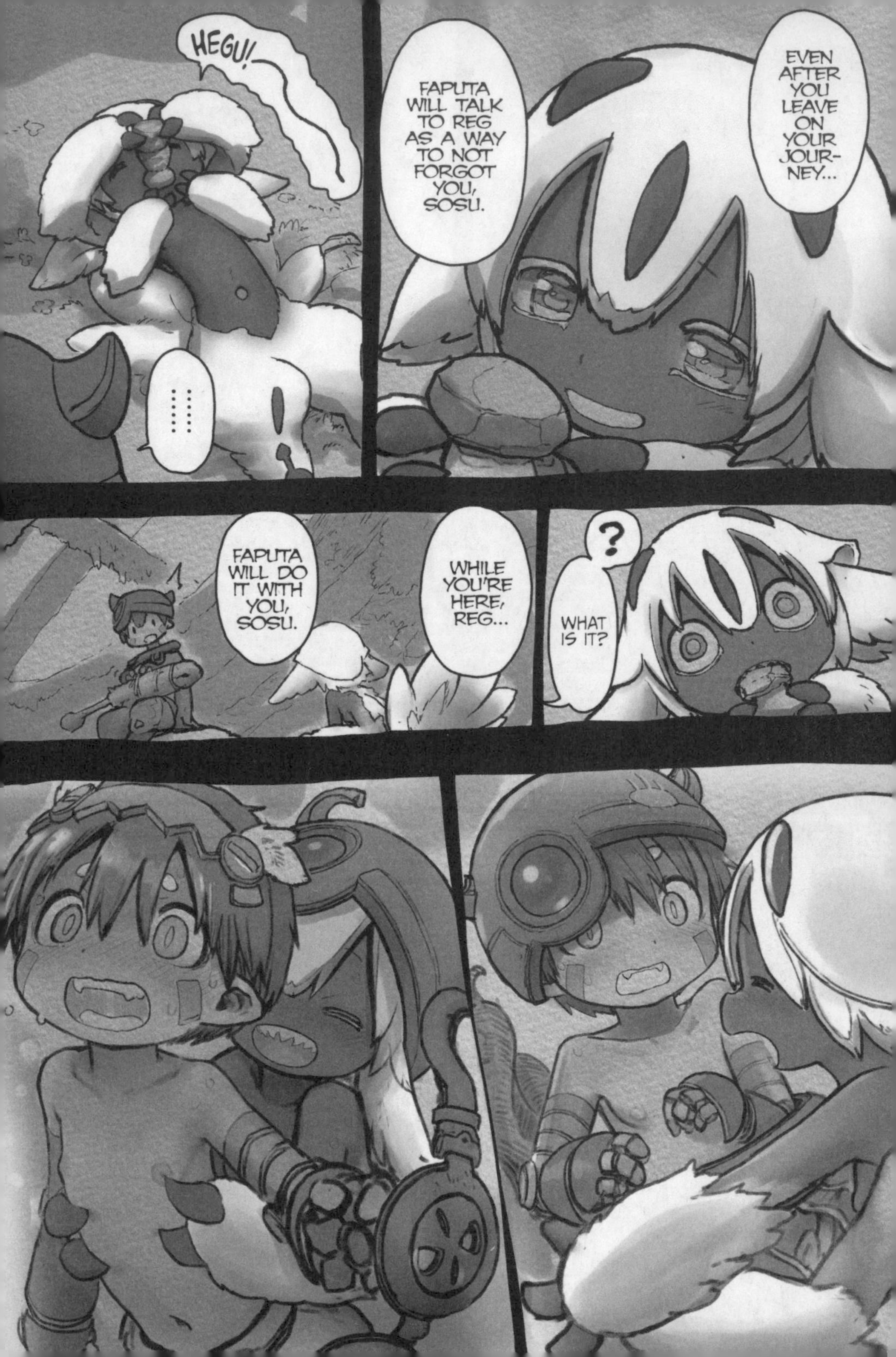
EVEN AFTER YOU LEAVE ON YOUR JOURNEY...
FAPUTA WILL TALK TO REG AS A WAY TO NOT FORGOT YOU, SOSU.
HEGU!
......
!
?
WHAT IS IT?
WHILE YOU'RE HERE, REG...
FAPUTA WILL DO IT WITH YOU, SOSU.

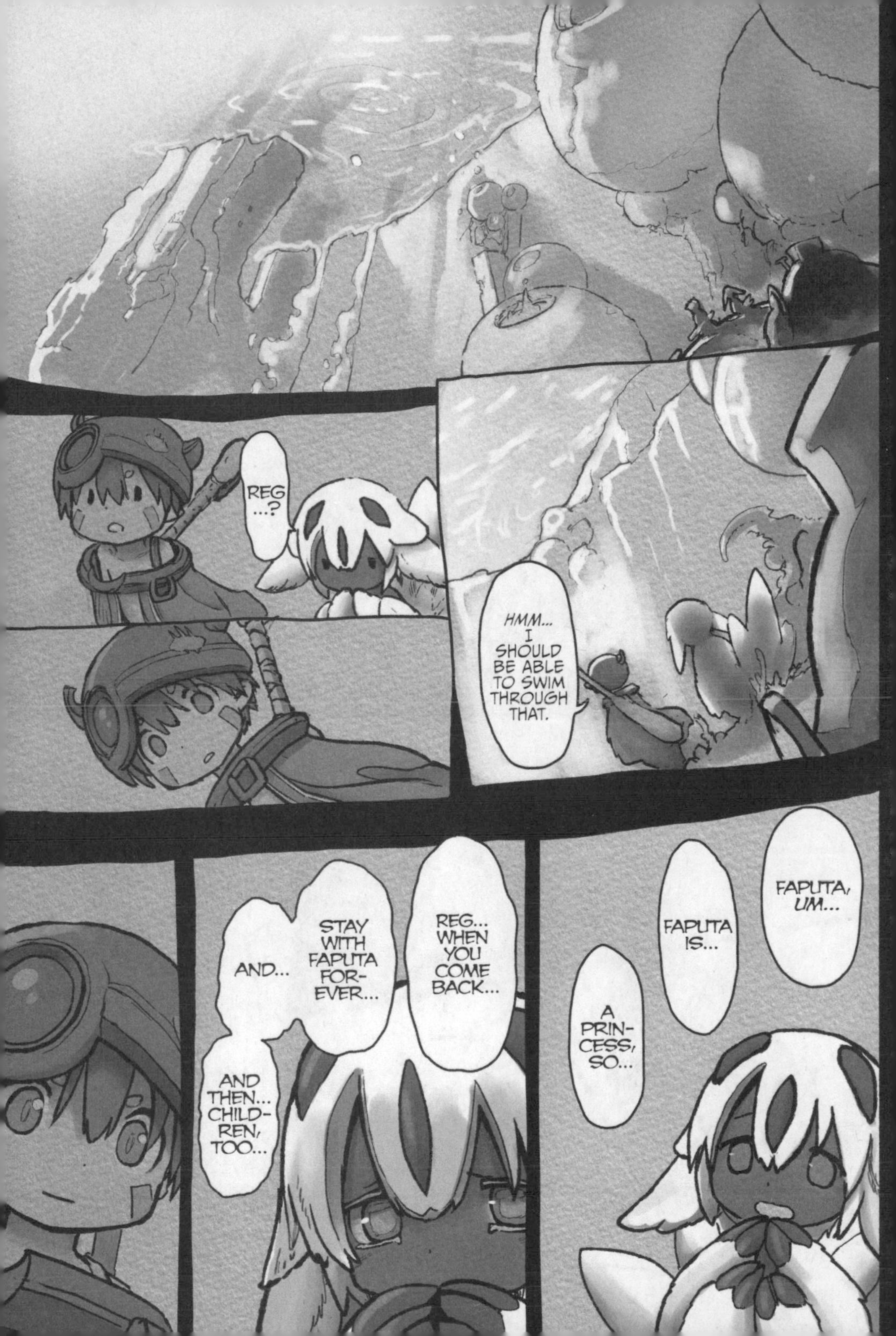
HMM... I SHOULD BE ABLE TO SWIM THROUGH THAT.
REG ...?
FAPUTA, UM...
FAPUTA IS...
A PRINCESS, SO...
REG... WHEN YOU COME BACK...
STAY WITH FAPUTA FOR-EVER...
AND...
AND THEN... CHILD-REN, TOO...

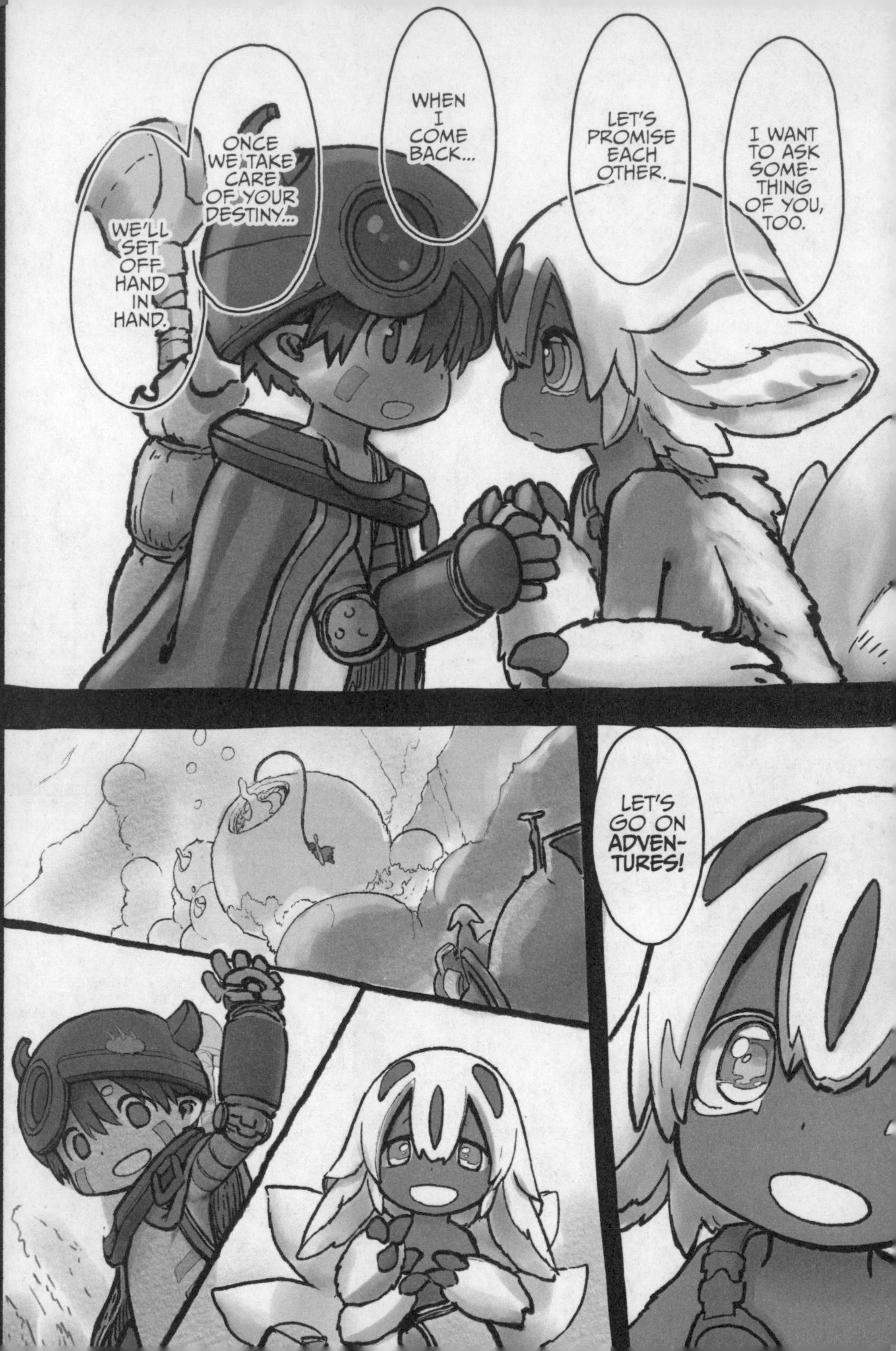
I WANT TO ASK SOME-THING OF YOU, TOO.
LET'S PROMISE EACH OTHER.
WHEN I COME BACK...
ONCE WE TAKE CARE OF YOUR DESTINY...
WE'LL SET OFF HAND IN HAND.
LET'S GO ON **ADVEN-TURES!**

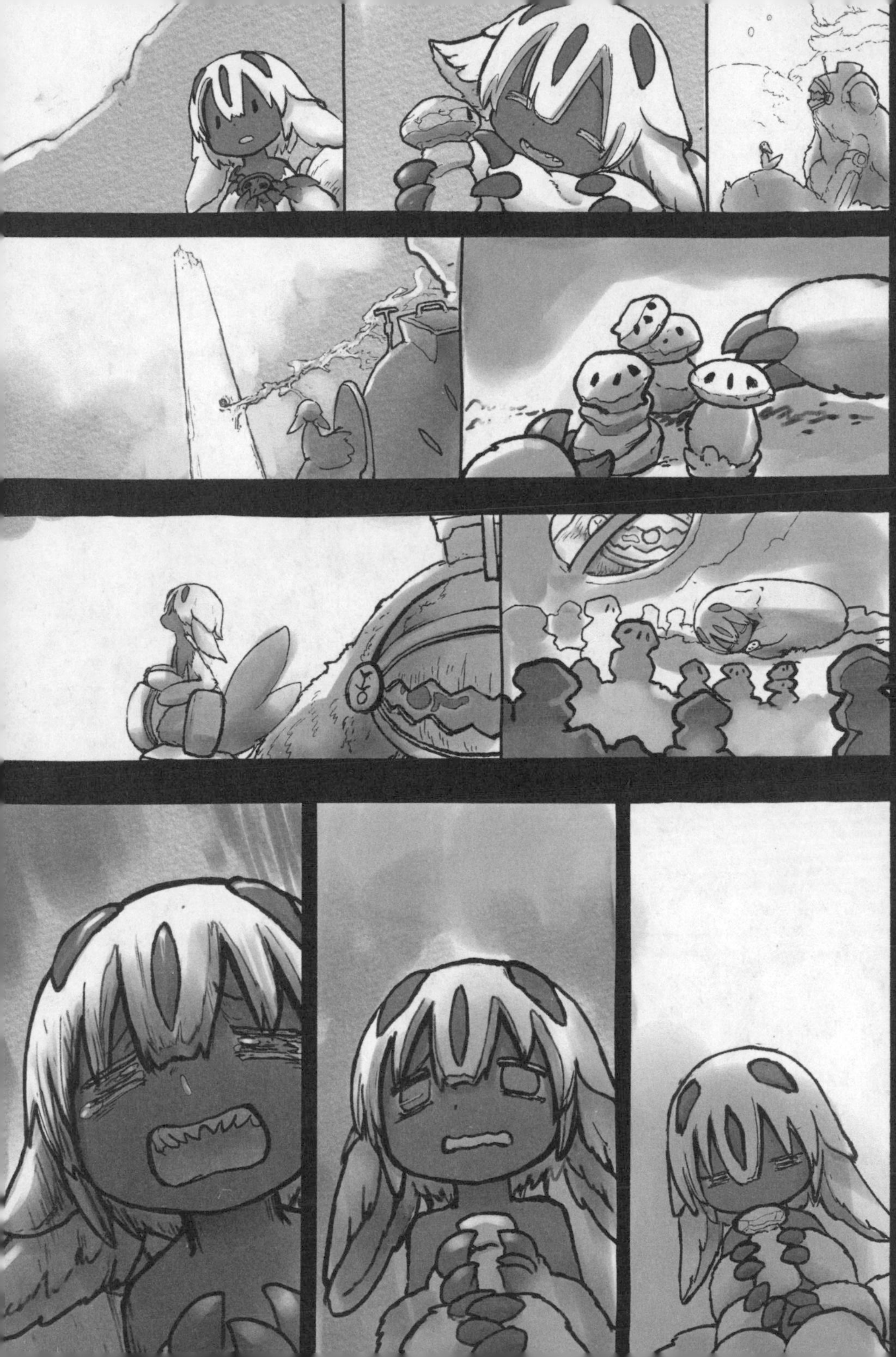

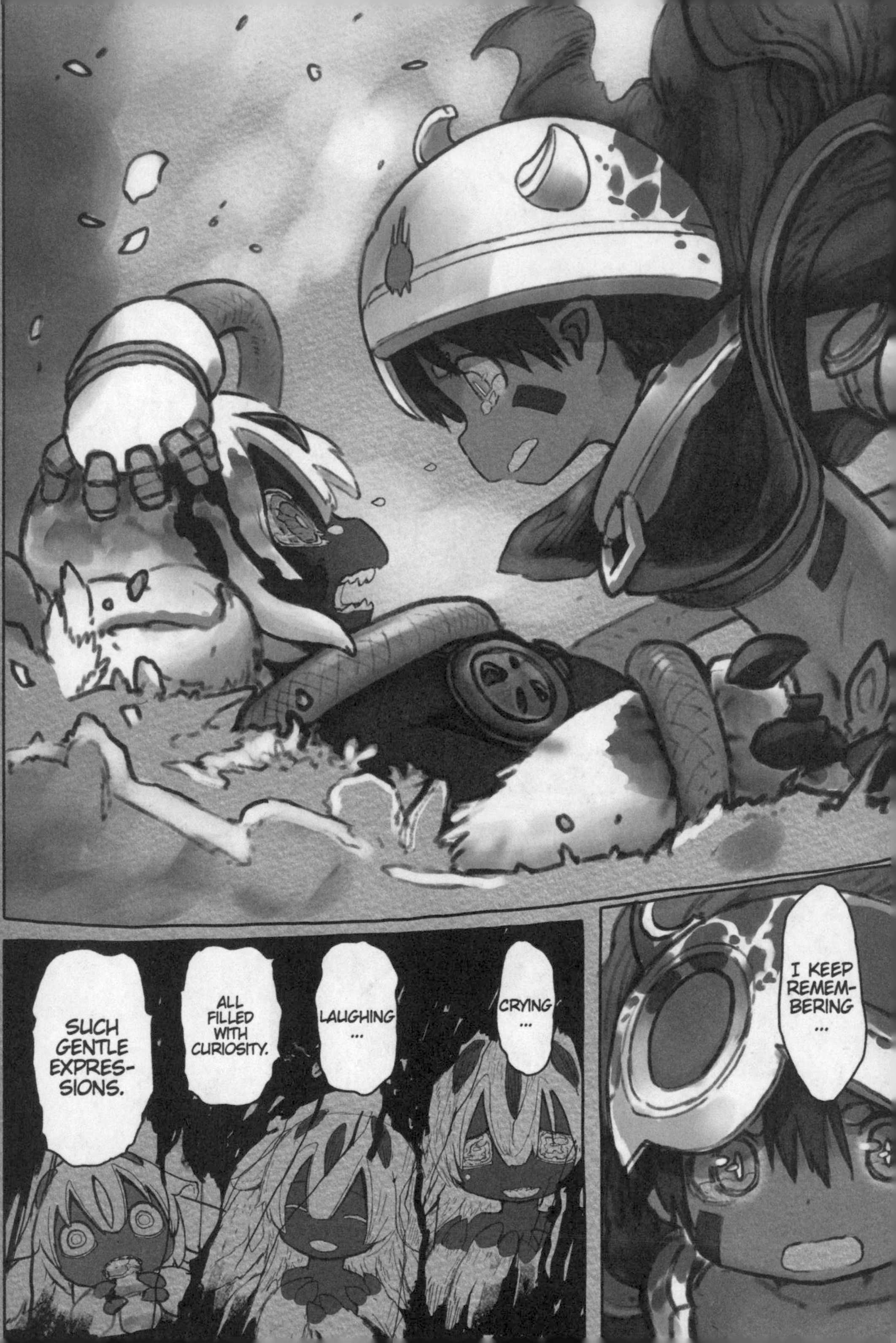
I KEEP REMEMBERING ...
CRYING ...
LAUGHING ...
ALL FILLED WITH CURIOSITY.
SUCH GENTLE EXPRESSIONS.

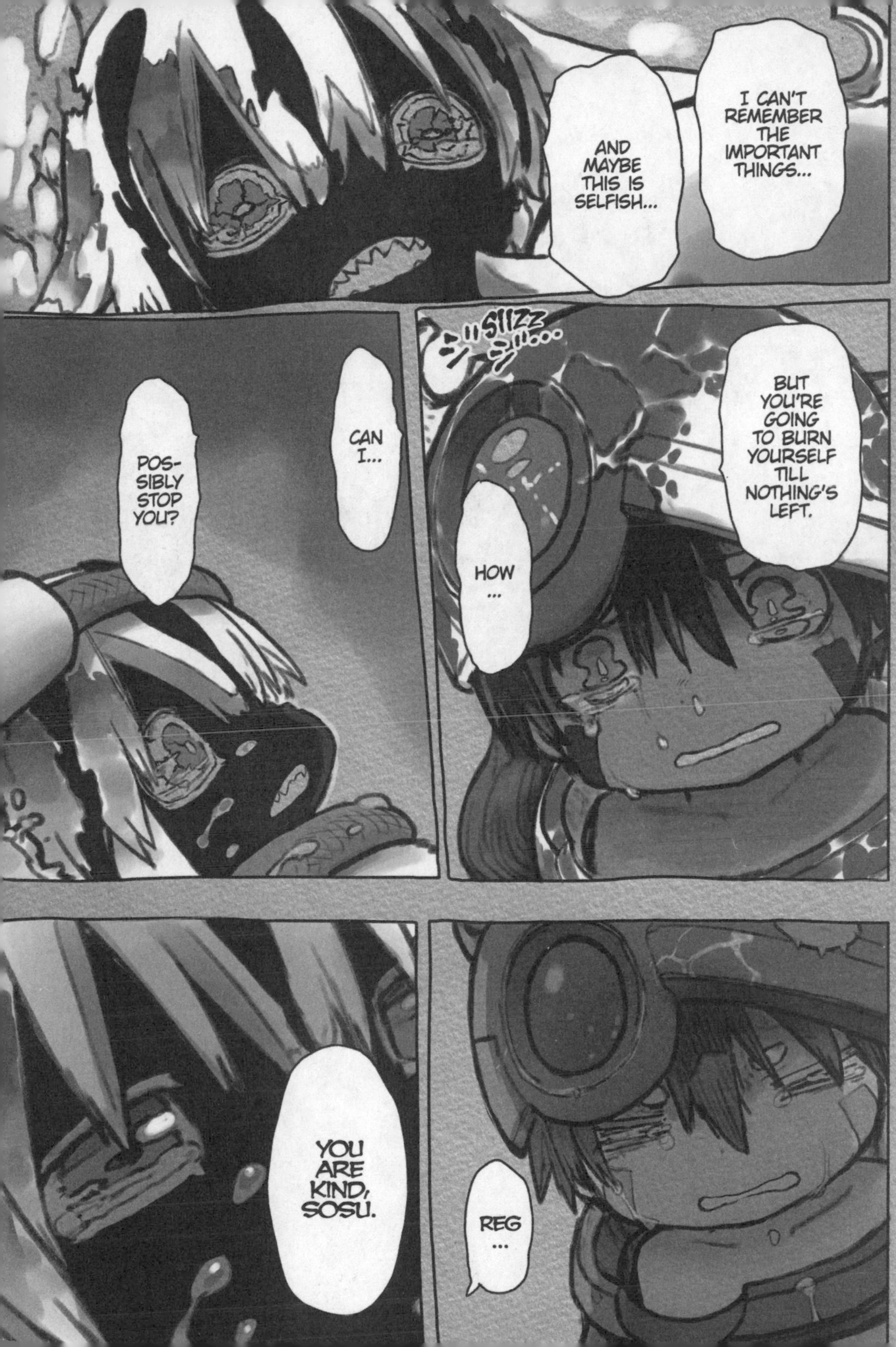
I CAN'T REMEMBER THE IMPORTANT THINGS...
AND MAYBE THIS IS SELFISH...
SIIZZ
BUT YOU'RE GOING TO BURN YOURSELF TILL NOTHING'S LEFT.
HOW ...
CAN I...
POS-SIBLY STOP YOU?
REG ...
YOU ARE KIND, SOSU.

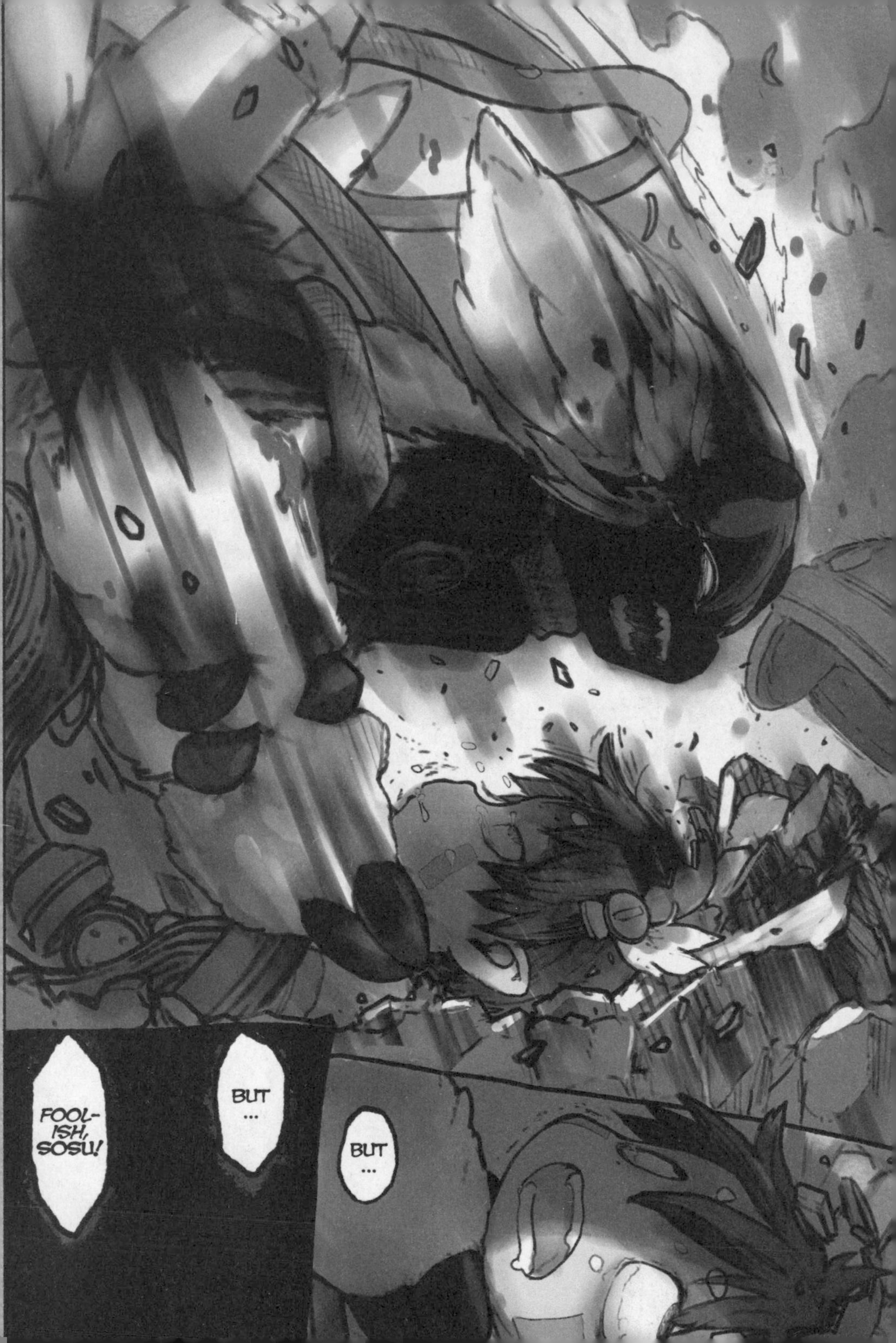
BUT ...
BUT ...
FOOL-ISH, SOSU!

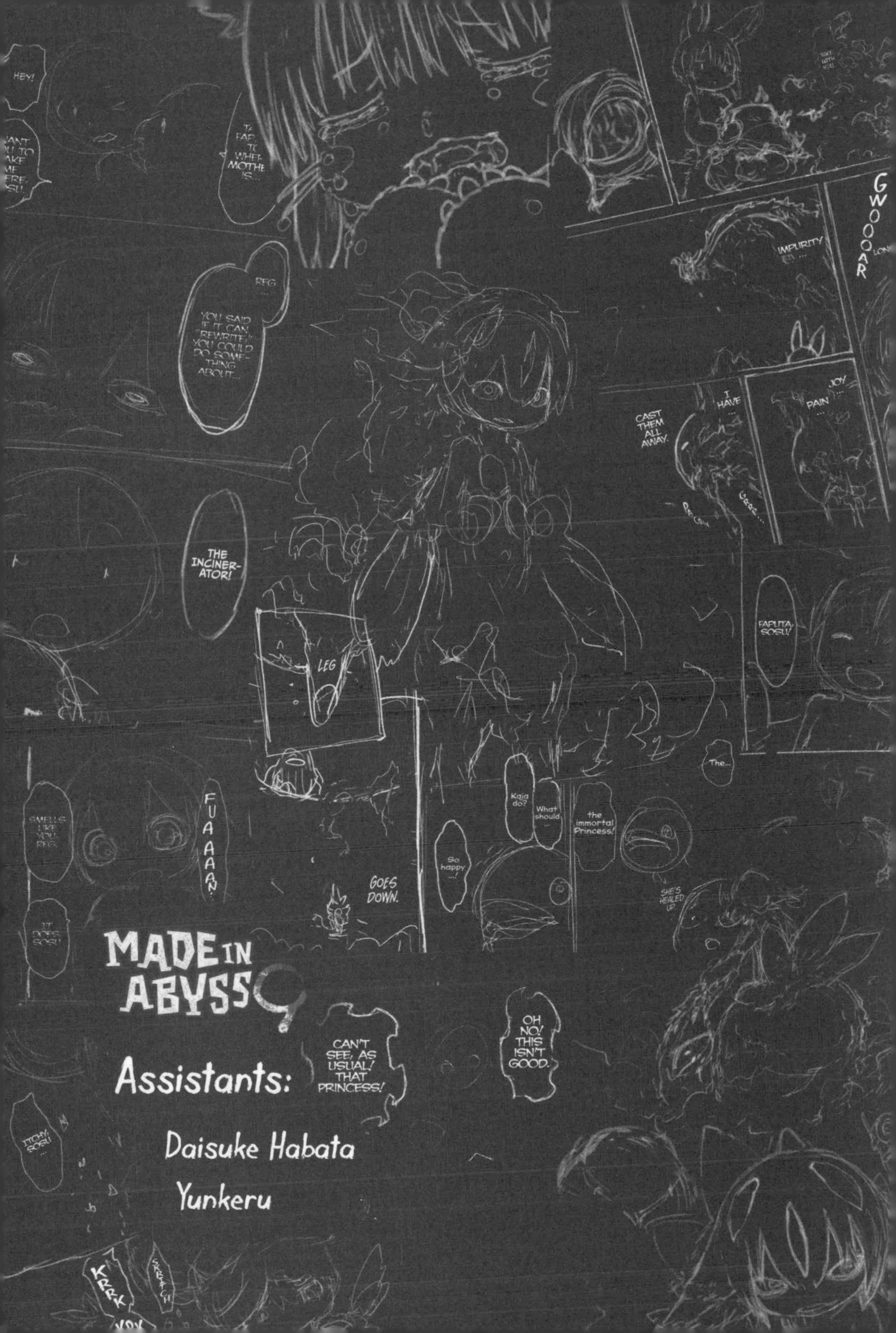
GWOOOAR
IMPURITY ...
JOY ...
PAIN ...
I HAVE ...
CAST THEM ALL AWAY.
FAPUTA, SOSU!
The...
REG ...
YOU SAID IF IT CAN "REWRITE," YOU COULD DO SOME-THING ABOUT...
HEY!
THE INCINER-ATOR!
LEG
the immortal Princess!
What should ...
Kaja do?
So happy ...
SHE'S HEALED UP
GOES DOWN.
FUAAAAAN
SMELLS LIKE YOU, REG.
IT DOES, SOSU!
OH NO! THIS ISN'T GOOD.
CAN'T SEE, AS USUAL! THAT PRINCESS!
ITCHY, SOSU ...
SKRTCH
KRRK

MADE IN ABYSS 9

Assistants:

Daisuke Habata

Yunkeru

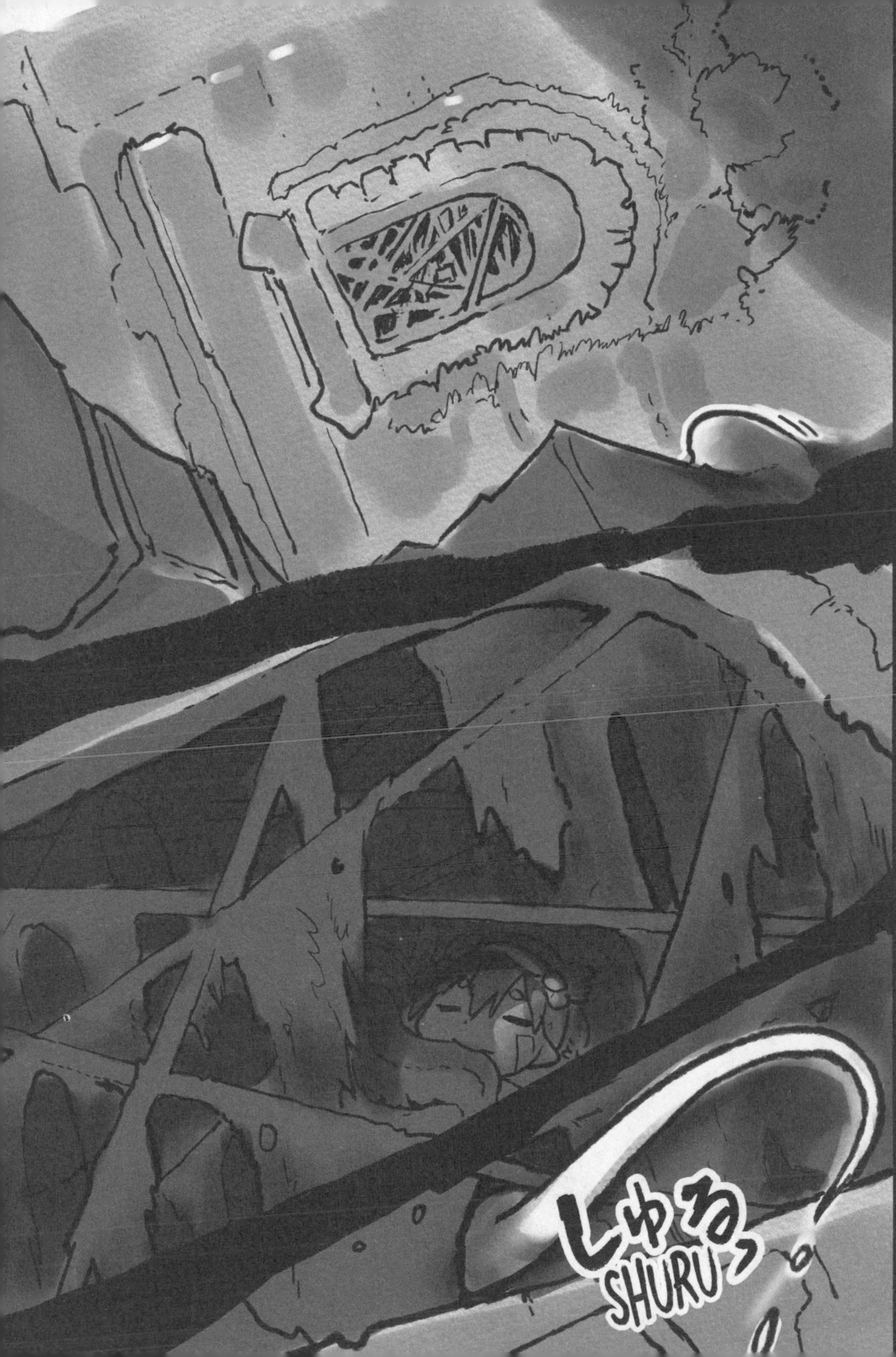
しゅるっ
SHURU

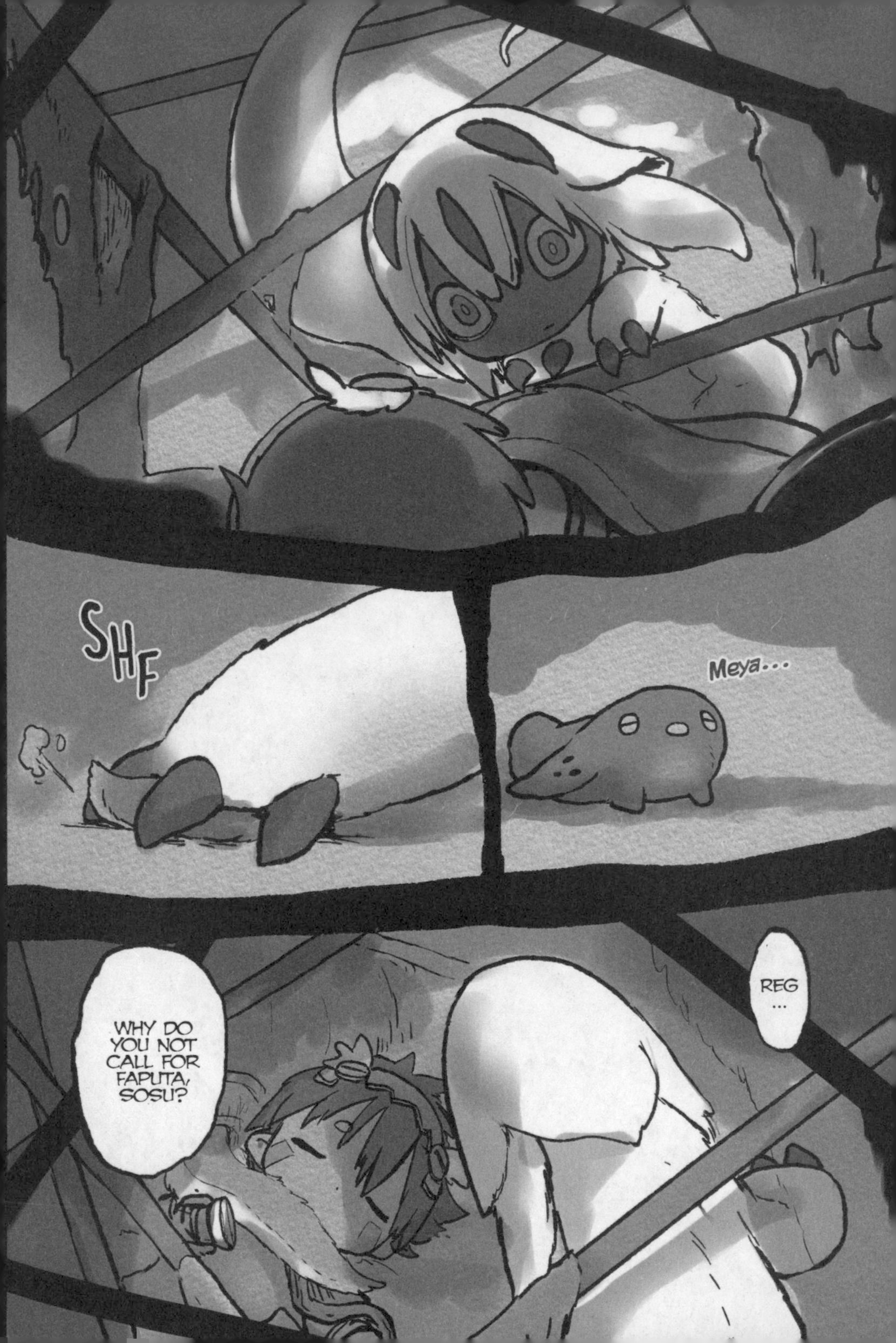
Meya...
SHF
REG ...
WHY DO YOU NOT CALL FOR FAPUTA, SOSU?

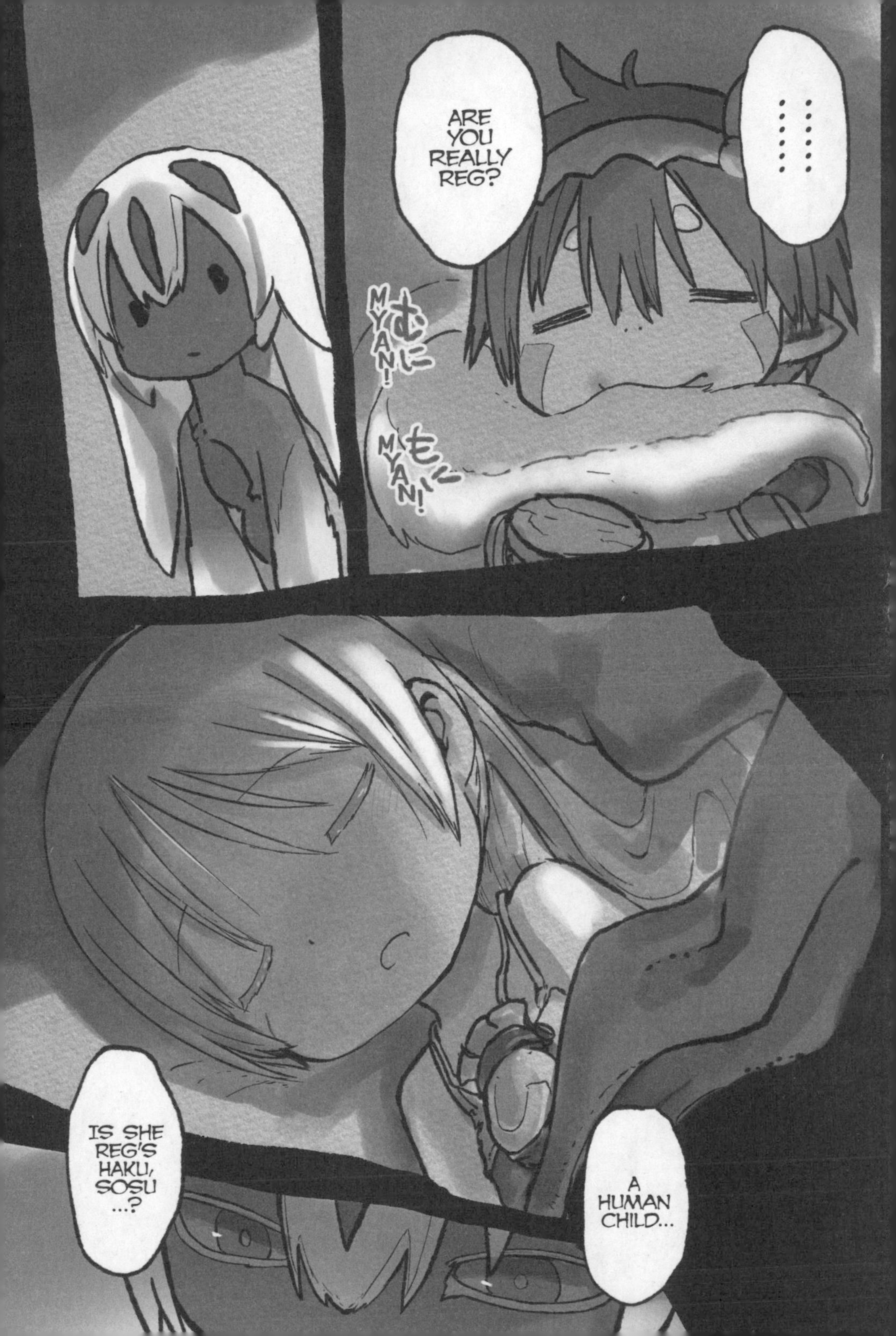
......
ARE YOU REALLY REG?
むに MYAN!
もに MYAN!
A HUMAN CHILD...
IS SHE REG'S HAKU, SOSU ...?

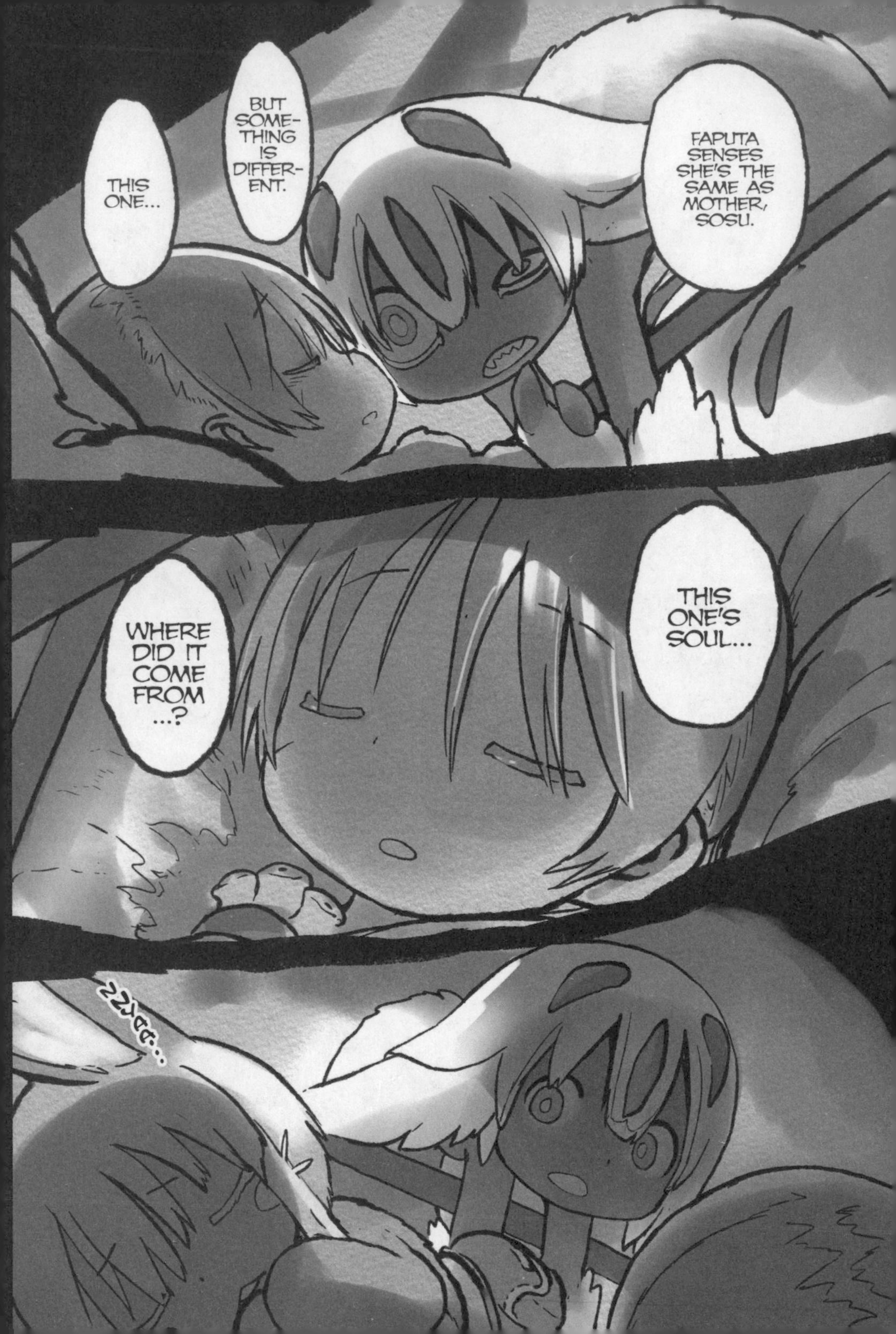
FAPUTA SENSES SHE'S THE SAME AS MOTHER, SOSU.
BUT SOME-THING IS DIFFER-ENT.
THIS ONE...
THIS ONE'S SOUL...
WHERE DID IT COME FROM ...?

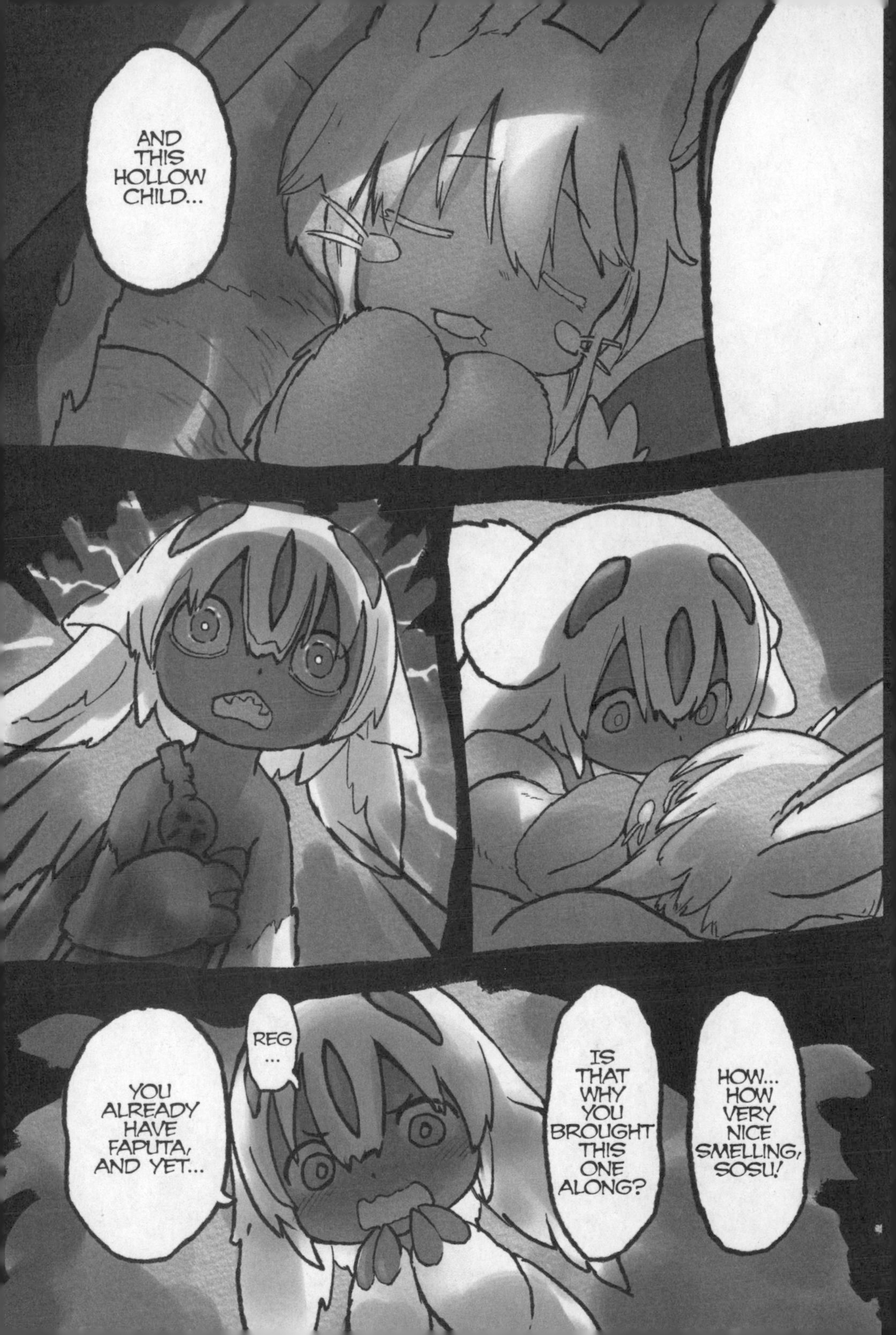
AND THIS HOLLOW CHILD...
HOW... HOW VERY NICE SMELLING, SOSU!
IS THAT WHY YOU BROUGHT THIS ONE ALONG?
REG...
YOU ALREADY HAVE FAPUTA, AND YET...

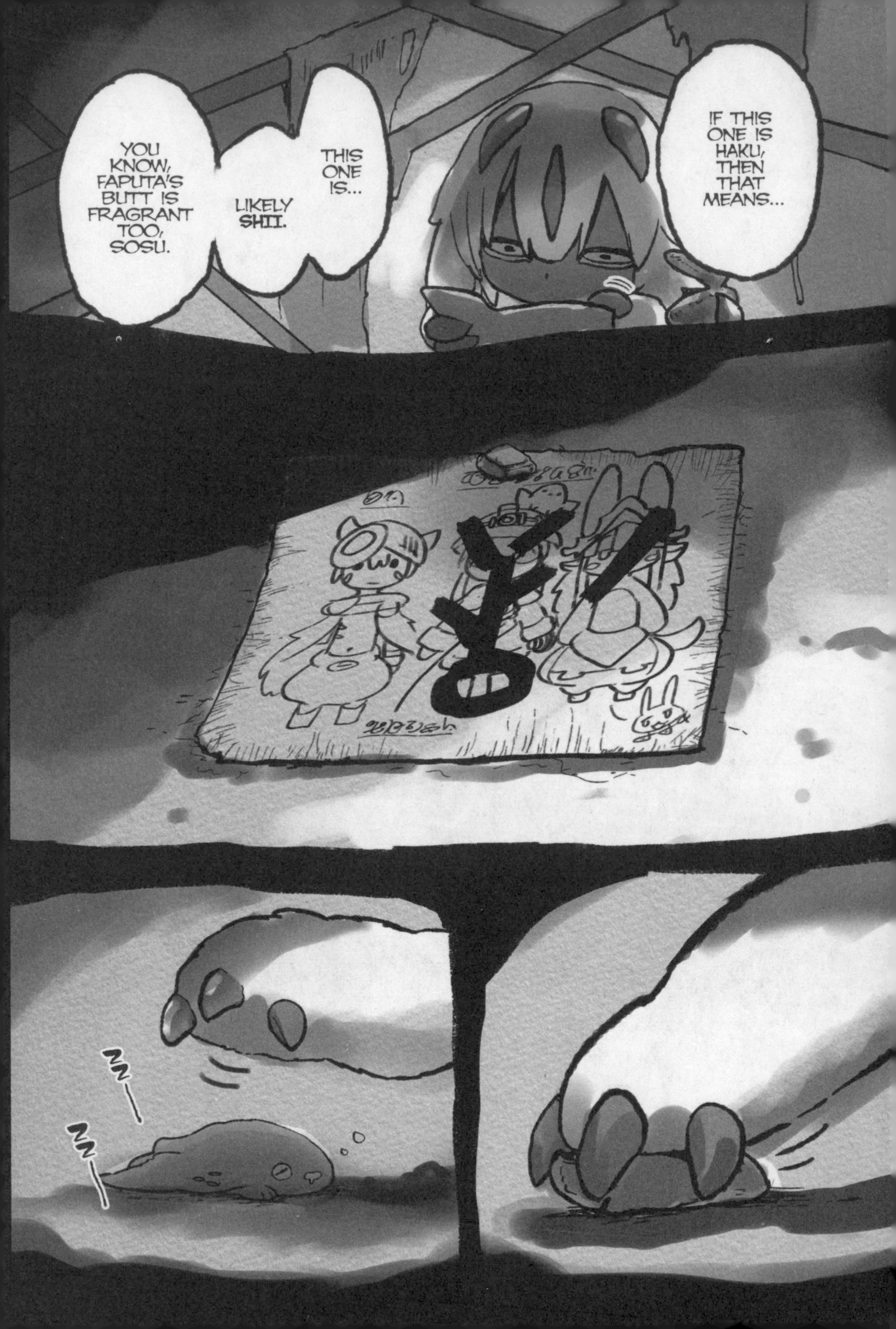
IF THIS ONE IS HAKU, THEN THAT MEANS...
THIS ONE IS...
LIKELY SHII.
YOU KNOW, FAPUTA'S BUTT IS FRAGRANT TOO, SOSU.
ZZ—
ZZ—

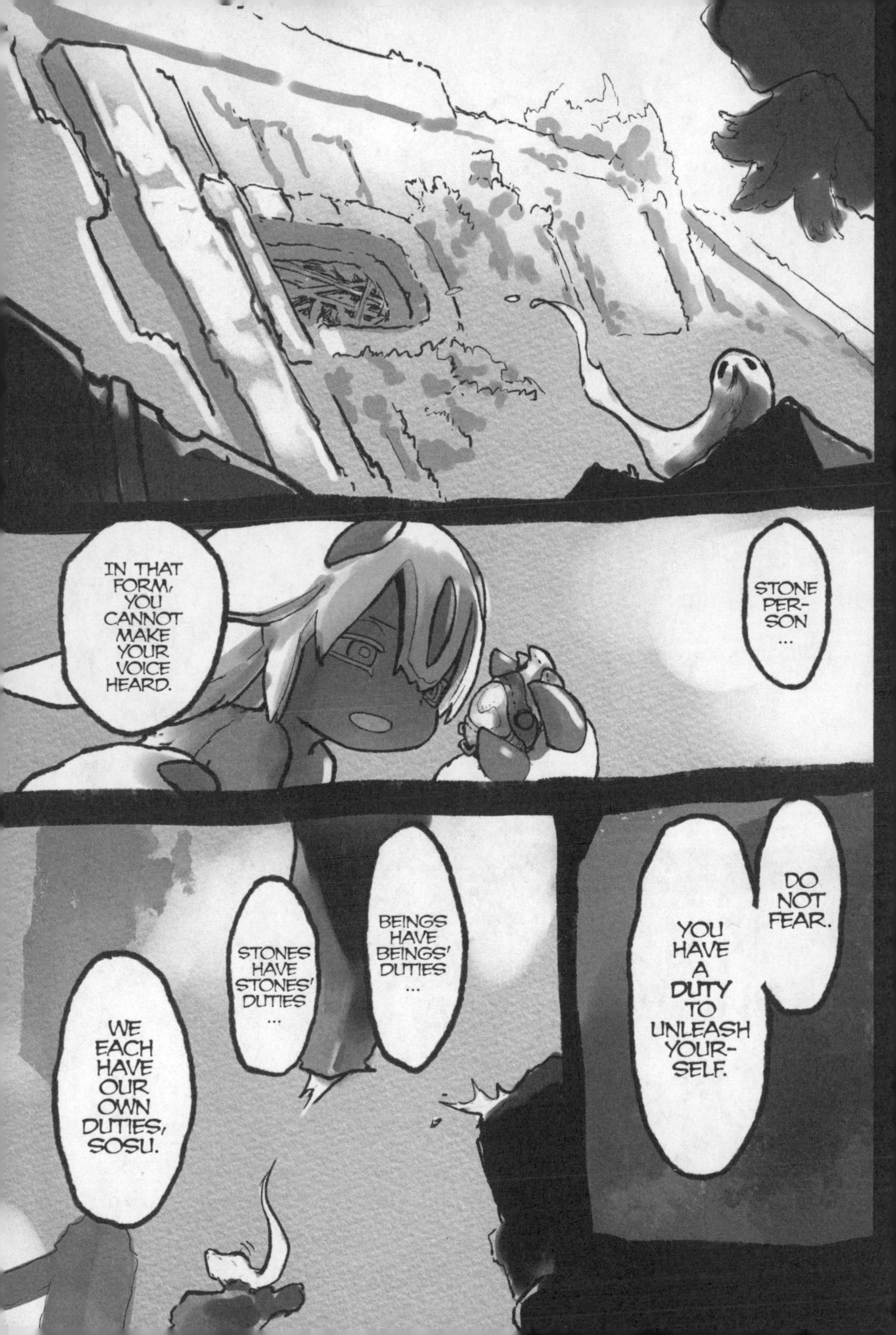
STONE PER-SON ...
IN THAT FORM, YOU CANNOT MAKE YOUR VOICE HEARD.
DO NOT FEAR.
YOU HAVE A DUTY TO UNLEASH YOUR-SELF.
BEINGS HAVE BEINGS' DUTIES ...
STONES HAVE STONES' DUTIES ...
WE EACH HAVE OUR OWN DUTIES, SOSU.

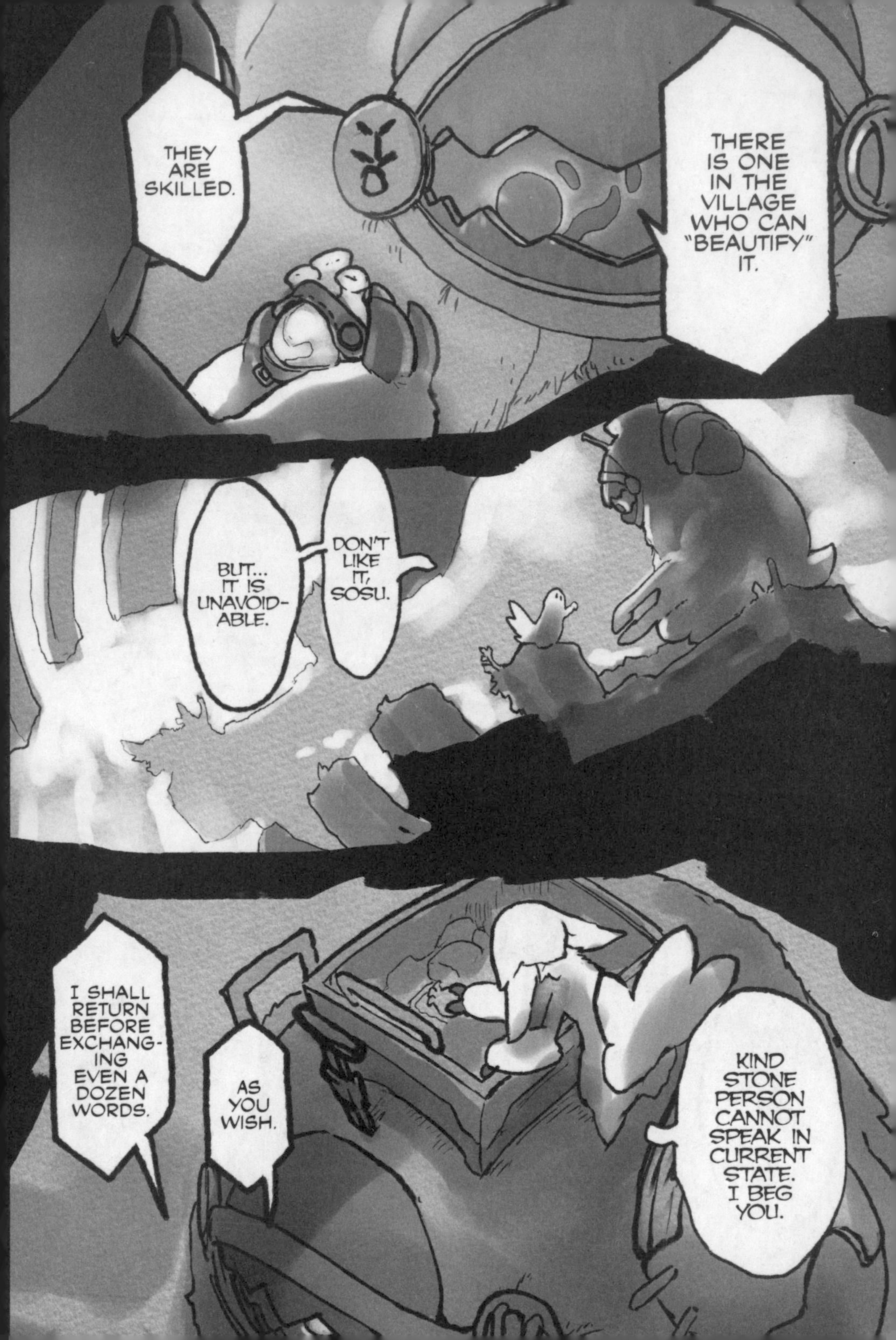
THERE IS ONE IN THE VILLAGE WHO CAN "BEAUTIFY" IT.
THEY ARE SKILLED.
DON'T LIKE IT, SOSU.
BUT... IT IS UNAVOIDABLE.
KIND STONE PERSON CANNOT SPEAK IN CURRENT STATE. I BEG YOU.
AS YOU WISH.
I SHALL RETURN BEFORE EXCHANGING EVEN A DOZEN WORDS.

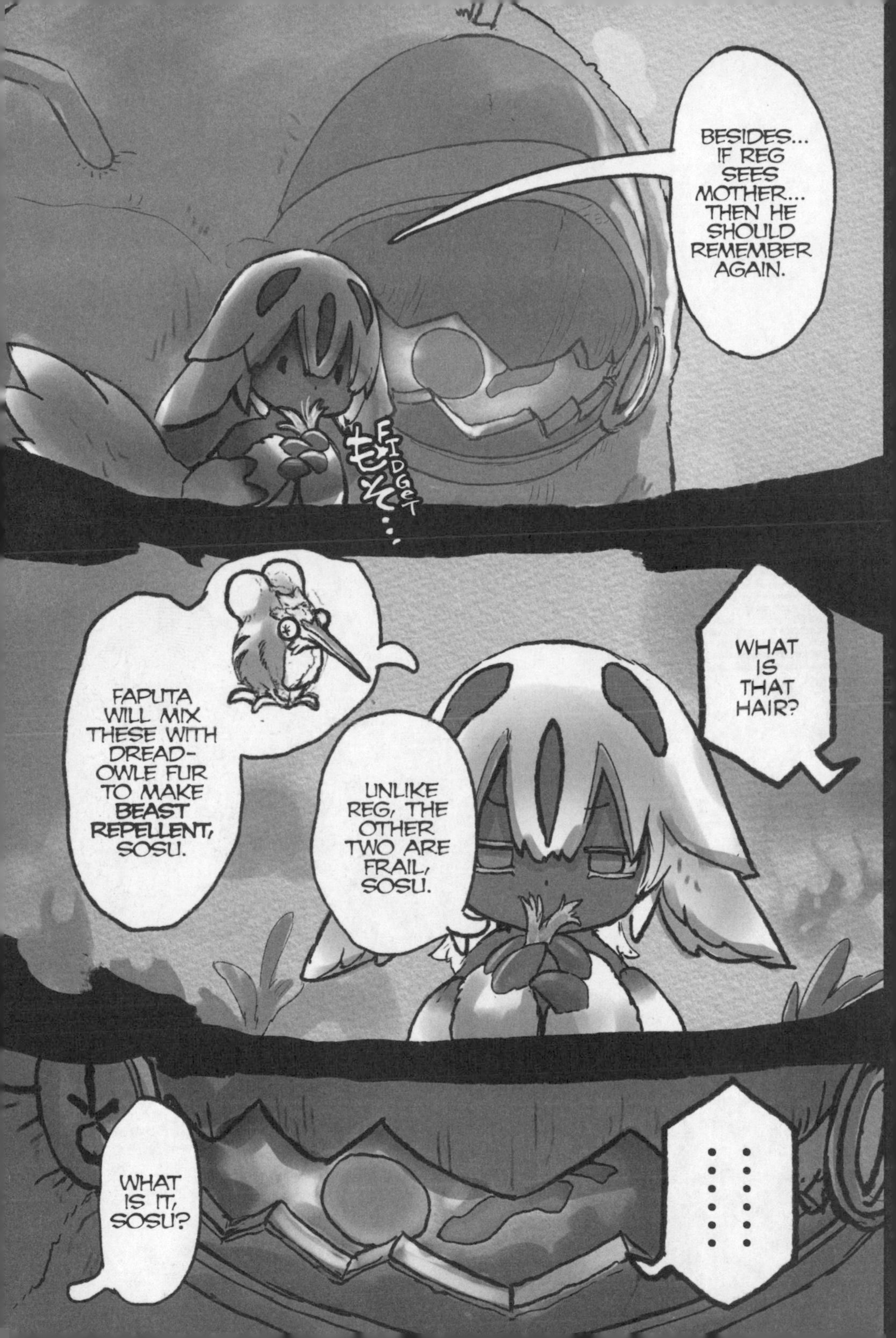
BESIDES... IF REG SEES MOTHER... THEN HE SHOULD REMEMBER AGAIN.
もそ もそ…
FIDGET
WHAT IS THAT HAIR?
UNLIKE REG, THE OTHER TWO ARE FRAIL, SOSU.
FAPUTA WILL MIX THESE WITH DREAD-OWLE FUR TO MAKE **BEAST REPELLENT,** SOSU.
......
WHAT IS IT, SOSU?

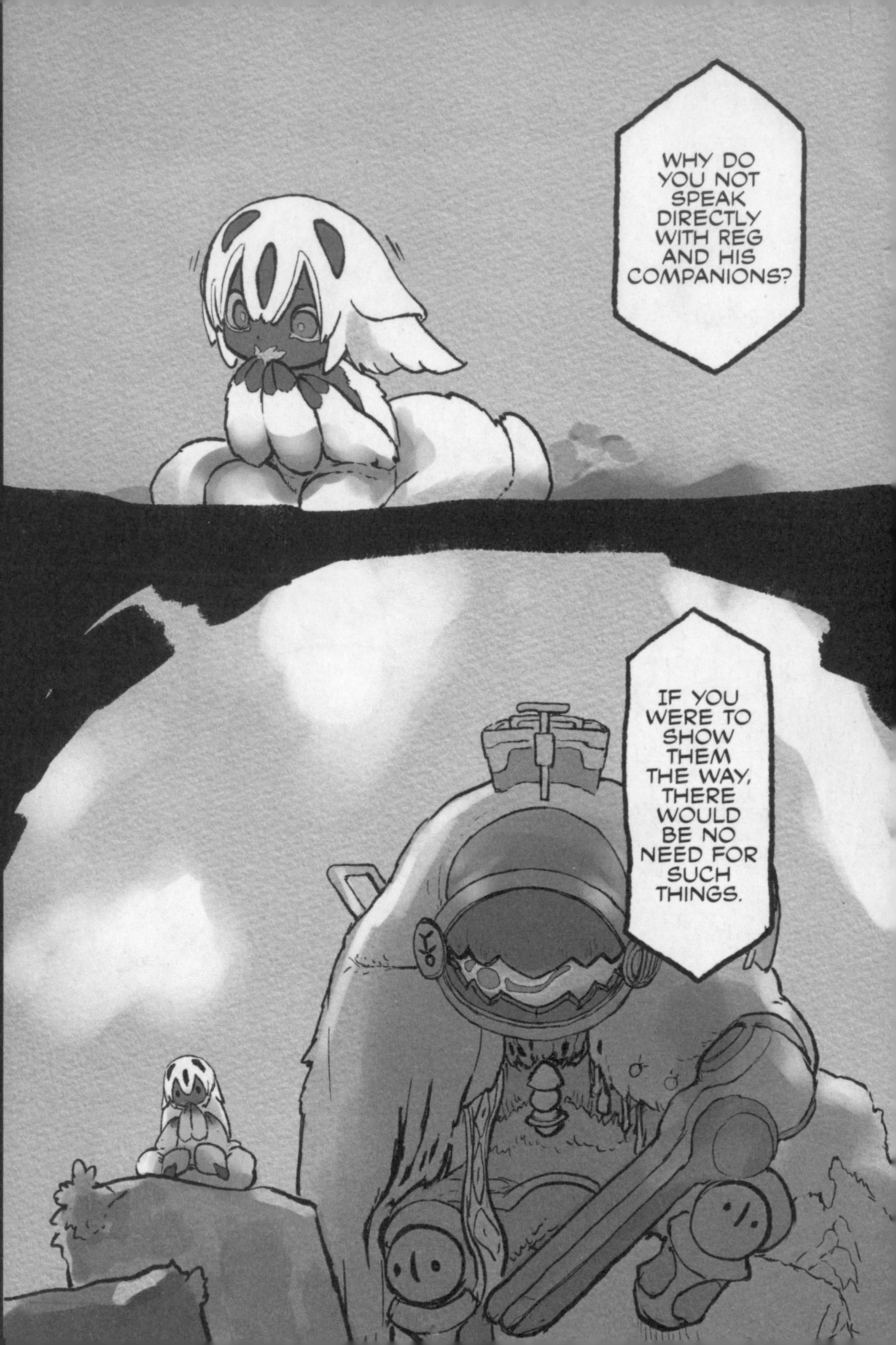
WHY DO YOU NOT SPEAK DIRECTLY WITH REG AND HIS COMPANIONS?
IF YOU WERE TO SHOW THEM THE WAY, THERE WOULD BE NO NEED FOR SUCH THINGS.

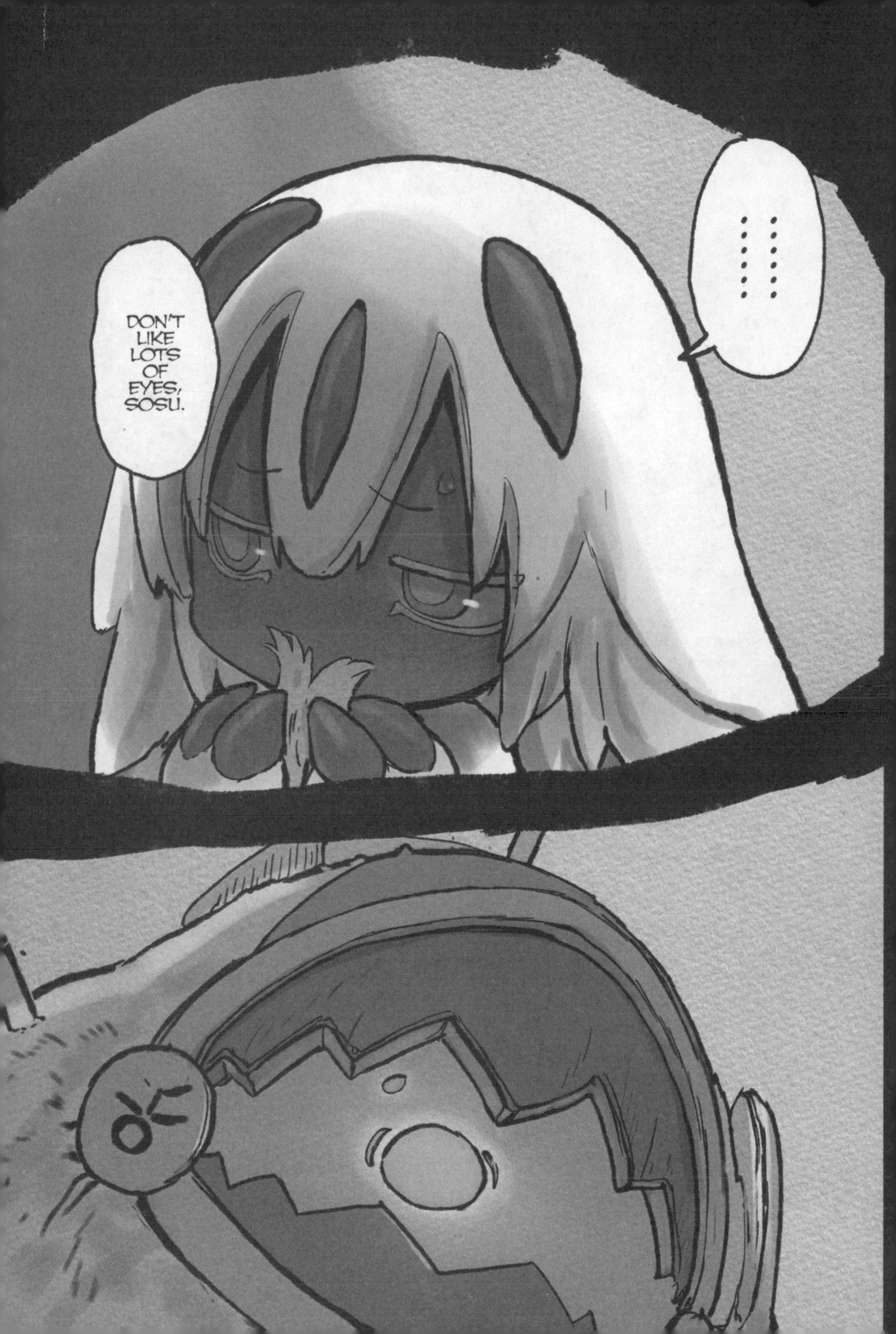
......
......
DON'T LIKE LOTS OF EYES, SOSU.

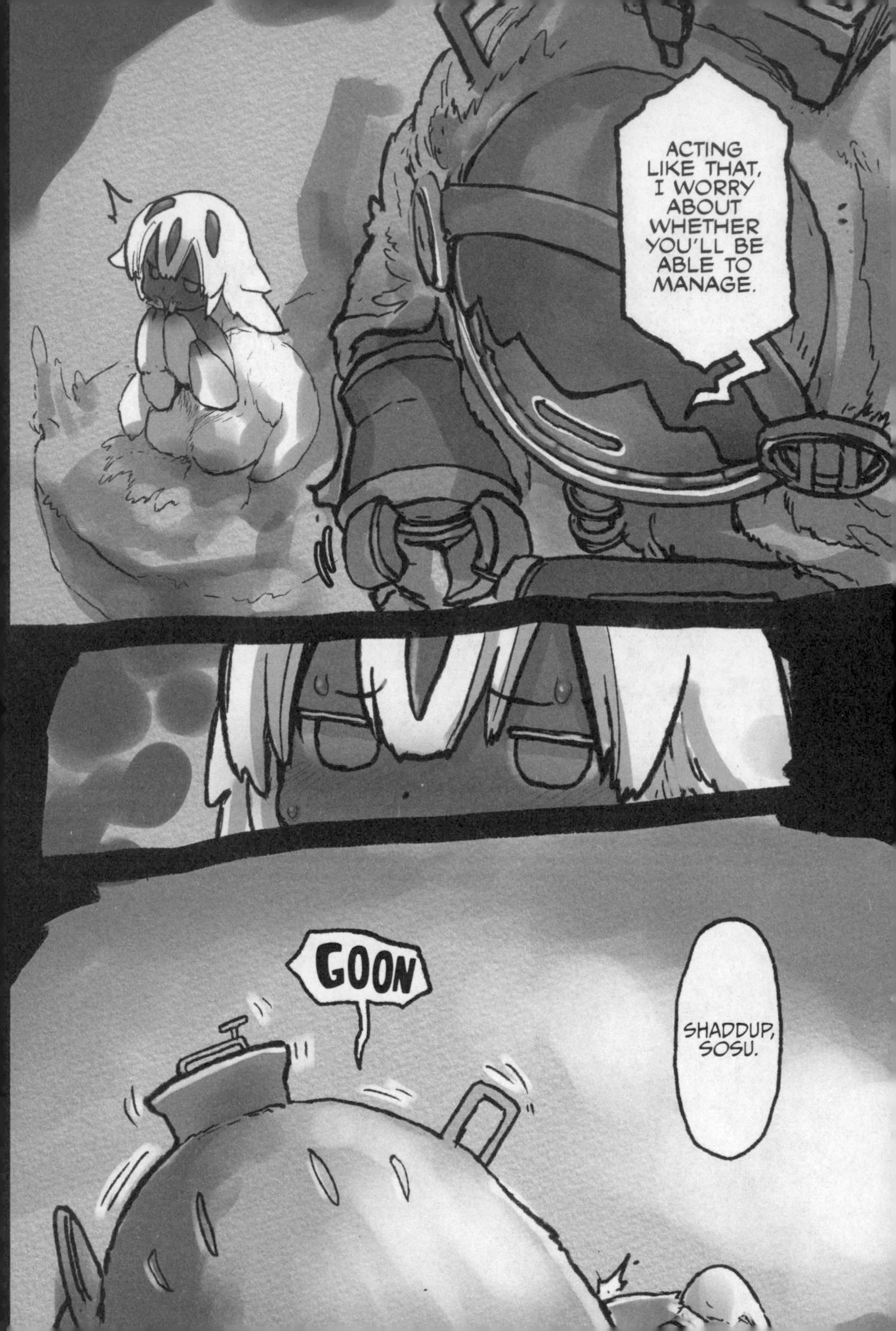
ACTING LIKE THAT, I WORRY ABOUT WHETHER YOU'LL BE ABLE TO MANAGE.
SHADDUP, SOSU.
GOON

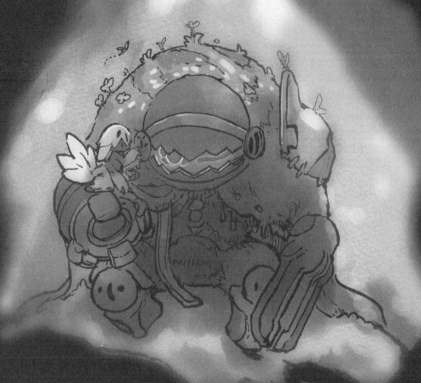

TO BE CONTINUED...

❀ MOON OUTFIT ❀

LONG-ESTABLISHED CHILDREN'S
CLOTHING IN THE FAR WESTERN
COUNTRY OF JISWEKU.

WITHIN THE ROYAL
FAMILY OF JISWEKU,
"CHILDREN OF THE SHADOWS,"
WHO ARE BY NATURE
SENSITIVE TO SUNLIGHT,
ARE OCCASIONALLY BORN.

CHILDREN OF THE SHADOWS
ARE SAID TO ONLY LIVE TO
THE AGE OF TEN. EVEN
AMONG THE ANCIENT TEXTS
OF JISWEKU, IT IS WRITTEN THAT
"THREE THOUSAND SUNS
WILL ELIMINATE A CHILD OF
THE SHADOWS."

THIS MOON OUTFIT
THEREFORE SERVES TO
CONCEAL CHILDREN OF THE
SHADOWS FROM THE SUN.

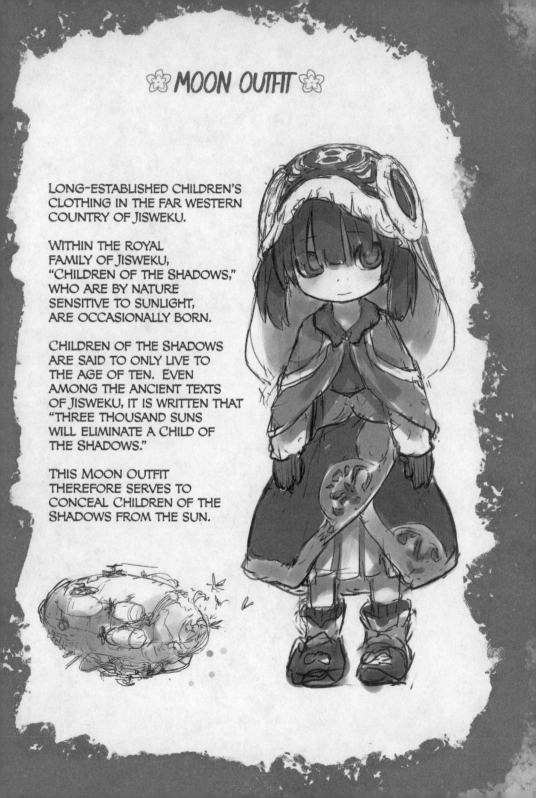